Iraq Between the Two World Wars

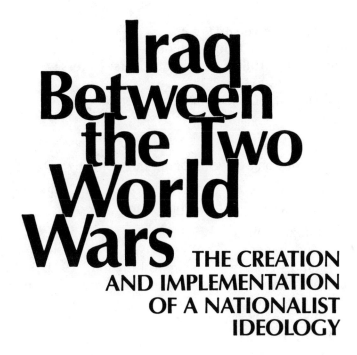

Iraq Between the Two World Wars

THE CREATION AND IMPLEMENTATION OF A NATIONALIST IDEOLOGY

Reeva S. Simon

COLUMBIA UNIVERSITY PRESS

New York   1986

Columbia University Press
New York   Guildford, Surrey
Copyright © 1986 Columbia University Press
Printed in the United States of America

Library of Congress Cataloging-in-Publication Data
Simon, Reeva S.
  Iraq between the two world wars.

  Bibliography: p.
  Includes index.
  1. Iraq—History—Hashimite Kingdom, 1921–1958.
2. Iraq—Armed Forces—Political activity.   3. Nationalism—Iraq—History.   I. Title.
DS79.S57   1986   956.7'04   85-29893
ISBN 0-231-06074-2

This book is Smyth-sewn.

For Sheldon

Contents

Introduction   xi
I.   The Creation of a State   1
II.   The Officers, Germany, and Nationalism   7
III.   The Officers in Iraq   45
IV.   Education   75
V.   The Army   115
VI.   The Rashid 'Ali Coup   145
VII. Conclusion   167

Appendixes
I.   The Hashimites   171
II.   Iraqi Cabinets 1921–1941   173
III.   Biographical Sketches   179

Notes   183

Bibliography   211

Index   229

Acknowledgments

It is customary and I am pleased to have the opportunity to express my gratitude to those who have contributed toward making this book possible. I wish to thank Professor Arnold Blumberg for transmitting his exhuberance for the study of history; Professor Irene Gendzier for introducing the perplexities of the history of the Middle East; and Professor Elie Kedourie for presenting the intricies of modern Iraqi history.

I have received generous assistance from a number of libraries and institutions. The staff of the Public Record Office in England, Mr. John Taylor and Mr. Frederick Pernell of the United States National Archives facilitated research while Dr. George N. Atiyeh of the United States Library of Congress, and Rev. Joseph A. Devenny, S.J. of the Western School of Theology made otherwise inaccessible Arabic materials available to me.

I appreciate the invaluable services of the Columbia University Libraries, most especially the Interlibrary Loan Department, and the support I received from the Middle East Institute.

I am grateful for the constructive criticism contributed by professors Istvan Déak, J. C. Hurewitz, Ergun Osbudun, and Michael Stanislawski, and by Philip Mattar and Muhammad Muslih who read the manuscript. I am most indebted to Professor Richard W. Bulliet for his continuous encouragement and to Professor Phebe A. Marr for her unceasing support and interest in my work.

Of course, the views expressed herein are solely my own. It has been a pleasure working with editors Kate Wittenberg and Joan McQuary of Columbia University Press.

Finally, my thanks to my parents, to Sheldon, Miriam, Benjamin, and Ezra Hanan Simon and to Jean Andrews, without whose patience and help this work never could have been attempted.

Transliteration

I have generally followed a modified transliteration system based on that of the *International Journal of Middle East Studies,* but which omits macrons and diacritical works for velarized consonants, and identifies the ʿayn only. Geographical names reflect current American usage.

Introduction

This is a book of historical interpretation. As such, it seeks to answer the question: Why did a group of army officers, who had seized control of the government of Iraq in 1941, proceed to wage a disastrously futile war against Great Britain? Why did these officers reject the British and liberal democratic values, turning instead to a militaristic Germany, whose political ideology stood at the extreme edge of Romantic nationalism?

On the surface, the answer seems obvious. As a victor in World War I, although responsible for the creation of the modern state of Iraq, Britain, in consort with France, was instrumental in dividing up the Arab areas of the former Ottoman Empire and of occupying Iraq. To the officers, educated in Istanbul and returning to Iraq to play a leading role in the new state, who were first and foremost pan-Arab nationalists, dreaming of the unity of an Arab nation encompassing the Fertile Crescent and Arabia, the situation was intolerable and smacked of betrayal by the same politicians in Whitehall who were ostensibly leading Iraq to full independence. For while the facade of independence and of political democracy existed, the British exerted control in the background—through the Embassy where the British ambassador reigned *primus inter pares* and via a covey of British advisors who were directly involved in areas from political administration to landholding adjudication and the suppression of tribal revolts. Thus, Iraq was only nominally independent, so when the opportunity arose and the British Empire seemed about to be overrun by the Axis powers in 1941, the Iraqis turned to Germany. The enemy of the enemy is a friend.

But why Germany? Why not Japan or Italy? To students in non-Western countries, Japan was the paradigm, admired as a state that industrialized and modernized in a remarkably short period of time and then actually defeated a Western power in the Russo-Japanese War of 1905. Japanese commercial and diplomatic ties with Iraq did increase during the 1930s. Similarly, there was a direct connection to Rome through the Italian Legation in Baghdad which became the conduit for funds to pro-Axis Iraqis, but the Italians were suspect because of Mussolini's designs on North Africa, Ethiopia, and parts farther East.

That left Germany, not by default, but because there were links to Germany which went back to the turn of the century, associations which, despite Germany's later adoption of National Socialism, were reactivated in the 1930s. To be sure, there were some pro-Nazi Iraqis, but the army officers who turned to Germany were not Nazis. Indeed, they tended to overlook the racial ideology that placed them one step above the Jews and looked instead to those areas of compatibility they had formed with the Germany of Wilhelm II when German ideas, especially cultural nationalism, reached them in Istanbul, at the military schools where the Iraqi officers received their first taste of Westernization at the hands of German military officers.

There, they imbibed the burgeoning nationalist philosophies while studying military maneuvers and tactics. A non-Turkish minority in the new Young Turk exclusively Turkish state, the Arab officers in the Ottoman army adapted the German example of unification of diverse elements into a nation based on a common language and history. When they returned to Iraq, this was the world view they transmitted through the schools and, as military officers, through the army, finally turning to Germany for arms and advice in an abortive first step of evicting the occupier and reuniting the Arab nation.

Education, therefore, as the means for the transmission of cultural values and political ideas is the key to analyzing the reasons for the German-Iraqi link in 1941, which, in essence, is the culmination of a process that began before World War I, continued during the political turbulence in Iraq in the 1930s, and ended with the defeat in May 1941. It is the story of the creation of a political ideology, of how it was implemented and inculcated in Iraq, and how the realization of the political goals was attempted in 1941.

It has long been a given in studies in political development that in developing countries, the educated become the political elite.[1] In prewar Iraq, this elite tended to consist of graduates of the law and military schools of the Ottoman Empire, with a preponderance of military officers.

The role of transmitting these new ideas was taken over by the schools (and the army), state institutions, because other cultural agencies either did not exist or could not compete in the secular socialization process. In Iraq, for example, the Shi'i were reluctant to send their children to the government schools or let them join the army for fear of Sunni indoctrination.

A child frequently became separated from his natural environment because boarding schools were common, and peers at schools became comrades for life. The gap between the Western educated elite and the traditional culture widened and the Westernized student came to depend on his newly acquired *Weltanschauung* and his comrades in arms with whom he had more in common than his family. The education received during the formative years extending through young adulthood and the developing social relationships formed during that period of the person's life had a lasting impact.[2]

The question that arises, therefore, is not whether or not the transmission of cultural values through education is a real factor in the socialization process, but to what degree does the content received during the education process influence a person later in life? All societies use education to inculcate or indoctrinate either indirectly or through direct methods such as citizenship training, teaching history from a particular vantage point, or paramilitary youth movements in the schools. After World War II, the Allies deemed the situation so acute in Japan, for example, that the curriculum was completely revised and democratized by the American occupation forces[3] as was the Iraqi curriculum by the British occupation forces which reoccupied the country after the abortive war in 1941. For education and the army were the two areas neglected by the British advisors in Iraq and these were the two means used by the Iraqi nationalists to implement the nationalist ideology they instituted in Iraq.

The answer to the question posed, therefore, is linked to the role that education played in the creation and the inculcation of nationalism in Iraq; first, as a legacy of the Ottoman education the Iraqi officers who returned to Iraq to rule had received in Istanbul; next, by the kind of political education they transmitted to the Iraqi youth; and finally, with the means they used to put these theoretical ideas into practice on the political stage.

Chapter 1 assesses the situation that faced the Iraqi officers returning to Iraq after World War I. Chapter 2 discusses the relationships forged between the Iraqis and Germany before World War I, analyzes the legacies of military training and the German example of cultural nationalism as it related to Arab nationalism, and describes the reactivization of the Iraqi-German relationship in the 1930s. Chapter 3 explores the political maneuverings that brought the officers to political power in Iraq and chapters 4 and 5 discuss the means they used to inculcate Arab nationalism—first, through education and then, the army. Once the army seized power in 1941 (chapter 6), it used the opportunity to put into play the tenets of political Arab nationalism, which the officers attempted through the Rashid 'Ali coup and the war with Britain in May 1941.

Iraqi history during this period between World War I and World War II should not be seen as merely the assimilation of the Iraqi officers into the existing social elite. The officers became a new elite, albeit one which took advantage of the existing economic system to ensure its own financial security and social status. And in this sense the officers were "co-opted" into an oligarchical society fostered by the British. But the officers implemented their own policy, in this case pan-Arabism, after seizing control from the indigenous nationalist groups in Iraq.

Recent studies on Middle East politics and analyses of elites have emphasized the class theory to the detriment of cultural factors operative in the actions of groups. Current writers such as Hanna Batatu and David Pool,[4] who approach Iraqi history from the vantage point of class analysis, acknowledge the importance of the educational background of the Iraqi officers, but do not analyze the cultural determinants. The kind of education these officers received and how their world view was played out on the Iraqi stage is what this book is about.

Iraq Between the Two World Wars

I. The Creation of a State

They were all there, the "Forty Thieves" as Winston Churchill called them. Actually, their number was thirty-eight including one woman, Gertrude Bell, and two Arabs—the best experts on the Middle East. Churchill, newly appointed minister at the Colonial Office, had summoned them to Cairo during the second week of March 1921 to reorganize the administration of British Middle East interests.

While Churchill sat at his easel sketching pictures of the Pyramids in the shadow of an armored car during his frequent absences from committee meetings,[1] the specialists at the Cairo Conference, as it was to be known, sketched from three provinces of the former Ottoman empire—Baghdad, Basra, and Mosul—what would become the kingdom of Iraq. And they provided a king: Faysal, second son of the Sharif of Mecca,[2] newly exiled from a temporary throne in Syria, who, after some persuasion by his former comrade-in-arms T. E. Lawrence and by Sir Kinahan Cornwallis of the Colonial Office, reluctantly agreed to take on the task of ruling the new country. Gertrude Bell, Oriental Secretary to the British High Commissioner, Sir Percy Cox, found the creation of the kingdom a satisfying but exhausting job. "You may rely on one thing," she wrote to her father on July 8, 1921, "I'll never engage in creating kings again;" "it's too great a strain."[3] By August, Faysal was crowned king and the process of governing began.

Faysal brought his own entourage to Iraq. Also known as the Sharifians, these were former Ottoman army officers, most of Iraqi origin, who had been the military backbone of the Arab revolt which Faysal had led during World War I and who would now serve as the officers and administrators of Iraq until the end of the monarchy in 1958. They "have risked their lives and their futures and those of their families, in volunteering their services during the war," Faysal told the British, "and at every period of the struggle they have served me loyally. . .

> to those who say that it is impossible to constitute such a [national] government owing to the lack of trained men, I will say that until now not the slightest effort has been made to collect them, for most of the highest posts in the Eastern Zone of the O.E.T. are filled by Baghdadis today. Doubtless among the tribes a great deal of assistance will be necessary and the Baghdadis would all be only too glad to undertake it.[4]

They were young men; their average age in 1921 was in the low thirties. Most were lower-middle-class Sunni Arabs from Baghdad and the north who were products of Ottoman military and bureaucratic education which had become available to provincial Arabs during the last half of the previous century and many of them were related to one another by blood and marriage. But they had neither a local following nor a power base in Iraq and so were dependent upon the government for position and livelihood, unlike the indigenous politically and socially prominent groups.

They came to rule a country whose literate population as late as 1955 numbered only some 400,000 of about 4 million people.[5] Most of them pastoralists, farmers, and villagers, organized by tribe, village, or faith. The capital city, Baghdad, which in essence represented Iraqi political history after 1932, had a population of 300,000 before World War II.

They returned to an artificially created entity, a mandate entrusted to Britain at the San Remo Conference in 1920 by the World War I victors. Britain had occupied Iraq during the war in order to safeguard the route to British India, blocking German encroachments from the north and Russian penetration from the east through Iran. Although the British did manage eventually to secure Mosul and its oil for Iraq, outmaneuvering both the Turks and the French who claimed the former Ottoman province, Iraq was but a piece of the territory that Faysal and the Sharifians believed promised to them during the war. France now controlled Syria, and Britain governed Palestine which was also declared to be a Jewish homeland.

As Sunni Arabs, the Sharifians were part of a minority compared with the Shi'is who comprised over 50 percent of the population. Their country was composed of relatively discrete areas of ethnic and religious diversification, exemplified by the provinces into which the Ottomans had divided the territory. Baghdad and the northwest were primarily Sunni Arab; Basra with a significant Sunni population was the largest city in the predominately Shi'i south; and Mosul, although Sunni, contained a large Turkman population. In the mountains to the northeast of Mosul lay Kurdistan, an area of Kurdish speaking non-Arab Sunni tribesmen divided among Iraq, Turkey, and Iran which aspired to autonomy or independence. There were also Yazidis, the center of whose religion, which combined elements of paganism, Zoroastrianism, Christianity, and Islam, lay in the mountains to the west of Mosul, and Sabians who practiced their baptismal rites in the marsh areas in the south. Christians and Jews lived for the most part in the cities, except for a large number of Assyrian (Nestorian) Christians brought to Iraq from north of Mosul to help the Allies. After the war the British resettled the refugees in Iraqi territory.

The three provinces had different orientations. Basra, which at one time had applied for autonomous rule, looked to the Gulf and to India for commerce and was separated from Baghdad by the virtually ungovernable marsh areas of the Shatt al-'Arab; Mosul lay on the trade route to Syria and Turkey; and Baghdad had been on the frontier between the Sunni Ottoman Empire and the Shi'i Safavid state of Iran. There was a constant population flow at the Iranian border because the Shi'i Holy Cities of al-Najaf and Karbala lay just to the south of Baghdad and pilgrims and students traveled there in large numbers.

Needless to say, there was no focus of nationalist identification at the time of Iraq's creation. As late as 1933 Faysal was to despair:

> In Iraq there is still—and I say this with a heart full of sorrow—no Iraqi people but unimaginable masses of human beings, devoid of any patriotic ideal, imbued with religious traditions and absurdities, connected by no common tie, giving ear to evil, prone to

anarchy, and perpetually ready to rise against any government whatsoever. Out of these masses we want to fashion a people which we would train, educate, and refine. . . The circumstances being what they are, the immenseness of the efforts needed for this (can be imagined).[6]

The people of Iraq had traditionally looked to the tribal shaykh, the village headman, and religious leader for guidance and allegiance and paid taxes to whoever could collect them—the Turks in the garrison towns, or the shaykhs the British used to control the tribes. The problem which the new rulers faced was how to create an identification—a nationalist ideology which could weld their fractured country into a state—while being occupied by a foreign power.

For what the British had taken as an imperial prize during the war turned out to be an expensive hornets' nest, requiring money and troops for internal pacification. Local reaction to the decisions at San Remo was a revolt in 1920 which cost the British more than four hundred lives and 40 million pounds. So, instead of direct rule and a complete British occupation, they devised a government with an "Arab façade" containing all of the external trappings and institutions of a constitutional monarchy, complete with cabinet, political parties, and parliament on the British model. After an eleven-year training period, the fledgling state became independent in 1932.

But the British did not leave. Instead, they attempted to control Iraq via a covey of British advisers who supervised and reported on Iraqi internal developments, and by a treaty signed in 1930 as a prerequisite for independence. It provided for an Anglo-Iraqi alliance and for full consultations between the two countries in all matters of foreign policy. The treaty which was to endure for twenty-five years granted Britain the right to use airbases near Basra and at al-Habbaniyyah, and the right to move troops across the country. Britain was supposed to sell Iraq arms.

To the British, this system whereby Iraq would finance and secure a protective shield for the British route to India and would control the strategic oil-producing areas and the pipeline—in operation pumping oil to refineries in Haifa by the mid-1930s—seemed ideal. And it satisfied wartime promises to their Hashimite allies: Faysal had gotten his kingdom after all.

For insurance they fostered alternative power groups to the Sharifians, whom they mistrusted; but aside from token Shi'i cabinet members, they virtually ignored the Shi'i majority whom they considered to be religious fanatics. Instead, the British sponsored the election of some Shi'i landlords, of tribal shaykhs and urban notables to parliament; and, after a slow start, parliamentary seats became popular as sources of lucrative prequisites and powerful local patronage. The shaykhs were given administrative positions and land grants. Huge tracts of land which had been the personal possession of Ottoman Sultan Abdulhamid II were now state lands, leased by the politicians and their supporters. Ownership of formerly communal tribal lands by absentee landlords who had acquired title under the Ottomans was guaranteed by the Land Settlement Law of 1932 which granted tenure to anyone who had usufruct of the land for a period of over fifteen years. And the peasant was tied to the land by the Law for the Rights and Duties of Cultivators (1933) which stipulated that only peasants free from debt could leave the land to find other employment.

Throughout the 1920s the king and the politicians busied themselves jockeying for power, assuring their personal financial security, negotiating and opposing the treaty with Britain, and participating in the institutions the British had imposed on them. But the British did not provide an ideology, a focus for loyalty and belief to replace the traditional values and religion which they challenged by supporting secular education and "westernization." A flag, new headgear, and a foreign king did not produce a national identity. The British could create an Iraqi state, but they did not introduce British values.

So in 1941 the British were shocked to find themselves at war with a pan-Arab nationalist Iraq which seemed to yearn for a German victory. The Sharifians had not merely assimilated themselves into the ruling elite,[7] but had, under British noses, provided the new country with an ideology, a focus for loyalty derived from their Ottoman educational experience. Despite the attraction of French liberal thought and political nationalism in the Ottoman Empire, the officers transmitted a cultural nationalism with a militaristic bent, influenced by German nationalism and the German militarist tradition they had encountered in Istanbul. Once the Sharifians had taken control of the government apparatus, they had proceeded to inculcate pan-Arab nationalism via education and the military, following the pattern of the French, the Germans, and the Japanese.

    This, then, is the story of the beginnings of an Iraqi nationalism which saw Iraq as part of a greater Arab whole and which subordinated a local Iraqi future to the evocation of a glorious Arab past, a nationalism that became the rallying cry for the Rashid 'Ali movement and the war with Britain, a second attempt at independence and Arab irredentism that failed. A description of the nationalist ideology and a discussion of who created it and how it was inculcated will be the subject of the following pages.

II. The Officers, Germany, and Nationalism

Returning to only a part of the territory they had envisioned ruling, the Iraqi officers drew upon their Ottoman educational experience for a model upon which to base their goals for resurgent Arab strength and unification. They rejected Britain because of her role in dividing the Arab world after World War I and because Britain ruled their country. And unlike the Ottoman civilian intellectuals who saw in European liberal thought, introduced into the Middle East after Napolean's invasion of Egypt in 1798, the prescription for the financial and political ills of the Ottoman Empire, the officers, for whom reform connoted military modernization, were impressed by Germany, which had achieved unification and military superiority in a short period of time.

Like their counterparts from all over the Empire, the Iraqi officers in the Ottoman army before World War I were educated during the early years of the twentieth century when German military officers organized, supervised, and taught in the Ottoman military schools. There they encountered modern military thought from von Clausewitz to von der Goltz, and they were exposed to the concept of cultural nationalism as a means for knitting back together the disparate elements of the Arab world.

From their side, the Wilhelmian Germans looked to the weak Ottoman Empire both as an area ripe for colonization through which they could compete with British and French imperialism, and as an area compatible for cultural propagation. They hoped to use control of education as a means for indoctrination and eventual diplomatic alliance.

Despite military defeat in World War I and the German adoption of the National Socialist ideology which placed the Arabs slightly above the Jews on the racial scale, links remained between the German military and Iraq during the postwar period. In Iraq, Germans, who had served in the Middle East during World War I, found fertile ground for the reactivation of anti-British propaganda, taking advantage of the steadily growing Iraqi anti-British sentiments. Thus, in 1940–1941 when the lines for an impending conflict between Iraq and Britain began to be drawn, the Iraqi officers, now in charge of the government, turned to Germany, seen once again as a model and possible strategic alley for another attempt at Arab unification and independence.

Before turning to the actual role of the Iraqi officers in politics, however, let us set the stage by discussing their educational background and the residual legacy of this education: namely, the creation of a cohesive officer corps which retained linkages long after service in the Ottoman army, the adoption of cultural nationalism as a model for Arab nationalism, and by illustrating how German operatives began to use Iraq as a base for anti-British propaganda in the Middle East during the 1930s, reactivating a policy set in motion by the Kaiser in World War I. The impact of German activities in Iraq will be taken up later.

The Ottomans Turn to Germany

Until the 1830s the Ottomans had turned to Europe intermittently for military technology and technicians. Various European soldiers of fortune, mercenaries, and eventually a French military mission in Istanbul advised the Ottomans. French became the second language in the Ottoman military schools.[1] But French defeat in 1870 and their refusal to renew the military mission in 1877, coupled with the Ottoman defeat in the Russo-Turkish War (1877–1878) led to a reassessment of the situation. In 1880 Ottoman Sultan Abdülhamid II (1876–1909) commissioned a study of Ottoman and foreign military capabilities and institutions. It recommended reform on the German model.[2]

The invitation to Germany to send a military mission to the Ottoman Empire initiated a German-Turkish relationship which endured through World War I and whose legacy persisted into interwar Iraq. For it was during this period that the Iraqi graduates of the Ottoman military school in Baghdad began to arrive in Istanbul to study in the military academy. Military education was free and included room and board. Thus the army became an ideal career for lower-class Iraqis from less prominent families. "Istanbul was the Mecca (Ka'ba) of ambitious Iraqis," writes Talib Mushtaq, who later taught in the Iraqi schools,

> for whoever wanted an important position filled his bag with expensive presents and hurried to Istanbul, and whoever wanted advancement and promotion filled his pockets with tens of gold liras and went to Istanbul; and those wealthy families who wanted to give their sons a higher education sent them [there]. . . the majority of these attended the College of Law and the Mulkiye Shahana, the College of Political and Administrative Sciences as it is now called. . . . As for poor families, they made their sons attend the military school in Baghdad so that it might lead to their completing their higher studies in the Military College in Istanbul and graduate as officers in the Ottoman Army.[3]

Each year from 1872 to World War I, thirty to forty Iraqi secondary-school graduates went on to Istanbul; in 1903 the Iraqis were 10 percent of the total number admitted to the military academy.[4] By 1912 some 1,200 had become Ottoman army officers.[5]

Germany was attractive then and remained a model not only for the Ottoman military but for the Iraqi officers who first encountered the Germans in Istanbul. Germany had achieved unity and a centralized regime—one of the goals of the reformers—in a short time. More important, however, after the Congress of Berlin in 1878, Germany emerged as the Ottoman Empire's true friend, one who was not outwardly concerned with the "minorities" question as was Britain, nor suspected of "landgrabbing."[6] Later, for example, the German Kaiser Wilhelm II reaffirmed Ottoman confidence when he visited Istanbul in 1898 at a time when no other European sovereign would have met Abdülhamid II the "Red (bloody) Sultan";[7] The visit elicited an "expression of admiration for the Kaiser's truly religious spirit and his deep understanding of the meaning of religion."[8]

For these reasons in 1880 the Sultan approached the German ambassador through his French military *aide de camp,* Colonel Dreysée, requesting German military advisers. It took two years of negotiations and an Ottoman delegation to Berlin at the end of 1881 before Bismarck consented to send a military mission. Although he told the Ottomans that he needed the time to select the most qualified officers, he was really occupied by diplomatic concerns with Austria-Hungary. Finally, in March 1882, the contracts were signed; and in May the first military contingent arrived.[9]

Its most famous member, Colmar Freiherr von der Goltz, commanded the German mission from 1885 to 1895.[10] Thereafter, von der Goltz returned to Turkey for short visits, was invited in 1909 by the Young Turks for more advice, and during World War I commanded the Sixth Army Corps at Baghdad, where he died in 1916. A steady stream of German advisors followed during the prewar decade, culminating in 1913 in the mission of General Otto Liman von Sanders wherein German advisors took command of selected Ottoman military units until the end of World War I.

German Interest in the Ottoman Empire

There had been German interest in the Ottoman Empire since the early part of the nineteenth century when German propagandists realized the potential for colonization and economic expansion in the East. Helmuth von Moltke, writing in the 1830s after his visit to Asia Minor, called the Ottoman Empire a "field for spoil."[11] After unification and victory over France in 1870, Germany, during the last part of the nineteenth century, sought to compete with the British and the French who had ready markets in their colonial empires. Germany, a new imperialist power, found in the Ottoman Empire an area unclaimed by her rivals and a suitable alternative to British interests in Egypt and India.

Foreign policy toward the Ottoman Empire changed dramatically from the Bismarck era to World War I. Bismarck's policy was one of consolidation of German power in Europe with observation and mediation abroad, building German prestige in 1878, for example, as intermediary at the Congress of Berlin. He consented reluctantly to the German military mission in 1882, and then only as insurance against Russia.[12] But by 1890 the Iron Chancellor had resigned over a foreign policy dispute with Kaiser Wilhelm II who encouraged the army to foster a new policy of energetic imperialism. In it, the German military missions in the Ottoman Empire were direct tools for the achievement of attempted German domination of the Ottomans. As the goals of the new German policy were expanded from merely economic exploitation to cultural manipulation and eventually direct control of Turkish foreign policy before the outbreak of World War I, the German officers and diplomats in Istanbul also worked toward these ends.

Their work was complemented by the writings of the conservative intellectuals who dominated the history and politics chairs at the prestigious German universities, expressing their views after 1896 in the *Preussiche Jahrbücher,* one of the most important journals in Germany. One of the editors, Theodor Schiemann, an advocate of preventive war and since 1892 a historian at the University of Berlin, had previously lectured at the German War Academy where he was acquainted with senior Prussian army officers, was in almost daily contact with members of the General Staff, and had good relations with the Foreign Ministry. Also, as political editor of the *Kreuzzeitung,* which presented regular political commentaries, he reached and did much to shape the view of politically influential conservatives, aristocrats, soldiers, senior civil servants, and industrialists.[13]

He was the mentor of members of the German General Staff, one of whom, General Alfred von Waldersee, was a close friend of von der Goltz. Another, General Friedrich von Bernhardi, influenced von der Goltz's work.[14] Other advocates of *Weltpolitik* played important roles in Istanbul after 1896. Marschall von Bieberstein, in that year German Foreign Secretary, was sent to the Ottoman Empire in 1897 as German ambassador where he promoted German economic and political interests. His successor, Baron Hans von Wangenheim, spent the next twenty years cultivating the Ottomans and eventually helped to bring the Sublime Porte into World War I on the side of Germany.

This policy, which dominated German foreign affairs until the war, was propagated by the pan-Germanists and those among them advocating a Central European economic union, which stressed the union of all Germans not only for economic benefit but in order to oppose the pan-Slavic Russian menace. This was the first step. They then looked to German domination of Central Europe in cooperation with Austria-Hungary, and, finally, saw the Ottoman Empire as a candidate for colonization or economic penetration, or perfect for the establishment of a protectorate over Asia Minor. In a pamphlet published in 1896, *Germany's Claims to the Heirship of Turkey,* the pan-Germanists laid claim to the Ottoman Empire because of the lack of interest of the other powers and because the people of Anatolia and the nomad Arab tribes of Mesopotamia and Syria would not oppose a German occupation of their lands if "it were made clear to them that their country would largely benefit thereby."[15] For, having effected an occupation, the Germans could then restore those lands to their former prosperity and Mesopotamia would become Germany's India. German determination would ensure the prize; it could not fall into the hands of others.

Paul Rohrbach, one of the most outspoken supporters of the movement, linked economic interests with the idea of a cultural mission, calling for the "active participation of the German mind in the current reshaping of the world!"[16] To him, it was impractical physically to colonize Turkey. "We must endeavor," he wrote in 1912, "to make the German language and German science, and all of the great positive values of our energetic civilization . . . active forces for the regeneration of Turkey by transplanting them into Turkey."[17]

It became the mission of Germany to perpetuate its culture and promote it abroad: two of the pan-Germanic goals were to purify the German language and to educate children in the Germanic sense.[18] By the 1890s a combination of these views and those of de Gobineau, Darwin, Houston Stewart Chamberlain, and Paul de Lagarde, confirming the biological and cultural superiority of the Aryan race as exemplified by Prussia *qua* Germany held sway among conservative circles in the military and foreign ministry, and were promoted by the Kaiser himself. To them, Germany's choice was either to dominate or to wither away; and domination meant economic, cultural, and political domination, even if it required preventive war.

Where Germany saw Asia Minor in Abdülhamid II's time as a field for economic exploitation, after 1908 and the Young Turk revolution, pan-Germanists realized cultural affinities between the two nations, and Turkey was considered a cultural satellite ripe for ideological manipulation as well. The Turkish inhabitants of Asia Minor "are largely . . . Asians and Indo-Germans," wrote Rohrbach in 1912; "the Turk is of strong military instincts and a soldierly mind." There are even some related traits between the Turkish and the German character, he continued, for did not von Moltke consider that the "Turk is the Gentleman of the East?"[19]

Rohrbach maintained that cultural transmission required a system of German schools and a cultural exchange program enabling Turkish journalists, soldiers, and bureaucrats to experience the superiority and progress of Germany. And, above all, the German impact had to be felt in the army. Baron Hans von Wangenheim, ambassador at Istanbul before World War I, saw control of the army as a means to retain a pro-German government in power. In addition, he thought that Germany would have "unbounded opportunity to imbue the Turkish people with the German spirit," if Germany were entrusted with the reform of education in Turkey as well.[20]

Wilhelm II reiterated this theme at a secret farewell audience in December 1913 to the departing Liman von Sanders mission. Of primary importance was the "Germanization of the Turkish army through [German] leadership and direct control of the organization of the Turkish Ministry of War." And, he con-

tinued, "it will be up to the mission's members to gain the sympathy of the Turkish soldiers and to create for me a strong new
army which obeys my orders." Finally, the Kaiser gave General
Otto Liman von Sanders, head of the new military mission, one
million marks annually to use as he wished (i.e., for bribes)
whereas the old military instructors had received 30,000 marks
at the most.[21]

The German Legacy: The Education of the Ottoman Officer Corps

The German military presence in the Ottoman Empire which
resulted from this confluence of interests achieved three con-
crete goals: First, it helped bring Turkey into World War I on the
side of Germany, a fact that both Ulrich Trumpener and Frank
Weber describe in intricate detail and that will not be elaborated
upon here. Second, the collaboration of the military mission
with German industry at home increased German involvement
in the Ottoman Empire, a situation analyzed thoroughly by
W. O. Henderson.[22] And third and most significant for this
study, the German military advisors reorganized and instituted a
system of military education on the German model which
trained over a generation of Ottoman officers and created a new
class in Ottoman society.

Before turning to the officer corps, however, a few
words on "defense contracts" should prove interesting as the
German military mission in the Ottoman Empire worked hand in
glove with the industrialists back home. By 1900 German en-
trepreneurs, expatriates, and investors were actively involved in
Istanbul. The Deutsche Palästina Bank had branches in Syria
and Palestine. German engineers found in Asia a wealth of met-
als, oils, and the capability of supplying German textile mills
with superior quality cotton, a granary for the expanding German population, and a promise for the development of a rich
market for German manufactured goods.[23]

More lucrative still were the military supply contracts which von der Goltz and his successors negotiated for Germany. In 1885 Krupp provided the Ottoman coastal defense works as the development of land forces was to take priority over the navy which Abdülhamid II allowed to deteriorate.[24] Then, in 1887, the German Mauser rifle was chosen to equip the entire regular and reserve forces of infantry and cavalry with over one-half million rifles. The Baghdad Railway Concession (1902), which allowed Germany to complete the Berlin to Baghdad Railway, was the culmination of these civilian and defense contracts.[25]

Both Abdülhamid II and von der Goltz gave priority to the creation of a new officers corps and the reform of military education in the interest of greater military effectiveness. Guided by different motives, the Sultan saw a younger, educated officer corps specifically loyal to him as a new type of Janissary corps which would ensure his security and would unite the diverse elements in the empire. He was fully aware of the fate of his predecessors: The Janissaries had mutinied when Sultan Selim II (1789–1807) tried to institute military reform and Mahmud II (1808–1839) was placed on the throne by provincial notables in exchange for increased local power. The problems of decentralization and nationalist uprisings within the empire led Abdülhamid II to the creation of his own loyal troops.[26] Nevertheless, wary of creating another potential threat to his regime, he instituted a spy system and morals lectures in the military academy to reinforce the cadets' gratitude for their Sultan's munificence: the schools were available to all as a consequence of the Recruitment Law of 1842; they were free and the best vehicle for social elevation within the empire.[27] But the rifles remained in their crates and practical maneuvers were kept to a bare minimum.

Von der Goltz, on the other hand, envisioned an officer corps trained and organized on the German model, namely an elite, homogeneous, unified group, albeit in this case drawn from the various ethnic and social groupings that made up the

Ottoman Empire. It would exist as a distinct social class and be the heart and soul of the army. The unity of its membership would not necessarily be through direct loyalty to the Sultan but rather through the sharing of common experience and profession.[28] Having common interests and common duties, the whole body would render itself responsible to each individual member. Thus, Iraqis who passed through the Ottoman military system maintained a bond even though they fought on different sides during World War I. Yasin al-Hashimi, for example, who had served with the Turks and was wounded in the fighting in Palestine, was rescued by Nuri al-Sa'id, who was fighting with the British, not only because Yasin was an Iraqi but because they were comrades-in-arms from the military academy.[29]

There is evidence that attendance at distinctive secondary schools was the most influential experience for many who later achieved political power in the Middle East. The shared schooling and experience, the friendships made during this period lasted into adulthood and determined the circle of persons with whom classmates stayed in contact throughout the remainder of their lives. P. J. Vatikiotis has written of such bonds for the Egyptian officers and M. van Dusen has found similar links in Syria as has Frederick Frey for Turkey.[30]

In interwar Iraq, these allegiances were even more pronounced as the Sunni officers, who returned to rule the country, filled civilian and military posts in the bureaucracy and government. Nine of the fourteen prime ministers from 1921 to 1932 were former Ottoman military officers as were thirty-two out of fifty-six major cabinet members.[31] And by 1936, among the Iraqi army officers holding posts of Commander and above in the new Iraqi army, fifty out of sixty-one were ex-Ottoman officers who received their education in Istanbul.[32]

In his reform of Ottoman military education, von der Goltz drew upon his own experience. The German model on which the Ottoman officer corps was based was a product of Prussian military education. Its role in Wilhelmian Germany was to preserve the established order, to uphold the authority of the Kaiser against any demands for democratization, and to be a

"School for the Nation": that is, to educate the German people to be loyal subjects of an authoritarian monarchical state. The army led by the officer corps was the unifying factor in the new Imperial Germany.[33]

Thus, in Germany, the military and especially the officer became the model for society. The bourgeoisie copied his style and the *nouveaux riches* tried to enter the ranks of the officer corps. When, by the turn of the century, it was feared that not enough aristocrats were entering the military, members of the middle class were allowed to begin the process; but they were rarely admitted to the General Staff, the great bastion of Prussian values and pan-German ideals. Standards, however, were never relaxed and everyone had to conform to the ideals and values of the corps.[34]

The military tried to limit the influx of non-aristocrats by developing the theory that character in an officer mattered more than intellect, because character was essentially an aristocratic virtue, whereas intellect was the mark of the "bourgeois." Too much intelligence was a bad thing for an officer, von der Goltz stressed, because it could lead to doubt and hesitation in giving an order. Heart and character should be the decisive criteria in selecting officers, not intellect or scientific achievement. In *Nation in Arms*, which he wrote in 1883, the same year he went to Turkey, and which was translated into some twelve languages including Turkish, von der Goltz repeated his view of the dichotomy of society and complained that the weakening of the aristocratic elements in the army would reduce the distinction between the officers and men and thus undermine military efficiency.[35]

This emphasis on the distinction between ruler and the ruled in Prussian society was also a basic tenet in the *Weltanschauung* of the German ambassador to Turkey during the prewar decade, Baron Hans von Wangenheim, here described just before World War I by Henry Morgenthau, United States ambassador at Istanbul:

Wangenheim divided mankind into two classes, the governing

and the governed; and he ridiculed the idea that the upper could ever be recruited from the lower. I recall with what unction and enthusiasm he used to describe the Emperor's caste organization of German estates; how he had made them non-transferable, and had even arranged it so that the possessors, or the prospective possessors, could not marry without the imperial consent. "In this way," Wangenheim would say, "we keep our governing classes pure, unmixed blood." Like all of his social order, Wangenheim worshipped the Prussian military system; his splendid bearing showed that he had himself served in the army, and in true German fashion, he regarded practically every situation in life from a military standpoint.[36]

Wangenheim's views were similar to those of von der Goltz. Considered the "Fatherland's greatest living soldier" in 1913 after he had been active in the military for most of his life, von der Goltz was appointed to head the newly created "Young Germany League," a youth movement designed to counteract the anti-militarist propaganda of the Social Democrats. His selection to the post was in recognition of his embodiment of the militarist spirit. In his German history of the nineteenth century he wrote that arms and war were the only source of German greatness. "Only so long as the cultivation of the warlike spirit keeps pace with general cultural development has a nation been able to maintain its place in history." His enduring support of the Turks despite their defeat during the Balkan Wars lasted because von der Goltz maintained that they had not abandoned faith in the inborn military virtues of Islam.[37]

Education was the key to the creation of the new Ottoman officer corps. Although a military academy had existed in Istanbul since 1834, there were few graduates and the entering students were ill-prepared. Most of the officers in the Ottoman army rose through the ranks; many were illiterate and reached their positions through patronage. In 1884 the total number of active officers was 9,810, while estimates of the total officer corps including reserve officers ranged up to 30,000.[38] Upon his arrival, therefore, von der Goltz began the process of

molding a new officer corps by increasing the number of pre-
paratory schools throughout the empire on three levels. Realiz-
ing the need for a system of primary schools to develop officer
potential, he modified the *rüşdiye* schools on the model of the
German cadet school which educated the child from ages eight
to ten. These were completely secular schools, directly under
the control of the German Staff and staffed entirely by military
officers. Instruction was in Turkish, not French as had previously
been the case. Entering students were required to have some
background in arithmetic and reading and for those who did not
know Turkish, an extra year was required to catch up. Discipline
was rigid.[39] In 1893 the army opened twenty-one new *rüşdiye*
schools, including schools in Baghdad, Tripoli, Damascus, and
Beirut. By 1911 there were twenty-two schools, all of them
exposing students to science as well as the traditional Ottoman
curriculum.

The *idadiye* or intermediate school came under the
jurisdiction of the local *ordu* (military division) commander and
was located in the provincial capital: Istanbul, Adrianople,
Manastir, Bursa, Erzerum, Damascus, and Baghdad. If there was
no school in his area, the promising student was sent directly to
Istanbul to attend a military school there. The course of study
lasted three years. By the time the cadet reached the *Harbiye*
(military academy) in the capital, he had studied one Western
language in addition to Turkish, some Arabic and Persian, as
well as scientific subjects.[40]

Soon after his arrival in Istanbul, von der Goltz took
personal control of the *Harbiye*. His goal was quality not quantity, and so from 1884 to 1889 the officer corps grew from some
10,000 to just over 18,000 in number. More significantly, however, the percentage of military college graduates in the entire
officer corps increased from 10 to 25 percent. *Harbiye* graduates
were studying German or Russian in addition to French, courses
in the history of war, weapons, military organization, strategy,
tactics, and military literature.[41] More and more officers were
sent to study in Germany rather than France, beginning with ten
officers sent to train with German military units in 1883.[42]

The German Legacy: Cultural Nationalism

During the nineteenth century, the Ottoman Empire was assaulted ideologically as well as militarily. Religion, the traditional focus of loyalty, was giving way to secular nationalism. As primarily Christian provinces, notably Greece (1821–1830) and the Balkan territories, revolted against the empire fighting for nationalist independence, the Ottomans reacted. Abdülhamid II fostered pan-Islamism—the union of all Muslims under the aegis of the Sultan/Caliph; the Young Ottomans advocated the equality of all groups within the empire; and Turkish nationalists promoted Turkification, imposing the Turkish language and culture on all peoples in an effort to safeguard what remained of a crumbling empire.

Like military reform, these attempted solutions were drawn from the West. By the latter part of the nineteenth century, various strains of nationalist thought had developed in Europe. Britain and France represented the liberal model, which assumed the existence of a state and emphasized political reform based upon individual liberty. French nationalism as defined by Renan's famous essay *Que est ce-qu'une nation?* (1882) stressed rational choice. There were no emotional, cultural, or biological determinants for nationalism; it was an individual's choice to reside in a particular entity whose inhabitants had formed themselves into a homogeneous group. Germany and the Central European countries, which did not have well-developed indigenous middle classes, turned to cultural nationalism, in part as a reaction to the West—the Romantics set out to prove a superior undiluted cultural heritage; and in part as a national liberation movement, in the case of Germany specifically, directed against the Napoleonic Wars of "liberation"/occupation. Orienting themselves to the glories of the past and emphasizing language and history, the Germans and later the Italians began the struggles for national unification and political hegemony which succeeded, despite, in Germany's case, the setback of World War I, in challenging England and France during the 1930s.

These ideas penetrated the Ottoman Empire during the period of Western imposed fiscal and political reform in the mid-nineteenth century known as the Tanzimat. In addition to decreeing equal opportunity, equal taxation, and compulsory military service for all ethnic and communal groups throughout the empire, the Sultan instituted a system of secular education for the civilian bureaucracy as well as for the military. Students were sent to Europe to study, in particular to France, where they imbibed the works of the Western Enlightenment which emphasized individual dignity, the limitation of the power of government, and secure civic rights. The apparent concomitant of these ideals was participatory democracy on the British and the French models.[43] Thus, the first group of Ottoman nationalists, the Young Ottomans and their successors within the civilian bureaucracy, advocated democratic reform within the framework of the Ottoman Empire, not its dissolution into ethnically based components.[44]

In the military, German direction of Ottoman education was complemented by the shift from "Ottoman" to "Turkish" historical study. Influenced by the Romantic "pan" nationalists of Germany, Central Europe, and Russia, whose nationalism emphasized the cultural rather than the political nationalism of the earlier Liberal thinkers, Turkish historiography became the means for discussion of Turkish nationalism in a society where the discussion of politics was interdicted. Turkish history began, after 1877, to emphasize the early Turkish and pre-Islamic Turkish antecedents, relegating Arab and Persian contributions to Ottoman culture to limited roles. Before then, the texts published for the *rüşdiye* did not mention the Turkish ancestry of the Ottomans, but afterward practically all of the texts emphasized that the ancestors of the Ottomans were from "Turkish tribes of Central Asia."[45] One history, written for the military schools at the turn of the century, identifies the Turks as the fathers of the Ottomans, Tatars, and Mongols. It also relates that the Huns and Scythians who had migrated to Europe in early times were Turks. In his history of the Turks, written about 1900, Necib Asim, graduate of the *Harbiye* and teacher there and in various military schools, stressed that the wars of the Turks were in self-defense, were fought in order to spread civilization, and were successful in that they allowed the Turks to remain in their original homeland despite constant attacks by their neighbors from which they always emerged victorious.[46]

Emphasis was now on racial traits and philology even more than on the Islamic faith. Turkish replaced French as the language of instruction in the schools and Arabic and Persian words were purged from the language in attempts to purify Ottoman Turkish and enrich it with additions from Chagatay and other Central Asian Turkish languages. Authors used studies by European Orientalists on the racial kinship between Aryans and Turks, and newspapers underlined the virtues of the Turks through frequent comparisons with Europeans, both as a mechanism for self-defense and for self-glorification. While pointing out Turkish military qualities, they were also eager to demonstrate that the Turk was not the "bloodthirsty creature" he was depicted to be.[47] In a society, then, where politics and discussions of revolution were prohibited, the military student studied military and cultural superiority as well as the Turkish Aryan kinship.

Some of these ideas were later incorporated into the nationalist philosophy of Ziya Gökalp, the theoretician of Turkish nationalism. Although the recipient of a military secondary education, Gökalp did not read German; but the ideas of Fichte, Hegel, Treitschke, and others appear in his works, having reached him through French translation. Gökalp rejected the idea of racial purity, but he was attracted by the similar problems that faced Germany in the nineteenth century and Turkey in the twentieth, namely ethnic unity and industrialization/modernization. And like a number of Ottoman writers in the nineteenth century, he was attracted by the Romantic nationalism which caused him to look to Turkish rather than to Islamic roots. Both he and his military protégé, Mustafa Kemal, looked to the concept of an elite which would educate the nation in the new Turkish nationalism, a variation of von der Goltz's "School for the Nation." Although Atatürk criticized Germany and German military advice during the war, one can detect a nexus in the concepts of the "Leader" and the elite pulling the nation into the twentieth century. Under Mustafa Kemal Atatürk's direction, Turkey underwent a massive cultural transformation: it was changed from the center of an Islamic Ottoman multi-ethnic empire into a Western secular Turkish state.[48]

The Officers in Politics

Some European observers of the Ottoman scene writing immediately after the Young Turk coup in 1908 claimed that the German legacy was negligible. From the German side, very few of the officers got along well with the Turks. Except for von der Goltz, Turkish admiration for whom persists to this day, the Germans, who did not understand their Turkish students and did not speak Turkish, taught through interpretors.[49] After the Balkan Wars, some even questioned the Turks as *Herrenvolk*. By the time General Otto Liman von Sanders arrived in 1913, confusion over his status and command of the mission and resentment by some Turkish officers of the German presence led to in-fighting not only between the Turks and the Germans but among the Germans themselves.[50]

There were reports that the German mission and Sultan Abdülhamid II were working at cross-purposes, resulting in illusory military reform. The Sultan, it was said, wanted a paper army "to throw dust in the eyes of Europe and his own people."[51] His spies interrupted lectures, seizing illustrative maps that just happened to depict the royal palace;[52] and, the prevention of practical maneuvers thwarted any progress in military reform. Von der Goltz himself considered the Sultan to be the chief impediment to military modernization. The result of Ottoman interference, one observer of the Turkish army wrote in 1907, was the complete absence of true cohesion, of an *esprit de corps* in the Imperial Army.[53]

Wilhelm II, however, saw the situation in a different light. In marginal notes on a diplomatic dispatch in 1908, he wrote that there was a direct German influence in the Young Turk revolution which overthrew Abdülhamid II. Crediting the revolt to the "German officers" educated in Germany, the Kaiser called them absolutely Germanophile.[54] In truth, however, the German officers training the Turks had no knowledge of nor were they accomplices in the first military coup in the Middle East in the twentieth century.

Nonetheless, historians writing on the period do perceive a direct link between the creation of an elite officer corps and the 1908 coup. Bearing in mind that the Ottoman army consisted of three groups: the rank and file of mostly illiterate recruits who could be swayed at any moment by the propaganda of a demagogue; senior officers who were loyal to the Sultan and determined to create an army free of politics; and the young junior officers who were the men trained in the military schools, one can see that this last group formed the most cohesive unit.[55] Its *esprit de corps,* inculcated from the time the officers were cadets, "furnished an essential prerequisite of political organization."[56] Abdülhamid II's policy of dispersing the young officers throughout the empire only strengthened their bonds and increased the nationalist sentiment they illegally acquired at home. Those assigned to the Balkans were especially vulnerable, as they were not only in contact with the nationalist aspirations of the Ottoman Empire's non-Turkish minorities but with Austro-Hungarian officers as well. For Turks such as Mustafa Kemal, who was stationed with the Third Army in Macedonia, constant mingling with the Europeans produced both admiration and jealousy. The Turkish officers, ashamed of their shabby uniforms, low pay, and menial status under Abdülhamid II, were at once grateful for the Sultan's generosity in providing free education and despondent at the slow pace of their education and military reform.[57] Thus, with the Western techniques learned in the military schools, this group, and not the Turkish literati in Paris nor the civilian bureaucracy, perpetrated the first of the military revolts that led to the establishment of the Turkish state.

The officers who were responsible for the Ottoman pro-German policy throughout World War I were products of

German education. From 1908 onward, all of the Ministers of War were graduates of the military college, had studied in Germany, and were themselves responsible for maintaining German involvement in the Ottoman military. Ali Riza, a graduate of the military academy in 1885, spent three years in Germany, returning to Istanbul to teach at his *alma mater* before assuming his cabinet post after the revolution.[58] His successor, Mahmud Shawkat, an Iraqi and one of the most powerful men in the Ottoman Empire from 1909 to 1913, spent nine years in Germany after graduation from the military academy in 1882.[59] He, and not a successor, Enver, who is usually credited, was responsible for the Liman von Sanders military mission.[60] After Shawkat's assassination, Ahmed Izzat, another graduate of the *Harbiye* and German resident from 1891 to 1894, where he worked with Liman von Sanders, became Minister of War, succeeded in turn by the most "notorious" of all of the pro-German officers.[61] Glen Swanson, in an article on Enver, attributes German influence via the *Harbiye*, either through von der Goltz's *A Nation in Arms*, the Turkish edition of which was in the library's holdings, or more directly through his teacher von der Goltz's protégé, Pertev Demirhan.[62] Demirhan taught general staff duties, applied tactics, and military history at the general staff school. Enver graduated the *Harbiye* in 1902 and spent 1909 as military attaché in Berlin. He remained in power until the end of the war.[63]

Although German cultural propaganda also infiltrated the civilian sector, influences was predominantly in the army. By the turn of the century, the pan-Germans had established in Istanbul numerous cultural and educational facilities, promoting the use of the German language by the Turks. In well-to-do families some knowledge of German had become *de rigueur* and attendance by Turkish children in German schools grew from zero in 1892 to almost three hundred ten years later. German was largely taught in the medical and military schools, while Turkish physicians were educated in Germany and military officers were sent there to serve in the army.[64]

It must be mentioned that among the civilian bureaucrats certainly French and *lycée* education were predominant,[65] but among the military members of the Grand National Assembly of 1920, for example, almost one-half of the members knew German in addition to or instead of French.[66] And the impact of Germany was not lost among the Turks themselves. Kemal Karpat has remarked that although French influenced politics, literature, the arts, philosophy, and social habits, German influence was strongly felt in the army.[67] This view was confirmed by H. E. Allen, writing in the 1930s: "Germany's influence with Turkey's military class both before and during the World War naturally caused many officers who were important in the government to look at the West through German eyes."[68]

Iraq and Germany

Similarly, the Iraqis maintained what Bassam Tibi calls an "emotional Germanophilia."[69] Trained by the Germans, these officers, most of whom entered the new Iraqi officer corps or took up civilian posts after the creation of the kingdom of Iraq, comprised the new state's educated elite. Both the Ottoman empire, with its focus on Islam, and the Arab provinces as they had known them, no longer existed. Secularly educated, the officers and the ex-Ottoman bureaucrats who joined them, drew upon their Istanbul educational experience and subsequent wartime events in order to devise their own ideology. Like their Turkish colleagues, they too turned to Germany as a model. For unlike the British and the French who deceived the Arabs during the war, the Germans neither colonized nor occupied the Middle East, nor were they responsible for the fragmentation of the area.

The Arabs had begun the process of politicization under Ottoman rule, becoming more activist in direct response to the Young Turks' policy of increasing Turkification of the Ottoman empire. The ideological underpinnings of what was later to become pan-Arabism was provided by Sati' al-Husri, who used Germany for his ideological paradigm just as the officers did for their political and military model.

Before 1908, Iraqis studying at the Istanbul *Harbiye* were comfortable in the Ottoman milieu. As Iraqi Sunni Arabs under Ottoman suzerainty for more than three hundred years, they had become acclimatized, accepting the spiritual and temporal leadership of the Ottoman sultan, looking to such Iraqis as Mahmud Shawkat, who had attained a high position in the Ottoman establishment, as an ideal example of upward mobility. They appreciated the opportunity to study in cosmopolitan Istanbul, a center of intellectual ferment despite the omniscient imperial espionage system.

Like the Turks, they were impressed with the technical and military education disseminated by their German teachers, by the General Staff system they instituted, which instilled order and respect for efficiency by elevating the methods of war to the level of a science, once again creating the possibility of Muslim military ascendance. And the Iraqis read von der Goltz's *The Nation in Arms* which influenced their thinking about the role of the army and education in society.

But they read other things as well. Like the Turks, the Arab students secretly read the works of Namik Kemal, the Ottoman Liberal, and they joined the Arab-Ottoman brotherhood societies which advocated equality for all members of the Ottoman Empire. In addition, 'Ali Jawdat, Iraqi prime minister in 1934, tells us he also read the books by 'Abd al-Haqq Hamid, who wrote in Turkish but who told the exciting tales of Arab heroes and of the Arab conquest of Spain. These stories awakened 'Ali Jawdat's Arab consciousness. He began to question Ottoman discrimination against the Arabs in the Ottoman Empire, and he found new respect and admiration for the Arabic language and Arab culture.[70]

The Young Turks' policy of imposing the Turkish language and culture on the Arabs, however, was a turning point in Arab-Ottoman relations. It, more than anything else, sparked the development of an antidote to Turkism; namely, Arab nationalism.

There had been cultural glimmerings of an incipient Arab nationalism as early as the end of the nineteenth century when such Syrian Christians as Faris al-Shidyak (1804–1887) and Butrus al-Bustani (1819–1885), influenced by Western cultural encroachments in the Levant after Egyptian viceroy Isma'il's conquest of the Syrian coast and his liberalization policy, revived Arab interest in the Arabic language and in Arab history. Then in anticipation of the later Arab secularist movements, the religious reformer Abd al-Rahman al-Kawakibi (1849–1903) advocated Arab cultural supremacy and the emergence of a spiritual caliphate which would remove the Ottoman usurpation of Islam.[71]

In Iraq, the poets Ma'ruf al-Rusafi (1875–1945) and Jamil al-Zahawi (1863–1936) criticized Hamidian injustices while remaining loyal Ottoman subjects. When the Young Turk revolt occurred, therefore, Iraqis saw the new regime as one of reform. Branches of the Turkish Committee of Union and Progress (CUP) were founded first in Basra by an Iraqi colonel in the Ottoman army, Rashid al-Khuja, and later in Baghdad and in Mosul. They sponsored meetings, lectures, and a daily Arabic-Turkish newspaper, *Baghdad*.[72]

But once the Turanists, who advocated the union of Turkish-speaking peoples, took control of Turkish policy, the Iraqi literati and the army officers began to reconsider their allegiances.[73] Some, like Mahmud Shawkat, served the regime, while others tried to accommodate Arab-Turkish interests. They resigned from the CUP to form in 1911 the more liberal Hizb al-Hurriyeh wa al-Itilaf (Party of Freedom and Cooperation) which worked for the equality of all Ottoman subjects. Iraqis returning from Istanbul established similar organizations in Iraq. Talib al-Naqib of Basra, a local notable, founded his own group under the same name. Composed of lawyers, traders, small landowners, and a few army officers, the party was widely recognized in souther Iraq and sent seven representatives to the 1913 session of the Ottoman parliament. The session never met; nevertheless, the numbers so startled the Turks that they decided to negotiate reform. Talib al-Naqib dissolved his party and formed the al-Jam'iyah al-Islahiyya (Reform Committee) in order to cooperate with the authorities. He demanded, however, that the government appointed administrator be an Iraqi native, that Arabic be the official language in all government departments and courts, and that all arts and sciences be taught in Arabic in the schools. The reform committee in Baghdad went even further. Formed in 1912, publishing a newspaper *Bayna al-Nahrayn* (Mesopotamia), it attacked the CUP for its Turanic policy and its unfriendly attitude towards the Arabs.

These liberals joined with the Paris based al-Fatat (Youth)—a Young Italy kind of movement which advocated Arab participation in an empire similar to the Austro-Hungarian—to hold an Arab Congress in 1913. It stressed Arab rights within the Ottoman Empire. Like the civilian Ottoman and Turkish reform groups before them, the Arab intellectuals in Paris included very few army officers and military cadets.

The career army men tended to join the short-lived secret societies for the spread of Arab identity and culture which emerged in Istanbul and were quickly suppressed by the government. These groups gradually became more nationalistic as their predecessors were dissolved, and included the al-Ikha al-'Arabi al-Uthmani (1908) (Arab-Ottoman Brotherhood), and al-Nadi al-'Adabi (1909) (Literary Club) for the spread of Arabic literature al-Qahtaniyya (1909), and the al-'Alam al-Akhdar (1912) (The Green Banner), which worked to strengthen national ties among Arab students. When the Green Banner was disbanded, its members, primarily medical students, formed the extremist al-Yad al-Sawda (1913) (The Black Hand). It too dissolved; but not because of government pressure. Its members could not decide which method of assassination to use in carrying out their objective: the "murder of treacherous statesmen who opposed Arab nationalism."[74]

The most important of these secret societies, al-'Ahd (October 1913) (The Covenant), was formed just before World War I. Not only did it regroup after the war, but the majority of its founders and members were Iraqi officers stationed in Istanbul who subsequently returned to Iraq with Faysal to rule the country. It was said that some 315 out of the total of 490 Arab officers stationed in Istanbul joined the al-'Ahd.[75] Founded by a charismatic Egyptian, 'Azziz 'Ali al-Misri, and twenty-five army officers, fourteen of them Iraqis,[76] the group advocated a dual Arab-Turkish monarchy while really working for Arab autonomy within the Ottoman Empire. Four months after its inception, the group was disbanded by the Turks who transferred all Arab officers stationed in the capital to European and Anatolian provinces, placed Turkish commanders in the Arab areas, abolished all Arab parties, and increased CUP propaganda in the Arab provinces. These measures did not prevent Taha al-Hashimi, one of the original members, from carrying the program with him on his travels where he created al-'Ahd cells in Syria and in Iraq.[77]

World War I and Faysal's rule in Syria provided the opportunity for the realization of Arab autonomy. For almost two years after their victorious march to Damascus in 1918, Faysal and his provisional government, composed of army officers and ex-Ottoman bureaucrats, ruled Syria in anticipation of an imperial kingdom governing the Fertile Crescent and Arabia. During these halcyon days of Arab independence, many Arabs who had previously been active in Ottoman life were drawn to Syria and to a new identity, where they had to make the ideological transition from Ottomanism to Arabism. One, who became the ideological theoretician of the pan-Arab movement, was Sati' al-Husri.

Sati' al-Husri (1882–1968) modified his name to Abu Khaldun Sati' al-Husri in order to connote his conversion to Arabism.[78] From a well-established commercial Aleppan family, his father was an Ottoman civil servant who was frequently transferred throughout the Ottoman Empire. The family traveled and al-Husri studied at home, never receiving the traditional religious (*madrasah*) education. Turkish was his first language and he later learned French and Arabic, acquiring the latter and actively using it when he was somewhat into middle age. He liked the natural sciences and mathematics, teaching those subjects and writings textbooks for use in Ottoman schools. Al-Husri graduated from the *Mulkiye Mektebi* in Istanbul—the school for Ottoman bureaucrats.

By 1908 Sati' al-Husri was recognized as one of the

most influential educators in the Ottoman Empire, having spent eight years teaching and working as an administrator in the Balkans. While there he became aware of nationalism and was impressed by the importance Balkan nationalists placed upon language, especially the use of a national language in education. It is because of his later writings on Arab nationalism that Sati' al-Husri is renowned today. He began this work after completing much of a full career in Ottoman service.

Al-Husri left Turkey in 1919 to join Faysal in Damascus. He had spent the war in Istanbul. William Cleveland, his biographer, asked al-Husri why he left Turkey to join the Arabs and al-Husri replied that "he was an Arab and that when the Arabs separated from the Ottoman Empire, he had no choice but to join them."[79] He spent the rest of his life working out a theory of Arab nationalism and implementing that theory via education.

Although he had studied in France, al-Husri rejected French theories of nationalism for both personal and practical reasons. He acquired a profound dislike for the French after his experience in negotiating for Faysal with General Gouraud in March 1920 and after the ensuing catastrophe at Maysalun, when French troops drove Faysal and his followers from Syria.[80] The liberation of Arab areas from the French, and later the British, was to be a central theme in his concept of nationalism. But even more, al-Husri could not accept the French nationalist concept that the existence of a nation was predicated upon the existence of a specific state, for the Arabs had no state of their own. Nevertheless, to al-Husri, they were a nation. Therefore, German nationalism—with its differentiation between the nation and the state, the cultural being distinct from the legal or the mechanical entity—became his model, the lack of a state now being irrelevant.

But how did one define an Arab? Before the dissolution of the Ottoman Empire, it was not necessary to define one's focus of loyalty. For Muslims it was the Ottoman sultan/caliph who assumed the dual function of head of the secular state and religious leader of the Muslims. Non-Muslims had local communal allegiances, paying taxes to the central government, whatever it was. Now, however, with an Arab entity encompassing former Ottoman territory, with secular nationalism replacing former communal allegiances, new foci were required as substitutes for religion. Here again, German history inspired. For before 1871 Germany had undergone the transformation of uniting multifaceted entities into one united whole, a process similar to the one the Arabs would have to undergo in order to reunite.

For his own theory, al-Husri drew upon the works of the German Romantics, specifically those of Herder, Fichte, and Ernst Moritz Arndt, which he combined with the concept of "solidarity" between groups or the concepts of 'asabiyyah of the fourteenth-century Arab historian philosopher Ibn Khaldun.[81] They emphasized language and history as the integral components of national identity. For Herder a state was unimportant—a national language transmitted culture; it was the intellect of the nation and the means through which political power could be exercised. But Herder did recognize that "people, nation, and nationality are synonymous, describing a group of people with a common language, and a common heritage which constitute a national history." Fichte, with his call for unity and liberation from the foreign oppressor, made the state the focus for loyalty, and Arndt gave the nation exclusivity.

In short, al-Husri asserted:

A common language and a common history is the basis of nation formation and nationalism. The union of these two spheres leads to a union of emotions and aims, sufferings, hopes, and culture. Thus the members of one group see themselves as members of a unitary nation, which distinguishes itself from others. However neither religion nor the state nor a shared economic life are the basic elements of a nation, and nor is common territory. . . . If we want to define the role of language and history for a nation we can say in short that the language is the soul and the life of the nation, but history is its memory and its consciousness.[82]

That history was the history of the Arabs, not of Islam; for Islam's role in history was to spread Arabism, to help to preserve the

Arab identity of the Arabs. It played a subordinate role in the history of the Arabs which began in pre-Islamic Arabia and spread with the Islamic conquest throughout the Middle East and North Africa. Thus, Arabism—or the acceptance of Arabic culture and the history of the Arabs as the focus of loyalty despite one's religious belief—transcended religious and communal ties.[83]

To al-Husri, German nationalism, with its emphasis upon language and history as unifying factors, was the perfect model for Arab nationalism, even though al-Husri rejected all racial theories. He sought a leading Arab state like Germany's Prussia around which to reunite the Arabs. Later, after his exile from Iraq, al-Husri turned to Egypt; but, as Bassam Tibi notes, most of Sati' al-Husri's writings on nationalism, although published in book form after World War II, were composed first in Iraq where he worked as an educator from 1921 to 1941. While there he wrote articles and delivered speeches at the nationalist clubs and teachers college. Al-Husri and others promoted Iraq as the Prussia of the Middle East, causing an Egyptian writer—while Egypt was in the throes of the Pharoanism debate (local nationalism versus pan-Arabism)—to remark:

> We mean by "Husrism" the feeling that to labour for the sake of Arabism requires the adoption of an inimical stance towards non-Arab elements whether these elements are found within the Arab environment or outside it. This Husrism which we have seen in Iraq weakens the Iraqi entity itself since it looks upon the Kurds with some hatred, and does not desire closer relations with the Iranians or other Muslims who neighbour the territories of the Arabic-speaking peoples.[84]

Nevertheless, al-Husri worked in Iraq throughout the 1920s and 1930s to promulgate pan-Arabism via education and militarism.

German Activities in Iraq

In the 1930s Germany, and to a lesser degree, Italy, because of its expansionist policies in the area, became the role model for

Iraq as it had for the Turks before World War I. Iraqis were impressed with the strong leadership, the militarism, and the policy of reform from the top. In addition, they were inspired both by the resurgence of German power after defeat and the imposition of the Versailles treaty and by Germany's intimidation of the rest of Europe.[85] When Iraqi interest in Palestine actively emerged in the 1930s as a result of British acquiescence to increased Jewish immigration, there was admiration for Germany's anti-Jewish policy and even limited interest in forming a local Nazi party under the title of "National Defense League."[86] Needless to say, those Iraqis overlooked the German racial policy, which installed the Arabs just above the Jews in status, and the early Nazi policy of encouraging Jewish immigration to Palestine in order to solve the German problem. Sensing fertile ground for operations, the local German agents, recognizing the enduring Germanophile sentiment, especially in the Iraqi army, continued the German policy of active propaganda and cultural indoctrination, set in motion by the Kaiser more than three decades before.

German overtures to the Arabs in the 1930s reactivated a propaganda policy initiated during World War I.[87] A memorandum from the German Ministry of Propaganda, written in 1934,[88] for example, reiterated the old imperialist policy of cultural propaganda directed at the destruction of British influence in the Middle East, this despite subsequent protestations by the German Foreign Ministry that Germany had no interest in the area and that certainly as early as 1934 she was not in conflict with Britain. German propaganda policy emanated from more than one source: the propaganda ministry under Goebbels began its work immediately, mistrusting the diplomats, while on the official, diplomatic level, it was only late in 1940 that Germany expressed support for the Arab nationalist movement. And only in mid-1941 do we find generals Helmuth Felmy and Walter Warlimont concerned with the use of propaganda in order to achieve active Iraqi support for Germany.[89]

The memorandum stressed the importance of cultural influence and noted that only after this was achieved could political influence be considered. "In countries deserving of our interest and which are developing a special culture of their own," R. Kurt Kohler, one of the authors, writes:

> cultural propaganda does not, as all who are cognisant of the facts know, march parallel with economic propaganda, it actually precedes it. Is there any need to prove the fact that Yugoslavians, Bulgarians, Turks, and Egyptians who have been to German schools or who have at least taken German lessons or studied at a German university are less costly and far more influential propagandists than the whole army of representatives and agents for German pharmaceutical goods?

Only cultural ties constitute a "positive, sound and permanent foundation for propaganda in countries with which we desire to establish economic relations."[90]

    His methods are specific. Do not present German culture as one to be copied, he tells us. On the contrary, show interest in the history, the folklore, and the geography of the country and thus win the confidence of the people. Send German scientists there to work on archaeological digs; for a man with a pick and shovel is as important as the construction of the Berlin to Baghdad Railway. Open schools, institute German language courses, subsidize the local press, sell cheap books, and do not neglect the "social propaganda": "to draw the responsible persons of foreign countries into an atmosphere favourable to our interests, by means of competent individuals who do not hold an official post and who passes a high cultural level and a great capacity for self-adaptation a means which has unfortunately been most neglected by Germany." And, above all, he stresses, "draw to Germany the youth of foreign countries and assure that they go back with sweet unforgettable memories." Students do not wish only to study technical subjects in German universities, they look to the specialists there in their own history and culture.[91]

    The German Ministry of Propaganda, which oversaw all propaganda activities, had a special section on the Middle East; it controlled all political activities, links with universities, businesses, German institutions abroad, and diplomatic personnel, all of which were means to transmit German propaganda abroad.[92] By 1934 it could allocate some twenty million marks for publications in Arabic and Middle Eastern dialects, for subsidizing German schools abroad, for social and cultural attachés in German embassies, and for expense-paid visits to Germany by foreign writers and politicians. These were hosted and entertained by their German counterparts. In addition, there was a sudden increase in scholarly journals and university chairs devoted to Middle East studies.[93]

Italy and Germany, and to a lesser extent Japan, used radio broadcasting extensively. The Italians used Radio Bari to transmit programs to the Middle East beginning in 1934–1935 in preparation for the war against Ethiopia, combining poetry and music with anti-British propaganda. Italy was presented as the real power in the Middle East, while Britain was depicted as "decadent," as an imperialist oppressor, and was accused of committing atrocities in Palestine. In 1938, after a gentleman's agreement, Italian propaganda broadcasts ceased until the war and France's defeat when they resumed with increased frequency.[94]

By then however, the Germans dominated the airwaves. German radio broadcasting began gradually with newscasts beamed to the Middle East from a radio station at Zeesen, outside of Berlin. Arabic language broadcasts increased before the war, using Arab lectures in German universities and, later, well-known exiles from the Arab world.[95] Yunis al-Bahri, an Iraqi journalist and announcer for the official Baghdad Broadcasting Station, began to broadcast from Berlin from May 1939.[96] He, the Jerusalem Mufti, al-Hajj Amin al-Husayni and Rashid 'Ali al-Kaylani, who arrived in Berlin after the 1941 revolt in Iraq, supplied and disseminated Axis propaganda to Iraq and the rest of the Arab world.

The broadcasts emphasized British imperialism and weakness—and defeatism once the war began—German strength, support for pan-Arabism and Palestine, and the Jewish question. Thus, the British power was passé, its navy was "dilapidated," and Britain suffered tremendous casualties inflicted by Germany. It was Germany, the broadcasts emphasized, who was fighting the Arabs' real enemy—Britain, and Britain was dominated by the Zionists. Britain, in turn, promised the Zionists lands as far east as the Euphrates and planned the "Judaization of Palestine," permitting the land to be inhabited by the "enemies of Islam."[97] There is reason to believe," concludes Seth Arsenian in his study or wartime propaganda, "that Axis broadcasts—the German and Italian—were the more popular. Their highly colored, emotional programs, making the most of the common tastes and beliefs of the masses, providing music and entertainment, had greater appeal and were listened to more frequently in the coffee houses and other assembly places than were the allied offerings."[98] The British agreed. In 1942 British Intelligence concluded that 95 percent of the Iraqis were pro-German;[99] they tardily tried to institute counterpropaganda.

German agents on the scene began to play increasingly important roles. Dr. Fritz Grobba arrived in Baghdad in February 1932 to become Germany's representative to Iraq until he was expelled shortly after the outbreak of World War II. Fluent in Arabic and Turkish, Grobba knew the Middle East well and had served in Palestine under General Kress von Kressenstein during World War I. In 1921 he joined the Foreign Ministry, was posted to Kabul two years later, and then to Iraq and Saudi Arabia.[100]

Majid Khadduri maintains that Grobba was not a Nazi and that his loyalty to the Nazi regime was in doubt.[101] Lord Birdwood, Nuri al-Sa'id's biographer, mentions that in 1936 the German envoy quietly criticized Hitler to Nuri and soon after he was recalled to Germany, returning to Iraq nine months later "successfully brainwashed." By the end of 1938 Nuri realized how well Grobba was intriguing with the army officers in pursuance of German interests and wished to have him declared *persona non grata* and recalled. But the German government protested on the grounds of damage to German prestige, and the British were reluctant to arouse German sensitivies. Grobba did go on leave but returned before the outbreak of World War

II.[102] After the death in April 1939 of King Ghazi who succeeded King Faysal in 1933, Grobba's influence was thought to be such as to cause the Americans and the British to remark that Dr. Grobba had been directing all German propaganda not only in Iraq but throughout the Middle East.[103]

During his sojourn in Iraq, Grobba sensitive to Iraqi grievances against the British, used all of the methods outlined in Dr. Kohler's report in order to retain and expand the already Germanophile and Anglophobic sentiments in Iraq. To this end he cultivated the army officers, tried to negotiate German-Iraqi arms contracts—at times without his superiors' knowledge[104]—and, finally, with war imminent, Grobba tried to wean Iraq from her treaty obligations with Britain.

He was assisted by Dr. Amin Ruwayha, the physician to the German Legation, who acted as the link among the Axis, the Iraqi army officers, and the Jerusalem Mufti, and by Dr. Julius Jordan. Dr. Jordan, a German archaeologist, was employed by the Baghdad Museum and acted as the archaeological attaché to the German legation.[105] He was frequently invited to speak at the Higher Teachers Training College where he lectured both on archaeology and Nazism. Nuri al-Sa'id expelled him from Iraq in 1939 for inciting the students to anti-British activity after Ghazi's death.[106]

Soon after his arrival, Dr. Grobba—with the aid of his able wife—began to ingratiate himself with both the British and the Iraqis. Gerald de Gaury, British chargé d'affaires to the regent, called the couple "able and indefatigable,"[107] and Sir Maurice Peterson, British ambassador (1938–1939), writes that they made it a policy to be more British than the British: attending the hunt—they pursued jackals instead of foxes across the desert—and sitting next to Peterson in the English church. Frau Grobba visited the British sick, all the while passing on disparaging anti-British rumors to the Iraqis.[108] The Grobbas gave frequent parties at the legation, open not only to diplomats but to students and minor government officials, where they offered expensive cigars, Munich beer, and champagne.[109] They presented concerts and showed such films as "Deutschland Erwacht" and "Tag der nationalen Arbeit" which vividly portrayed the "strength, unanimity, and enthusiasm behind the Nazi movement in Germany."[110]

Both the Italians and the Germans generously awarded decorations to deserving Iraqis. In 1935 Ghazi received the highest award—the Star of the Order of the German Red Cross—from Germany and an automobile from Mussolini, and the next year various classifications of the Order of Honor of the German Red Cross were bestowed upon the secretary to King Ghazi, the Master of Ceremonies at the Royal Palace, and four officials in the Iraqi Foreign Office, in addition to educators Dr. Sami Shawkat and Dr. Muhammad Fadhil al-Jamali.[111]

The German legation distributed attractively illustrated books and pamphlets on request to students and to newspapers and supplied journalists with articles and photographs which were reproduced in the Iraqi press. It subsidized newspapers by promoting advertising by German and Italian companies and by outright grants. One paper, al-'Alam al-'Arabi, was said to be controlled by the legation. Publishing a daily anti-British column of "International Politics," it also serialized Mein Kampf in Arabic.[112]

Grobba sent journalists to the German Olympic games and lawyers and doctors on visits to Germany.[113] In 1937 the Director General of Education, Dr. Muhammad Fadhil al-Jamali, was invited by the German government to study education in Germany.

Special efforts were directed toward Iraqi youth. A German kindergarten was established in Baghdad for German and Iraqi children, and in 1936 German became the second foreign language studied in the Baghdad Central Secondary School, replacing French. The Germans who taught there had taken courses in the Deutsche Akademie in Munich which prepared teachers for cultural indoctrination. They spread Nazi propaganda in class and frequently taught private students without charge.[114] When the Iraqi Medical School was recognized by the Royal College in Edinburgh and London, Grobba tried to steer students to Germany for post-graduate study and offered the Iraqis a German technical school.[115] Peterson quickly got the British to make a counter offer. There was constant competition for students to be sent to Germany and to England; the Germans lowered standards for easy admission and in 1937 Jamali negotiated for a comparable British policy.[116]

Nevertheless, more and more students went to Germany. Taha al-Hashimi, when he was Director General of Education in 1935, sent some twenty students; and, although there were only some forty-three students studying in German during the ten years from 1929 to 1939, they returned to Iraq to important posts.[117] Five of them, known to be followers of Arab nationalist Darwish al-Miqdadi who had spent time in Germany working with Iraqi students there, denounced the British staff and disparaged the British equipment;[118] for, while in Germany, a British report tells us, students were subject to intensive propaganda. The Iraqi students were persuaded to join political societies organized by the Nazis and to participate in political activities which, although nominally inspired by Arab nationalist ideas, were in fact aimed at furthering German interests.[119]

The culmination of the youth-oriented propaganda occurred in December 1937. Baldur von Schirach, German Youth leader, visited Baghdad, Damascus, Tehran, and Ankara. Von Schirach told journalists in Damascus that German youth was interested in the activities of youth all over the world, especially in those countries which aspired for freedom. Germany wished to consolidate relations with these groups and to unite them with their Nazi counterparts. He emphasized the similarity between the pan-Arab renaissance and the German racial awakening which attempted to unite Germans from all over *Deutschtum*.[120] His visit to Baghdad resulted in an invitation to a group of Iraqi youth to attend the Nuremberg games the next year and in the formal institution of a movement similar to the Hitler Youth in Iraq.

Grobba, less of a Nazi propagandist and more sensitive to Arab nationalist, anti-British sentiments in the army, urged Germany to exploit this ideal opportunity. Arab friendship for Germany is "almost instinctive" he wrote in December 1937, after the installation of two sympathetic governments in Iraq. The Arabs remember the past, he told his superiors: Wilhelm II's speech at the grave of Salah al-Din in Damascus when the Kaiser declared Cermany's friendship for the Arabs, and the German-Turkish "brotherhood of arms," which is still active in the ruling classes of Iraq, Syria, and Palestine. More than twenty years later, Grobba writes, Germany is still the model for national unity; it has no colonial ambitions as does Italy, and the Feuhrer is highly respected. Grobba told Berlin that the Arabs already confide their secret plans to Germany, turn to Germany for arms and as an ally in their struggle for Palestine. "Even if Arab friendship towards Germany is determined above all by the Arab's own interest," he concludes, "it is an important factor for Germany, which we can make both political and economic use of."[121]

By this time Grobba had already begun to negotiate arms deals with Iraqi governments in contravention of Iraq's treaty with Britain, and it seems that he was certainly privy to, and may have had a hand in, the Bakr Sidqi coup of October 1936, which initiated military political activity in Iraq. H. H. Kopietz in his analysis of the German diplomatic documents, reports that both perpetrators, Hikmat Sulayman, who was Young Turk General Mahmud Shawkat's half-brother, and General Bakr Sidqi, an Ottoman military school graduate and Germanophile, were in constant contact with Grobba before the coup. Unlike the British who were totally surprised by the events in Baghdad, Grobba wrote to Berlin soon after the coup that Hikmat had confided "great sympathies for Germany" and that his government was inspired by the National Socialist ideology.[122]

Grobba worked diligently during the next two governments of prime ministers Hikmat Sulayman and Jamil al-Midfaʿi, and even confided that, had Nuri not been in power at the time, he could have influenced Iraq not to declare war on Germany. But when Nuri returned to Baghdad at the end of 1938, Grobba curtailed his activities. Nevertheless, he was credited with the spread of anti-British propaganda after Ghazi's death, which resulted in the incitement of a mob in Mosul and the death of the British consul G. E. A. C. Monck-Mason on April 5, 1939.

Ghazi, under the influence of alcohol, lost control of his car while driving at high speed on April 4, 1939. The car crashed into an electric pole, which fell on the king and fractured his skull. His two companions, who were in the back seat, died instantly and King Ghazi died soon after.

Dr. Harry C. Sinderson, the king's physician, and his colleague Dr. Noel Braham, attended the king, but Sinderson Pasha insisted that Dr. Saib Shawkat, an Iraqi colleague (brother of Dr. Sami Shawkat and an Arab nationalist) be present because, as Sinderson reveals, in his memoirs, "I was fearful lest, if no Iraqi doctor was in attendance, anglophobic mischief-makers might originate canards to the effect that Breham and I were responsible for the king's demise."[123] All three physicians signed the death certificate and the British left the car on display in order to convince people that the death was in truth accidental.[124] But the government's initial announcement was only that the king was dead; there was a delay in officially declaring it an accident, and rumors began to spread that the British killed the king. Sinderson reports that Grobba told the American minister Paul Knabenshue: "I hear that Sinderson did not let him live."[125]

The next day an excited mob, mostly students, marched on the British consulate in Mosul. There were anti-British speeches, and while he was attempting to explain the facts to the crowd, the British consul was fatally assaulted from behind with a pickax.

The British found anti-British and anti-Nuri leaflets on the scene and arrested several young men with typewritten handbills who were linked to the German legation and to Dr. Jordan, the "local agent of the Nazi party."[126] Peterson and de Gaury reported that the Germans incited the mob. Grobba, on the contrary, contends in his memoirs that Ghazi's death was a British plot to turn Iraqis against Germany, that the arrested students were really teachers and perhaps were not even German but Swiss, and that there was only one resident German in Mosul—a German-Jewish opthamologist who hated Hitler. He agreed with Sami Shawkat who claimed that there was no German propaganda and that the British and the Jews were trying to incite the Iraqis against the Germans.[127]

Nevertheless, the nationalists maintain to this day that Ghazi's death was not accidental and that both the British and Nuri conspired to kill the king because of his anti-British activities:[128] for example, using a radio transmitter in the palace to broadcast anti-British propaganda and to incite Iraqi designs on Kuwait. German propaganda made frequent use of the incident throughout World War II, especially on anniversaries of Ghazi's death. Radio broadcasters discussed "King Ghazi the Martyr" who died at the hands of the British because he opposed British actions in Iraq.[129] And Ghazi became the symbol of the pan-Arab movement which, by 1941, had turned once again to Germany, this despite the continuous British presence in Iraq since World War I.

For the British occupied Iraq and had reneged on their promises for an independent Arab state, a situation intolerable to the nationalists. Consequently, Germany, which had ties with the Iraqi officers dating back to World War I, was able to exploit Iraqi grievances over the British role in their country and in Palestine and attempted to wean Iraq from British influence. This process, resulting in the Rashid 'Ali coup of 1941, could be implemented only after the officers attained political power in Iraq. Their road to power, begun soon after the officers returned to Iraq in 1921, will be the subject of the next chapter.

III. The Officers in Iraq

The Iraqi Ottoman officers who joined the pre-World War I Arab nationalist societies in Istanbul advocated the revival of an Arab state whose unity was to be intact but whose borders were not clearly delineated. The sudden dismemberment and occupation of this area after World War I left the Iraqi officers with a piece of the territory—Iraq. While there were indigenous groups, notably the Shi'i tribes and a local intelligensia which had been working all the while for local control and the eviction of the British, they, by the mid-1920s, had lost all effective strength as a united political force and relinquished control of the country to the pan-Arab officers. With independence in 1932, the pan-Arabs turned from fighting the British and the treaty, which bound them in mutual alliance, to charting Iraq's role in the Arab world as the leader of a reunited Arab state.

Iraq and World War I

World War I caught the Arab nationalists without any coordinated plans. Except for 'Aziz 'Ali al-Misri, who had been tried and convicted by the Ottomans for bribery—camouflaging his true nationalist activities—and who escaped to Cairo, most of the officers began World War I fighting with the Ottoman Empire. Aziz 'Ali approached the British twice, offering Arab assistance, but he was rebuffed once because the Ottoman Empire was not yet a belligerent and Britain hoped to keep her neutral, and then because of the dissension in the British command which was to obfuscate postwar policy.[1] While British officers in Cairo favored an Arab uprising and had begun negotiations with the Hashimite Sharif of Mecca in 1915 supporting Arab proposals for an independent Arab state, the British officers of the India command opposed Arab control of Iraq. From their vantage point on the Persian Gulf, the British in India moved quickly during the fall of 1914 to invade Iraq, capture Basra, and promulgate the desire to annex all of Mesopotamia, thus precluding a Turkish-German *jihad,* which could stir up Muslims in India, Persia, and Afghanistan, and assuring British control of the gateway to the Persian Gulf and the oil which had begun trickling out of Abadan. These conflicting British policies—support for Arab nationalist aspirations versus direct British control of Mesopotamia—resulted in confusion and an indecisive British policy toward the status of Iraq providing Arab nationalists working in Iraq and Syria with five years to regroup and formulate their own plans.

The British began their conquest of Iraq without anticipated Arab support; for despite the premeditated Ottoman policy of destroying tribal authority by centralizing the Ottoman regime in Iraq, which they had begun at the end of the nineteenth century, the Turks now turned to these shaykhs with bribes and medals for support in a *jihad* against the Christian infidel. Shi'i and Sunni tribal leaders provided an estimated force of 11,000 to 18,000 tribesmen.[2] But their effect was marginal because as the British pushed north to defeat the Ottomans, first at Basra in November 1914 and then disastrously at Shu'aybah in April 1915, the tribesmen began to harrass the retreating Ottomans rather than the advancing British. Some Iraqi Ottoman officers who had begun the fight on the Turkish side, deserted to the British—notably, Mawlud Mukhlis, 'Ali Jawdat, and 'Abdullah al-Dulaymi. Nuri al-Sa'id had left Istanbul before the war, making his way from Cairo to Basra where he was captured by the British and sent on to India. Ja'far al-'Askari was captured in North Africa and Jamil al-Midfa'i escaped to British lines from Syria.[3]

Yasin al-Hashimi was a notable exception. Sent to Syria in command of an Iraqi division at the beginning of the war, he met Faysal and members of the Arab nationalist group al-Fatat in Syria during Faysal's recruiting visits there in March and May 1915; but he was not impressed with the son of the sharif of Mecca. He never joined the Hijaz campaign, but spent the rest of World War I fighting in Gallipoli, in Galicia against the Russians, and in Palestine. Wilhelm II decorated him for his admirable military career. Yasin, like many others, found himself with the Sharifians toward the end of the war, in his case because he was wounded during the fighting in Palestine and was rescued by fellow Iraqis.[4]

Initially, only some fifty Iraqi officers accompanied Faysal in 1915 on his campaign north to Syria from the Hijaz in what came to be known as the Arab Revolt.[5] Many joined involuntarily. The British recruited Faysal's soldiers from the prisoner-of-war camps in India, requesting that the India command send the Arab prisoners to the Hijaz, which they began to do in 1916.[6] Many Iraqis were not informed of their destination nor were they given advance briefing, so that of the 132 prisoners who arrived in June 1916, for example, 102 officers and soldiers refused to fight the Turks; of the eleven officers, only three joined the Sharifians.[7] After the fall of Baghdad and the ensuing British occupation, more Iraqis joined the Sharifians, swelling their numbers to 190 according to the British, and causing Husayn to condition their acceptance by 1917 upon political and military suitability. By August 1917 most of the Sharifian officers were Iraqis and former al-'Ahd members.[8]

Like the war, the armistice of October 1918 left the Iraqis in a quandary. The British occupied Mesopotamia and began to cultivate the support of the local tribal shaykhs, the landlords, and the non-Muslim minorities, placing them and Indian immigrants in the newly installed bureaucracy, but never delineating Iraq's postwar fate. Ignoring the ex-Ottoman civil servants ("efendis") and the army officers, the British left them unemployed and susceptible to the pan-Arab propaganda emanating from Damascus, which was now independent and in Arab hands. The officers joined the Hashimites, and the "efendis" had imposed leisure to consider alternatives to British rule.[9]

At first, the British, especially under Sir Arnold Wilson, who was Acting Civil Commissioner from April 1918 to October 1920 while Sir Percy Cox served in Persia,[10] considered making Mesopotamia a British protectorate like Egypt, to be an adjunct of India staffed by Indian immigrants in reward for their service in the war. Cox had wanted an Arab façade, but Wilson swamped the Foreign Office with correspondence advocating his policies. The country had rich agricultural and mineral potential and was strategically important. To Wilson, an imperialist of the old school, Britain's duty lay in the spread of Christian civilization in the East, and as the Arabs were not capable of ruling themselves, His Majesty's Government was charged to instruct them. Wilson's ideas conflicted with the pro-Arab British officers in Cairo, who were similarly inundating London with proposals to fashion some sort of self-rule for the Arabs. International events and pan-Arab activity in Syria ultimately swung London by the fall of 1919 to Cairo's view.

With Russia's withdrawal from the conflict and the publication of wartime secret agreements after the Russian Revolution, and the declaration of U.S. President Woodrow Wilson's Fourteen Points, which emphasized independence for the former territories of the defeated Ottoman Empire, the Arabs felt deceived by the British but hopeful of beneficial effects from American pressure. The Anglo-French Declaration of November 1918, promising Anglo-French support for Arab self-government in Syria and Iraq, which replaced the Sykes-Picot Agreement signed in 1916—it delineated future control of the Middle East by the British and the French governments—provided a focus for subsequent political activity in the Arab areas. The British cited "special interests" in Baghdad and Basra provinces in the Husayn-MacMahon correspondence on the basis of which Sharif Husayn authorized the Arab revolt. Now Iraqis in Damascus worked not only for Syrian-Palestinian independence but also for Iraqi independence from British occupation and for unity with Syria.

There was still fighting in trans-Jordan when Yasin al-Hashimi reconstituted the Arab nationalist societies there in 1917. The following year al-Fatat emerged publicly when the Arabs took Damascus and installed a British-sponsored provisional government, its leaders assuming the major posts and the group transforming itself into the political party, al-Hizb al-Isti-qlal al-'Arabi (Arab Independence Party), to work for Arab independence from foreign rule.[11] Composed of members from Iraq, Syria, and Palestine, many of the political activists working in Damascus during the years 1918 to 1920 were later to reconvene in Baghdad after 1939 to continue the work after the failure of Arab uprisings against the French and the British in Syria and in Palestine. Of the Iraqis in Damascus in 1918, Ja'far al-'Askari became governor of Aleppo, Nuri al-Sa'id and Taha al-Hashimi "operated near the center of civil and military power," and Yasin al-Hashimi became Chief of Staff of the Arab army. Non-Iraqis who later appeared in Baghdad included the pedagogue Sati' al-Husri, Muhammad Izzat Darwazah of Nablus, secretary of al-Fatat and leading member of al-Istiqlal, and al-Hajj Muhammad Amin al-Husayni—soon to become the Jerusalem mufti and a leader of the Palestine Arab nationalists—who arrived in Damascus in April 1920.

Al-'Ahd was composed primarily of army officers in Faysal's army. Syrian enmity of the preponderant Iraqi role in Syrian affairs led the society to split into Iraqi and Syrian components. Yasin, disillusioned with the results of the Versailles peace conference, took advantage of Faysal's absence to use the group to spread anti-British and anti-French propaganda in his own campaign to liberate the Arab areas from foreign rule.[12] There were, for example, al-'Ahd branches in Baghdad and in Mosul which were galvanized to thwart a plebiscite planned by Sir Arnold Wilson for late 1918, early 1919.

Wilson, in an attempt to prove to London that Iraqis overwhelmingly supported direct British rule, proposed a plebiscite as an antidote to the Anglo-French declaration of November 1918. The result was unclear, depending upon conflicting responses, but there was definite support for a unified state of Iraq consisting of the former Ottoman provinces of Basra, Baghdad, and Mosul to be ruled by an Arab amir with British guidance—not quite what Wilson expected. Some notables from Hilla wanted Sir Percy Cox to be king of Iraq[13] and in the Shi'i Holy Cities, the Naqib of al-Najaf advocated direct British rule; but ten shaykhs from that city signed petitions calling for independence under a son of the Sharif of Mecca; and the chief religious leader of Karbala issued a *fatwa* (declaration) to that effect. Direct efforts by al-'Ahd members to spread Arab nationalist materials—letters and pamphlets from Syria—in the coffee houses, to use the mosques for anti-British speeches, and to pack political meetings with their supporters resulted in anti-British responses in Baghdad and in Mosul.[14]

Nevertheless, conditions in Iraq were inhospitable for demobilized Iraqi veterans—Wilson considered them enemies of the new regime—and many of them went to Syria where they were hardly welcome. The Iraqi al-'Ahd represented by Mawlud Mukhlis, Naji al-Suwaydi, Thabit 'Abd al-Nur, and Naji al-'Asil wrote to Cairo and to London early in 1919 appealing for a change in British policy and calling for an independent Iraq under a son of the Sharif of Mecca. At the March 1920 Syrian Congress, Faysal was proclaimed king of Syria. Simultaneously, some Iraqis, regrouping in the Mu'tamar al-'Iraqi (Mesopotamian League), which emerged to consider Iraqi interests specifically, advocated an independent Iraq to be ruled by Faysal's brother Abdullah. The Iraqi declaration was signed by twenty-nine members of the Iraqi community in Syria; the chairman was Tawfiq al-Suwaydi, and his associates included Ja'far al-'Askari, Naji al-Suwaydi, and Jamil al-Midfa'i.[15] Although Nuri al-Sa'id was not a signatory, he told his biographer, Lord Birdwood, that the group met at his house in Damascus; the Iraqis wanted to emphasize that Syria was not their only concern.[16] Both declarations stressed cooperation with the Allies in the area.

The 1920 Revolt

In April 1920 the victors met at San Remo and assigned the mandates—Syria to the French and Iraq to the British. By July Faysal was forced to flee Damascus and trouble for the British was brewing in Iraq.

Details of San Remo reached Iraq in May. In June, a shaykh, known for his nationalistic activities, was imprisoned at Rumaytha by the British authorities for refusal to pay a debt. His colleagues freed him from the mud jail the next day and, destroying nearby railroad tracks and bridges, initiated a revolt which spread throughout the tribal areas of the Euphrates and to regions north and east of Baghdad, leaving one-third of the country ungovernable for more than three months. The British were forced to bring in reinforcements from Iran; they used Royal Air Force (RAF) squadrons to bomb al-Kufah; and they laid siege to al-Najaf and Karbala. When the 1920 revolt ended, it had cost the British more than 400 lives and 40 million pounds, emphasizing to the British public the expense of the now discredited India policy of direct rule.[17] While London had already veered towards Cox's Arab "façade," the British now had to find a suitable Arab.

Was the 1920 revolt a nationalist uprising? Wilson called it a "chaotic insurrection by anarchist tribes, incited by Hashimite agents trained and financed by the Cairo Bureau,"[18] a conclusion mirroring his general view of the Iraqi scene and his competition with Cairo. While admitting to the "ideological-clerical composition of its command", the nationalist view at the other extreme, expounded by the official Ba'th party interpretation of events emphasized the popular nationalist struggle of the "130,000 rebels composed of farmers, bedouins and common citizens [who] took up arms in face of one of the mightiest imperialistic powers at that time and fought its overpowering forces in numbers and equipment for more than five months with unprecedented bravery." "The national force in Iraq," the *Encyclopedia of Modern Iraq continues:*

> look upon [the] 1920 revolution as a sign of national pride for its great struggle of independence. The daring feat of the farmers in this revolution have been as flaming torches to carry on the struggle by the crowds towards national independence and social progress. Despite the conviction and execution of so many nationalists who took part in it, the occupying British could not kill the Iraqi will to attain its lawful targets and goals.[19]

Elie Kedourie notes the significant Shi'i leadership and support and holds that the uprising was a Shi'i attempt to establish an Islamic state;[20] and Fa'riq al-Fir'aun, a member of the leading clan of the Fatla tribe which played a considerable role in the hostilities, finds the 1920 revolt to be a regional tribal insurrection against heavy taxation and foreign rule.[21]

It seems most likely, however, as Amal Vinogradov concludes in her retrospective study of events, that all of these forces coalesced with events in Syria and anti-British demonstrations in Egypt to incite the eruption. Local Iraqi opposition to British rule incited by San Remo, by the results of the plebiscite, and by propaganda from Syria led to the establishment in 1919 of a political coalition whose headquarters was in Baghdad but which had links throughout the country, especially in Shi'i areas. More locally oriented than al-Ahd, the Haras al-Istiqlal al-'Iraqiyyin (Iraqi Guards of Independence) attempted to unite Sunni and Shi'i and was composed of members of old established Iraqi families, ex-officials, officers, and educated young men who, although working for Iraqi control of Iraqi affairs, nevertheless, advocated the kingship of a son of the Sharif of Mecca.[22] As his rule was to be secular, Shi'i had few problems with the candidacy of a Hashimite prince. Political grievances in addition to heavy-handed British occupation, changing socioeconomic conditions, and heavy taxation were the catalysts for this "primitive" nationalist uprising.

Most interesting was the fact that the Syrian-based Iraqi officers played a marginal role in the revolt after their own abortive military escapades against the British earlier in the spring. They were too involved with Faysal's fate at Maysalun and, after his defeat, too disorganized and despondent to join their countrymen. The British tried to prevent those who wished to return to participate from entering Iraq. Some Sharifian officers did train tribesmen in the use of artillery, but the urban nationalists in Baghdad and Mosul limited their role to the spread of propaganda leaflets and demonstrations. The active leaders and supporters of the revolt were tribal leaders of the middle Euphrates, merchants, landowners, and statesmen in Baghdad, merchants in Hillah, and religious figures in al-Najaf and Karbala—these last being in control of the propaganda apparatus.[23] The tribes bore the brunt of the fighting and, as a result, they were removed as an effective opposition to British policy in Iraq. Now London moved quickly to establish a stable government.

Faysal and the Treaty

Faysal had expressed interest in Iraq as a suitable substitute for his lost throne a month after his flight from Syria, but only if his brother, 'Abdallah, were to relinquish his claim.[24] The British provided 'Abdallah with Transjordan and began preparing the way for Faysal's triumphal march to Baghdad. In the spring of 1921 they reorganized colonial administration—henceforth the Colonial Office, staffed primarily by the pro-Sharifian British, would deal with Iraq—and, at the Cairo Conference in April,[25] the British decided that Britain would administer the country by treaty rather than by fiat and that Faysal was malleable enough to negotiate a treaty providing the mandatory power with military and economic control.

To be sure, Faysal had support in the country in addition to that of his returning Iraqi entourage. He was acceptable to most Shi'is because of his lineage and his leadership of the Arab nationalist cause, even though there was a local Shi'i candidate for the throne, the Shaykh of Muhammarah, who was quickly "nudged" to drop his candidacy.[26] Other local personalities also declined: the Naqib of Baghdad was considered too old and Sayyid Talib, remembered for his "notoriety dating back to Turkish times," was considered too politically ambitious and not suitable for the Shi'is because of his Basra Sunni background. Fearing his successful opposition to their candidate, the British physically removed him from the scene. It was said that at a private dinner party he had threatened armed uprising; Sayyid Talib of Basra was subsequently detained after taking tea with Lady Cox at the British Residency and deported.[27]

Nevertheless, the British were to claim that 96 percent of the population supported Faysal. Disregarding much of the opposition, they were reluctant to reveal that the referendum they had engineered to confirm support for Faysal showed that there were Euphrates provinces that requested continued British control, as did many of the minorities; that the Kurds of Sulaymaniyyah abstained from the voting; and, that Kirkuk rejected the amir completely.[28] The now familiar story is told of the administrator in Kirkuk who, when asked to draw up a petition in favor of Faysal, drew up two, one for and one against the candidate, and presented both to the British. After hearing a rumor that the British had changed their minds, the man wanted to be on the safe side.[29] Faysal himself was bitterly disappointed by the lack of overwhelming popular support which greeted his arrival in 1921.[30]

The treaty negotiations, which began almost immediately, did not end until the Constituent Assembly ratified the first version in 1924, and then its renegotiation continued until independence in 1932. British-sponsored leaders such 'Abd al-Muhsin al-Sa'dun, a tribal leader, educated in Istanbul, who was Faysal's antagonist during the treaty debate, urban notables from Basra who saw the British safeguarding their interests, and the majority of the Christian and Jewish population supported British control via the treaty, while Arab nationalists, who soon realized that actual independence was not to be, joined with Shi'i support and fought the treaty through political parties and the press. Faysal procrastinated to the point where the British regretted their choice and even considered replacing him: "Faysal should be under no delusions in this matter," Churchill commented. "He will be a long time looking for a third throne."[31] Faysal was in constant touch with the Shi'i leaders who incited demonstrations during May, June, and July, and only Faysal's appendicitis attack and hospitalization in August 1922 gave Cox the opportunity to seize control, arrest the opposition, and convince the Naqib of Baghdad to sign the treaty.

Opposition continued. Shi'i religious leaders issued pronouncements against the upcoming elections to the Assembly; and when the government deported the leader to Iran, many of his followers accompanied him in a calculated protest which misfired. It, in effect, marked the end of the Shi'is as a united political force. Rather than influence the elections, this act alienated both the British and the Sunni Arabs. The Sunnis, opposing Shi'i appeal to a foreign power—Iran—no longer trusted them as Arab nationalists. Thus, from the early 1920s there were few Shi'i administrators: no Shi'i were appointed among the ten *mutasarrifs,* thirty-five *qa'imaqams* and eighty-five *mudirs,* except in the Holy Cities,[32] and only the education portfolio in the cabinet was to be traditionally allotted to a Shi'i. The conscription issue in 1927–1928 brought united Shi'i opposition (see chapter 5), and after that different Shi'i groups and politicians were to be used by the Sunni Arabs to further their own ends.

For by the end of the 1920s, three basic political groups emerged—anti-British nationalists, those politicians of Faysal's immediate circle, and the Shi'i—most of whose members either opposed one another or worked together when the situation suited them. The king received his crown from the British and derived his support from British planes and, primarily, from the clique of Ottoman-trained Arab Sunni army officers who had shared a common background of school, military service, and the experience of Faysal's provisional government in Syria. They, in turn, subdivided into smaller groups, which attempted to gain political support from the various elements of the indigenous population. Some, such as Nuri al-Sa'id, garnered political allegiance or personal fealty from members of the newly-formed Iraqi army, which he was charged to create, or from groups of tribal shaykhs in exchange for the possibilities of increased land acquisition and cash payment. Others, such as Yasin al-Hashimi, acquired their own followings of tribal shaykhs in addition to Shi'i leaders who alternately supported and left him as his cooperation with the British waxed and waned and as his personal policies and ambitions coincided with theirs. No one looked to the Iraqi peasant, the growing urban unemployed, the younger generation of recently commissioned army officers, the newly educated bureaucrat, or the numerous minorities; nor did anyone evince any real interest in the basic problems these groups presented to the new state.

Consequently, the ruling elite, by independence in

1932, consisted of personalities rather than political forces or ideologies although some of the politicians used ideology to advance their careers. But, in truth, there was little difference in the ideological goals of these men—all were Arab nationalists of the pan-Arab persuasion who wanted, after Iraq's independence, Iraqi leadership in the Arab world whether it be by federation of independent states or union under a common king on the British, German, or Italian model. They differed in method, not in outlook.

This elite used the constitution and the parliamentary system of government which the British imposed on them in order to rule the country. Parliament existed as the legislative body but was used in reality to rubber stamp executive fiat. It was a body of political forces brought together to enact the platform which the king and his cabinet, with the British in the background, wished to legitimatize. For Faysal had the constitutional power to call for new elections and to create and dismiss cabinets and prime ministers when he wished, and he used these powers to his own advantage. Consequently, toward the end of his rule there existed a multi-faceted political power struggle: the king atttempted to centralize and to concentrate more power in his own hands; the politicians competed for power among themselves and against the king; and the king changed supporters from among the politicians as his strategies required. As soon as individuals achieved stature in their own right, they lost royal support.

Specifically, between 1920 and 1936 there were no fewer than twenty-one cabinets but only fifty-seven office-holders; and, of these men, Nuri had held office fourteen times. Upon close examination, however, the actual number of personalities serving in the top posts of the government—prime minister, ministers of defense, interior, finance—numbered only twenty-seven and of these, fourteen held office more than three times. The true ruling elite of Iraq could be said to have consisted of about fourteen men who changed cabinet posts frequently and were constantly scheming to get back into power if they happened to be out. The king controlled the game of musical chairs.[33]

In 1929, in compliance with the British decision to sponsor early Iraqi admission to the League of Nations in 1932 and independence, the treaty was renegotiated. This time the opposition was organized around the "anti-British" Arab nationalists under the leadership of Yasin al-Hashimi, whose use of the tribes and the Shi'i to support his newly formed political party al-Ikha al-Watani (National Brotherhood), presaged the political tactics of the 1930s. Faysal called upon Nuri al-Sa'id to suppress the opposition-incited strikes and demonstrations and to see the treaty safely to completion. Nuri's successful handling of the treaty and its ratification by his newly elected parliament left an anti-British and an anti-foreign legacy which persisted throughout the monarchy.

The treaty virtually gave the British control of Iraqi foreign policy, as Iraq was obligated to consult closely with its ally on foreign affairs. This alliance included mutual help in wartime and stipulated that in exchange for British aid, equipment, and training of the Iraqi armed forces, the British were entitled to use all Iraqi facilities and assistance including railways, ports, and airports in time of war. In addition, the British were permitted to lease two airbases to be guarded by Iraqis at British expense. Any advisors and experts Iraq required were to be British, and the high commissioner was to be replaced by an ambassador who was to take precedence over others.[34]

Once the treaty was ratified and ceased to be a focal point for political activity, politicians turned first to personal political maneuvering and then to Iraq's role in the Arab world.

Personal Politics 1932–1936: Nuri al-Sa'id and Yasin al-Hashimi

By the early 1930s it had become evident to the politicians that the treaty would be passed, Iraq would be independent, and that Faysal would try to dominate the government.[35] So, instead of the treaty and the British, the politicians attacked the king who, after returning from Europe in 1930, "quite evidently began to emulate Mussolini whom he had met on a trip," and whose politics he admired, and whose special portrait surrounded and adorned by an exquisite silver frame was later presented to Faysal by the Italian chargé d'affaires in Baghdad.[36] Yasin, for example, now directed his party, al-Ikha, which he speedily reorganized, to present warnings to the Iraqis about the imminent danger.[37] Faysal in turn suppressed the party press when its editors did not "cease their foolish and persistent criticism" as the king had warned.[38] That is not to say, however, that Yasin, himself, was averse to playing a dominant role in a strong government or reluctant to conspire with the king in order to remove his greatest rival, Nuri al-Sa'id, from power.

Nuri had been Faysal's staunchest supporter throughout the struggle for independence of the previous decade, but the king did not hesitate to remove him from power in 1932 and replace him with Yasin, who had spent the 1920s bobbing and weaving on the issue of the treaty, generally opposing it but sometimes supporting it when it was to his political advantage. But by 1932 Nuri had achieved such political acclaim and international stature that he began to overshadow the king.

The collision occurred in 1932. The year before, Yasin's political party had supported a general strike while Yasin toured the country advocating the foundation of a republic with himself as president.[39] Nuri, prime minister at the time, was in Geneva preparing the way for Iraq's entrance into the League of Nations. He returned to Iraq and settled the strike, despite Yasin's attempts to persuade the leaders to continue.[40]

By this time Faysal was ready to shunt Nuri into the background. In June 1932 he offered the government to Yasin, but was prevented by the British from deposing Nuri until the Prime Minister had guided Iraq safely into the League. While Nuri was in Cairo en route to Baghdad from Geneva in October, he received a telegram from Faysal informing him that he was no longer in power. The conspirators had the delicacy not to install Yasin's Ikha government immediately, and Yasin had also to maneuver some kind of support for the recently signed treaty which he had spent his political career loudly opposing. Therefore, an interim government held power until early in 1933 when Yasin was able to form a government.[41] He took the finance portfolio, working with Rashid 'Ali al-Kaylani who became the prime minister.

Nuri, for his part, used his time out of power to complain to the British about Faysal, the man he had supported through thick and thin since 1915. He "stoutly affirmed" that he would not accept cabinet responsibility in Iraq again, unless there were a complete change of heart on the part of King Faysal, whose political intrigues and continued interference in the day-to-day business of government rendered the position of any cabinet intolerable. In conversations with the British representative in Geneva, he even went so far as to refuse to accept the premiership as long as Faysal was king since the king was now too old to change. Nuri saw little hope for improvement when Faysal's son, Ghazi, would succeed him, and began to discuss with the British other possible Hashimite candidates for the throne of Iraq.[42]

He changed his mind soon after, however, for he became Foreign Minister in Rashid 'Ali's government. But while in power, Nuri did not prevent his supporters from attempting to subvert the government. In June 1933, for example, an associate of his, 'Abd al-Razzaq al-Hassan, the former editor of Nuri's party newspaper, published a pamphlet called *Arab Nationalism in the Scale* in which he claimed that the Shi'is of Iraq were more Persian than Arab and was highly doubtful of their ability to dissolve sectarian loyalties in a larger Arab nationalism.[43] Shi'i attempts to respond to such charges in the press soon escalated into impassioned demonstrations and armed uprisings against the government in al-Najaf, Karbala, and other Shi'i Iraqi cities to such an extent that three predominately Shi'i provinces in the south were virtually ungovernable. Although the author was imprisoned and copies of his work confiscated, the punishment was considered inadequate for what the Shi'is believed was a Sunni attack against them.[44] Ordinarily this revolt would have been sufficient cause for the resignation of the government, but it was also involved with the Assyrian crisis which erupted at the same time and the impact of Faysal's untimely death (see chapter 5).

When Faysal died in August 1933, the political align-ments and alliances changed. The symbol of unity had disappeared, leaving a political vacuum. Ghazi was a political unknown when he succeeded Faysal, but because of his complete lack of resemblance to his father, he became a pawn rather than a manipulator in the political game.

Faysal had been a mature man of international renown and experience when he became king of Iraq, politically aware and able to compete with the politicians for power. He was at ease dealing with the British and liked to travel to Europe where he engaged in the social life in which he could not indulge in Iraq. He was cosmopolitan even though he was raised among the bedouin as a child. A transitional figure, he operated in Western society, but at the same time understood and liked the tribal shaykhs whose support among both the Sunni and Shi'i he courted and received. And he was respected by the leaders of the different elements of Iraqi society for his lineage and for his role in World War I. Although the politicians conspired against him at the end of his life, they respected his political abilities.

The growing urban population was not as supportive. Faysal was never fully accepted as an "Iraqi" while he was alive and was not popular. The American minister, writing in 1932, noted that when Faysal appeared on the streets of Baghdad in his automobile, there was no indication that his presence was noted. "I," he wrote, "have seen him pass along New Street time after time but the only people who seemed to pay attention to his passing were the foreigners who as a rule paused and lifted their hats."[45] By the end of the following year, after the army's campaign against the Assyrians, support for Faysal by the urban crowds was completely eclipsed by the adulation for his son, Gahzi.

From 1933, when Ghazi became king, until 1936, the two personalities who had emerged as political leaders, Yasin al-Hashimi and Nuri al-Sa'id, first competed for the king's support; then, when it became abundantly clear that Ghazi was not his father, each politician tried to concentrate more power unto himself.

Both of these men came from similar backgrounds and had similar views concerning Iraq's role within the Arab world, but they differed on the methods to be used in achieving Iraqi independence from the British. Born into lower-middle-class Arab Sunni Baghdadi families in the last quarter of the nineteenth century, Yasin and Nuri took the path to personal advancement open to Arabs under Ottoman rule, through the government educational system and into a military career. They both attended the Istanbul Military College and later the Staff College, finally serving in the Ottoman army until the outbreak of World War I.

Although they were both Arab nationalists and members of al-Ahd, their wartime careers followed different paths. Nuri deserted the Ottomans, certain that their alliance with Germany would bring defeat, and fled to Iraq. There, he worked with the Iraqi nationalists and later with the British and Faysal whom he saw as natural allies in the struggle for Arab independence, a real possibility since the Ottomans seemed certain to lose the war. Nuri was decorated by the British and depended upon them for support until his death in 1958.[46]

Yasin's wartime career has already been described. He reluctantly joined the Hashimites only after he was wounded in Palestine, forced to flee to Damascus one step ahead of the advancing Sharifian forces. There, he was rescued by Nuri and the other former Ottoman military colleagues who were later to become Iraqi prime ministers, and they finally convinced him to join Faysal. Faysal immediately made the former Ottoman Major General Chief of Staff of the Arab forces and President of the Military Advisory Council of Faysal's provisional government in Syria.

But Yasin had his own plans. While Faysal and Nuri were in Paris, he began to fight against the British and the French and simultaneously conspired against Faysal and Nuri for working with the victorious powers. Organizing and mobilizing the Arab forces under his command, Yasin attacked the British, instituted a pro-Turkish anti-Sharifian propaganda campaign, drew up military plans to fight the French forces landing in Syria, and joined with the indigenous Iraqi politicians who instigated the 1920 revolt against the British occupation.[47]

These wartime events had lasting effects on the later careers of both men. Yasin was never trusted by Faysal, because he had deserted the king in his most trying hour and did not have the common war experience of the other Iraqi officers who formed the coterie around the new Iraqi king. The latter immediately received important government posts. Although given a job as a provincial administrator upon his return to Iraq in 1922—the British being determined to keep him away from the new Iraqi army—Yasin was disgusted at his exclusion from the center of power and soon resigned.[48] He spent the rest of the decade struggling for political power through his campaign against the British and, by implication, Faysal and Nuri, using the treaty issue as his vehicle and gaining a reputation for political expediency which eventually led to his downfall.

Nuri's career during this early period lies in shadow. His biographers go into great detail about Nuri's wartime career, his association with Faysal and general support of Faysal's policies, but provide only small glimpses of the man who would achieve international stature in the late 1930s. He used his post as Chief of Staff of the new Iraqi army to create a following in the military which he would later use politically, doing just what the British were successful in preventing Yasin from doing. He went through a "picaresque period" in those days, according to Gerald de Gaury, "when he was guarded day and night by a selected gang of toughs, some in the uniform of the Iraqi Military Police." He was said to have been privy to the assassination in 1924 of Tawfiq al-Khalidi, senator and former minister of justice, [49] and is reported to have gone around with a bomb in his pocket during the debates in the Constituent Assembly of that year, presumably in order to discourage opponents of the treaty.[50] He used his support in the army for political intrigue and the promotion of anti-British demonstrations as he did during the visit of Lord Melchet in 1928, an anti-Zionist event, but in reality used to influence the outcome of the upcoming elections.[51] "At work he was full of nervous energy and high inquisitiveness usually concealed by a statesmanlike reticence while in official European circles." Nuri cultivated the British, liked to play bridge, and was invited to many social events at the British Residence. But his inner insecurity showed through when he sometimes appeared with his two pistols showing beneath his clothes, accompanied by a gang of toughs.[52]

The two men had different personalities. Yasin was enigmatic, a loner, cool under pressure, but incapable of communicating well, a trait which often generated mistrust. Nuri was garrulous and verbose, often to the point of incoherence, especially when he was excited. Yasin had not initially socialized with the British, running to them with every problem as Nuri habitually did, but he began to cultivate them once he was in power when their usefullness to him became apparent. His interests ran to economics, Nuri's to foreign affairs. Both men were consummate, skillful, driven politicians, who persevered on their determined courses no matter what the criticism and submerged their differences when they decided that a coalition of forces would benefit each other's personal ambition.[53]

Although Yasin could not trust Nuri to stay out of political mischief when he was in the government, it was much safer having him expend his excess energies working in foreign affairs than intriguing against the government. Consequently, Yasin—with British support—included Nuri in his cabinet which came to power in 1935. Nuri, for his part, wanted to spend more time working in foreign affairs "where he knew he could do his best work"; and, although as he told British ambassador Sir Archibald Clark-Kerr, "he was by no means happy . . . he saw no combination that could be better for Iraq than the present one and that there was no question of his deserting Yasin until something better was in sight and that would be unlikely for a long time to come.[54]

Yasin had prepared his way to power well, taking a number of steps after Faysal's death to create for himself the image of a strong leader in order to clear the path for his suspected dictatorial ambitions. There was a rumor, for example, that as soon as Ghazi became king, Yasin proposed the marriage of his eldest daughter to the young king in order to align himself permanently to the Crown. Shortly thereafter, the engagement of Ghazi to the daughter of 'Abdallah of Transjordan was announced. The queen wasted no time in establishing her opposition to a marriage coalition with Yasin.[55] Having failed in this attempt, Yasin turned next to the British, whom he had been fighting militarily and politically for most of his career. He began to cultivate the British ambassador in Baghdad, Sir Francis Humphreys, engaging in long discussions about his plans for Iraq and the importance of British advice in the achievement of his goals for the country. Needless to say the ambassador was impressed and his positive impressions were transmitted in diplomatic correspondence to London by his successor Sir Archibald Clark-Kerr, who found Yasin to be more stable in his handling of the crisis which befell Iraq in 1936 than the perennial British protégé Nuri.

Once in power in 1935, Yasin al-Hashimi worked quickly to consolidate control. The pro-Yasin newspapers began writing editorials supporting a more authoritarian regime, while Yasin neutralized the opposition by controlling parliament, disbanding and abolishing political parties including his own, in order to "assimilate the parties in one organization." He instituted a spy system against the Leftist Ahali organization, his strongest competitor for political power,[56] and purged the civil service except for the ministries of defense and foreign affairs, strongholds of Nuri's supporters. He brutally suppressed a Yazidi uprising against military conscription and placed areas of Shi'i revolt in the country under martial law with the Iraqi military, which he expanded, the army being doubled and the air force growing from a few planes to three squadrons. He failed to renew the contracts of several high-ranking British advisors and concluded trade agreements with Japan and Germany and an arms deal with Czechoslovakia. Iraqi national pride was strengthened by these measures and by the formation of paramilitary youth organizations, military training programs in the schools, and veterans organizations for servicemen who had participated in World War I. After a little more than one year in office, Yasin had prepared the country for an Arab nationalist government.[57]

The government took great pains to show the international community, especially in the wake of the Assyrian crisis of 1933, its moderation toward minorities. Muhammad Fadhil al-Jamali, the Shi'i Director General of Education, ordained that all student communal identification (Shi'i-Sunni) be removed from school records and that no sectarian propaganda be practiced in the schools.[58] But, concurrently throughout the decade, the government passed public morality laws characterized by the American representative in Baghdad as anti-Western and xenophobic.[59] The government passed laws against the sale of liquor near houses of worship and against Jewish and Christian public use of tobacco during Ramadan. It opposed lewd dancing in nightclubs and forbade cabaret artists to wear evening dress—costumes had to be long-sleeved and buttoned to the neck, causing Paul Knabenhue, the American minister, to remark that soon only veiled dancers would be seen in Baghdad. These laws and the ordinances for separate seating of the sexes during cinema performances were attempts to enforce Muslim morality.[60]

In the nationalist cause, street names and names of hotels were rewritten in Arabic, and Arabic subtitles for foreign films had to appear on the film itself, not on a side screen. Foreign tourists were not permitted to take pictures of uncomplimentary views of the country, and Iraqi young men were enjoined not to marry foreign girls, except those from Arab countries. In this case, al-Istiqlal, the nationalist newspaper, quoted the example of the German racial purity laws.[61]

Pan-Arabism in Iraq:
The Issue of Palestine

Now Iraq began to assert its role in Arab affairs. To be sure, Faysal had never lost the memory of his brief rule in Syria and had worked for Iraqi-Syrian unity under Hashimite aegis throughout his life. He dabbled in Syrian subversion in 1931, for example, hinting to the Syrians in a speech at Damascus that, if they had listened to his advice, they would be enjoying independence like the Iraqis.[62] But it was his brother 'Abdallah of Transjordan who continued the Hashimite unity program for the Fertile Crescent; and, after his death, 'Abd al-Ilah, the regent for Faysal II of Iraq, Ghazi's successor after 1939, continued to nourish the flame albeit with his own personal royal ambitions in mind.[63]

During Faysal's lifetime specific interest in the affairs of Palestine was limited to matters which overlapped with pan-Arabism or Arab unity. Faysal was not overly concerned with Zionism in Palestine because he thought that an agreement with the Jews would be reached and that even though Palestine Arabs strongly resented the presence of the Jews in the country, there could be an accommodation. For once a confederation of Arab states had been established, Faysal was convinced that there would no longer be an objection to the Jews because they would again be a minority within a larger entity.[64] As late as 1933, just before his death, he reiterated this view in a discussion with the British during his state visit to London. He was concerned about the question of Jewish immigration and thought that a final limit should be placed on it, but he was troubled more by the situation in Transjordan. "The Arabs would never permit the Jews to penetrate into Transjordan without a struggle," he said, "and unless the movement which had begun were stopped, bloodshed would certainly result."[65] Not only was he worried about the possibility of Arab-Jewish strife, but Faysal stressed his concern over the problem of future Iraqi-British relations if this struggle were to come about.

It is significant, therefore, that the two incidents of anti-Jewish demonstrations that occurred in Iraq before 1936—one coinciding with British Zionist Lord Melchett's visit to Iraq in 1928 and the second in reaction to the Wailing Wall incident in Palestine in 1929—were, according to British historian Peter Sluglett, more political than anti-British and anti-Zionist.[66] The speakers at the Friday service in the Hayderkhana Mosque in Baghdad took great pains in 1929 to state that they bore no enmity toward the Baghdad Jews. The government quickly suppressed the ensuing riots and temporarily suspended the publication of two nationalist newspapers.[67]

After Faysal's death, however, Iraqi pan-Arabism shifted direction. Unlike Nuri, who continued from time to time to advocate a Hashimite-dominated confederation as he did in 1938 under King Ghazi, [68] other Iraqi nationalists, notably Yasin and his successors, worked to develop a strong Iraq as a center of an eventual federation of Arab states. Yasin's vision of Iraq was that of a "Prussianized" state, a strongly centralized regime which would eventually bring other Arab states under its influence, just as Prussia controlled the rest of Germany. To this end, his government continued and expanded the strengthening of Iraqi pan-Arab consciousness via a strong spirit of militarism. Combined with pressure from Syrians and Palestinians, who saw Iraq as their protector against the British and the French, this effort ultimately led to the 1941 Rashid 'Ali coup.

Throughout the 1930s, while the governments walked a fine line on official policy concerning Palestine in order to avoid treading on British sensibilities, they simultaneously fostered unofficial support for the Arab cause in Palestine. Repeatedly, beginning with Yasin's government which sent Nuri al-Sa'id to negotiate the end of the Palestine Arab strike in 1936, Iraqi regimes warned Britain of Iraqi pro-Palestinian sentiments, but were careful not to take any overt action to rupture Anglo-Iraqi relations.[69] Thus, for example, Yasin's governments supported the mediation attempts by the Arab governments to solve the Palestine Arab strike in 1936; Hikmat Sulayman's government (1936–1937) filed a protest against the British Royal Commission Report (1937) that recommended the partition of Palestine, but did not send an official delegation to the Bludan Conference called in September 1937 to oppose partition.[70] Although Naji al-Suwaydi, an active pan-Arab, attended the conference, he worked to tone down the conference resolutions. And moderates Tawfiq al-Suwaydi and Nuri represented

Iraq at the London Conference which met in 1939 to discuss Palestine.[71]

Unofficially, however, beginning in 1936 during the Arab strike in Palestine and throughout the Palestine Arab revolt (1936–1939), Iraq increasingly became a center for pan-Arab anti-British activity. Iraqis encouraged political interchange among Egyptians, Syrians, and Palestinian nationalists. Early in 1936 high ranking nationalists from Palestine and Cairo visited Iraq and were generously entertained by Arab and Islamic clubs and associations where they addressed audiences on pan-Arab ideals.[72] Among them was Emile Ghury, a prominent Palestinian publicist who established close contacts in political circles. The Ministry of Education recruited Palestinian teachers who were given a warm welcome as symbols of the growing and close understanding between Arab countries. And parties of Iraqi notables and politicians, as well as a group of over thirty students from the Baghdad Law College and Teachers Training College, toured Egypt, Syria, and Palestine. In Palestine, at the receptions given in their honor, the groups had "frequent opportunities to pledge the support of their countrymen to the Arabs of Palestine in their struggle against Zionism.[73]

In this climate, despite the government's official position of noninvolvement in Palestine and its attempt to "keep the lid" on the emotional sympathies of the Iraqi public, Iraqis reacted strongly to the plight of their brethren in Palestine. This cause was a natural outlet for the Arab nationalist ideology fostered by the government through the schools and the army. Throughout the summer, emotional momentum built up so that by the end of September 1936, the government had lost control.

The protests, which began in April 1936 with newspaper articles attacking the British, were parried by the British Embassy. Ambassador Clark-Kerr had his staff brief the Iraqi government daily on the situation in Palestine in order to counteract the "influence of false rumours which have been in circulation." Nevertheless, he felt it necessary to appeal to Prime Minister Yasin al-Hashimi, drawing his attention to newspaper articles which were deliberately distorting the facts and requesting that Yasin "restrain the press from publishing further tendencious matter of this kind."[74]

The articles ceased, but on April 30 the newspapers published the text of a protest addressed to the League of Nations by the Muslim Defense League of Baghdad, and a deputation of Iraqi senators and deputies presented a memorandum to the British ambassador, expressing anxiety and concern over the future of the Arabs of Palestine whose economic and political rights they felt could only be safeguarded by a limit on Jewish immigration. It was natural and inevitable, said Naji al-Suwaydi, the group's spokesman, "that the Arabs of Iraq should take the greatest interest in the political, social, and economic welfare of the Arabs in the adjacent countries and that, in consequence, any events which brought distress to their neighbors and brothers must also deeply stir public feeling in Iraq."[75] All in all, British Ambassador Sir Archibald Clark-Kerr was satisfied that the visit was cordial and friendly and that the delegates wished that, in the best interests of Anglo-Iraqi relations, the Palestine problem be settled speedily and happily.[76]

Throughout the month of May the British received protests and letters from Iraqi groups such as the Muslim Youth Society and the students of the Baghdad Law College.[77] These protests emphasized the detrimental effect that the Palestine problem could have on Anglo-Muslim relations if Jewish immigration to Palestine were not stopped. Although the Iraqi government forbade demonstrations and public meetings, days of mourning were declared, prayers were recited for the souls of all who perished in Palestine, and newspapers appeared bordered in black. There were flag days and in many towns subscriptions opened; schoolboys collected money and several thousand pounds were sent to Palestine.[78]

In June, a representative of the Arab Higher Committee in Palestine visited Iraq; "enthusiasm for the Arab cause was stimulated at the meetings which were held in his honour by the principal organizations in Baghdad."[79] There were attempts to coordinate the fundraising and volunteer activities of the various groups in Iraq, Syria, and Palestine. In September, the nationalists directly involved the Jewish community in Baghdad.[80]

Incidents began in September 1936 when Muslim youths began to solicit funds from Jews for the relief of suffering Muslims in Palestine. Anti-Jewish agitation, especially by the Committee for the Defense of Palestine, increased and meetings were held in the mosques of Baghdad. Two Jews were shot in the street by "unknown persons" either for personal or political motives; one died in hospital. After another Jew was killed in October, the community requested police protection and the government complied. Local newspapers requested the Jewish community to publish a statement denying all ties with the Jews of Palestine and with international Jewry; and, in hopes of ending the anti-Jewish reaction, the Chief Rabbi announced that the Jewish community of Baghdad did not support the Zionist movement in Palestine.[81]

On October 12 meetings to "explain" the Palestine situation were organized in Baghdad mosques after prayers commemorating the Ascent of the Prophet. Before the service, however, the announcement was made that the Palestinian strike had been settled. The services were "informative and devoid of political implications," quite possibly because of the large numbers of plainclothes policemen in attendance. It is not improbable, wrote the American representative, "that an order from the Government was more effective in rendering the meeting innocuous than the settlement of the Palestinian strike."[82] subsequent incidents, such as the attempted bombing of Jewish social clubs in August 1938 were seen to be political moves to discredit the al-Midfa'i regime.[83]

Two groups became the foci for Iraqi pan-Arab activity: the Palestine Defense Committee and the Muthanna Club. Both organizations, fostered by Yasin's brother, General Taha al-Hashimi, became conduits for financial and ideological commitment to Palestine throughout this period. Taha, later succeeded by Sa'id Thabit, formed the Society for the Defense of Palestine in 1936 during the initial stages of the Palestine Arab revolt in order to serve the cause of the Arabs in Palestine. Its goals were not only to send charitable contributions to the Arab "mujahidin," but also to organize the religious leadership around the cause, to explain the seriousness of the situation, and to foster religious pronouncements and support for the struggle *(jihad)*, both in terms of Arab nationalism and Islam— hence the continuous attacks upon the British and the Jews for atrocities committed against the Arabs.[84] In 1936 the committee collected more than two million Iraqi dinars, some of the money coming from Baghdad Jews who were strongly advised by Thabit to contribute.[85] He later went to Palestine with a group of Iraqis in order to transfer the funds for arms purchases.[86] The group continued its speaking activities and collections throughout the Palestine revolt, expressed its opposition to the British White Paper on Palestine (1939),[87] and sponsored Palestinian speakers and fund raisers, and was one of the Jerusalem Mufti's main support institutions when he arrived in Baghdad in 1939.

Consistently, Iraqi governments denied sending arms to Palestine, but there is evidence that they supported private operations. On one occasion Yasin had Sa'id Thabit and a group of Iraqis stopped at the border;[88] but he nevertheless encouraged the gun-smuggling escapades of Yunis al-Sab'awi and Salah al-Din al-Sabbagh.[89] Even Nuri's government in 1939 did not prevent German supplied weapons from leaving the country. The British representative in Jidda tells us that German agent Dr. Amin Ruwayha reported in February 1939 that he could evade Iraqi customs because the Minister of the Interior arranged for the absence of a given border policeman at a specific time; he had men and guns at the ready.[90]

The leader of the Palestine Arab guerrilla force, Fawzi al-Qawuqji, was a Syrian former Ottoman military officer who had fled Syria after working with the Syrian rebels against the French. He held a military commission in the Iraqi army and a position in the Royal Military College.[91] In August 1936 he resigned from his post to take a contingent of some fifty armed men to Palestine. "Despite the vigilance of the Iraqi Government he managed to take with him a considerable quantity of rifles and ammunition, and he soon became a conspicious figure in the fighting which followed his arrival."[92] In Palestine he coordinated the guerrilla activities in the north, organized military training of the Palestine Arabs, and managed to smuggle Axis weapons into the country.[93] He returned to Iraq, was detained in Kirkuk for six months by Hikmat Sulayman's government (1936-1937), for fear of his links with Yasin's supporters. After Bakr Sidqi's death (1937), he returned to Baghdad and became, in 1939, the commander of the Mufti's forces in his mini-government in Baghdad.[94]

In addition to denying provisioning, the Iraqi government denied training non-Iraqis for service in Palestine. Although it was against Iraqi law for non-Iraqis to be admitted to the military college, the British protested to Nuri in 1940 that Palestinians were receiving training in Iraqi military camps. The British ambassador, Sir Basil Newton, in spite of Nuri's denials, advised the Prime Minister that he had heard from several sources that about twenty educated Palestinians had been attached for four months to the reserve officers training courses at the military college. These men, the ambassador continued, had been "chosen by the Palestinian organizations in Iraq as being likely to make insurgent leaders for Palestine, and included six men who had been employed as teachers by the Ministry of Education."[95]

Teachers, however, were more active in the pro-Arab Muthanna Club, named for the Muslim conqueror of southern Iraq al-Muthanna bin Haritha al-Shaybani,[96] which became the intellectual focus not only for pan-Arabism but increasingly for the expression of pro-German sentiments. Its founders and most outspoken members included Dr. Sa'ib Shawkat, brother of Dr. Sami Shawkat, the Director General of Education, and Palestinian teachers Darwish al-Miqdadi and Akram Zu'aytir, to whom the French refused a visa in 1939 because of his stridently anti-British speeches at the memorial service for Ghazi.[97] Sa'id Thabit was on the executive committee, as was Dr. Amin Ruwayha. Its goals, as described by one of the founders, Muhammad Mahdi Kubba, were to provide a forum for the discussion of pan-Arabism and Palestine, to awaken nationalist spirit among the youth, and to spread Arab culture, especially knowledge of the history of the Arabs.[98] It was not to enter into internal Iraqi politics. The club invited pan-Arab speakers to address the membership and Sati' al-Husri frequently spoke there.[99] King Ghazi supported the club and in 1936 gave it a parcel of land, which was then sold, the proceeds going to Palestine.[100] Along with the Palestine Defense Society, the Muthanna Club sent protests against the partition plan and sent a delegation to the Bludan Congress, after which the speeches and publications became noticeably more anti-British and more anti-Jewish, in conformity with the propaganda protocols set by the conference.[101]

Unofficial support for Palestine, which increased throughout the 1930s, was accompanied by the promulgation of Arab unity in the schools. For despite the British presence in the country and the frequent Iraqi cabinet changes, the goal of the men who wrote curricula and appointed teachers was to use education as a mechanism for the inculcation of pan-Arabism.

IV. Education

In the 1930s the Iraqis, like the French, the Germans, and the Japanese used the schools to inculcate nationalism. Although established and instituted under the British mandate, the Iraqi curriculum emphasized Arab nationalism and Iraq's important role in a pan-Arab union. Throughout the 1920s, as independence from Britain and the treaty issue preoccupied the politicians, these were the topics discussed in the classroom, while the educators within the Ministry of Education clashed over methods and political control. Increasingly, throughout the 1930s, pan-Arab issues emerged, and with the recruitment of Syrian and Palestinian teachers, their concerns with independence from France and Britain were expressed in Iraqi school texts and in classroom discussion.

Although the Minister of Education was traditionally a token Shi'i political appointee, the directors general and the inspectors general wielded real power in a centralized system whose authority emanated from Baghdad. From 1920 until 1941 the three men instrumental in forging educational policy and implanting a nationalist ideology in the schools were Sati' al-Husri, Muhammad Fadhil al-Jamali, and Sami Shawkat.

Faysal gave Sati' al-Husri the opportunity to realize his nationalist theory in pedagogical terms. Appointed Director General of Education in 1921, a position immune from frequent cabinet changes, unlike that of Minister of Education whose incumbent arrived and departed at the whim of the Prime Minister, al-Husri had continuity of tenure and independence of action in the administration of Iraqi education until he was successfully challenged by Muhammad Fadhil al-Jamali. Rightly called the "Father of Iraqi public education,"[1] al-Husri was directly responsible for creating and instituting the curriculum, implementing teaching methods, choosing textbooks and teachers for primary and secondary schools, establishing a teacher training program, and inculcating in students a pan-Arab ideology. He accomplished this either through the course of study itself or by speeches delivered at the teachers college, law school, and Muthanna Club and articles published regularly in Baghdad newspapers and his pedagogical journals *al-Tarbiyya wa-al-Ta'lim* ("Education and Instruction") and *al-Mu'allim al-Jadid* ("The New Teacher").

By 1919 when al-Husri joined the Hashimites in Damascus, his reputation as an Ottoman educator had been made, and he had modified his educational policy to fit his newly emergent Arab nationalist views.[2] Before World War I, al-Husri's Ottoman bureaucratic education and his subseqeunt research and study in Europe reinforced a liberal Ottoman philosophy—belief in the value of the Western scientific tradition, the role of the individual in reform of society, and reform of the Ottoman state rahter than its transformation along national lines—to the point where he published prolifically in education, psychology, sociology, and the natural sciences and neglected politics. Al-Husri never did join the Young Turks, although he was sympathetic to their goals, especially after observing Balkan nationalism at work.

In 1911, as one of the most influential educators in the Ottoman Empire, he debated Ziya Gökalp, the Turkish ideologue, over the role of education in the Empire. These debates are significant as they illustrate al-Husri's later shift in thinking. He tried to demonstrate to Gökalp, who advocated Turkish nationalist indoctrination for the entire society, the efficacy of Western liberal moral concepts, the importance of educating the individual in a multi-ethnic and multi-religious society, and reform of the Ottoman Empire without resorting to a narrow Turkish nationalism. It was a debate of "Spencerian individualism versus Durkeheim's collectivism," psychology versus sociology.[3]

But by 1918–1919 al-Husri had arrived at an Arab nationalist position almost mirroring Gökalp's Turkish nationalist views. Now he saw language—Arabic—and history—history of the Arabs—as the keys to Arab unity. Al-Husri left Anatolia and joined Faysal in Syria in 1919 to become Director General of Education in Faysal's provisional government where he tried to Arabize the schools. When Faysal left for Baghdad, al-Husri followed him.

Throughout his residence in Iraq, 1921–1941, al-Husri remained aloof from local party politics, maintaining that education was a more productive means for achieving Arab unity. To him there were two levels of politics: "secondary politics" influenced by party positions and changes of government which should be kept out of the classroom, and a higher politics—the achievement of fundamental national goals, among them the fostering of patriotism and nationalism. He tirelessly devoted his energy and skills as an educator to achieving the latter. "I will employ every means," he said, "to strengthen the feeling of nationalism among the sons of Iraq to spread the belief in the unity of the Arab nation. And I shall do this without joining any of the political parties which will eventually be formed."[4]

Instead of the home and the family, the school would become the social and cultural educator. It would teach the superiority of the community, order, discipline, cooperation, love of fatherland, and the role of the individual in service to the nation. The school was to be not only a place for study but also the theater of a new life, the mechanism for social change, by which al-Husri meant indoctrination in an Arab nationalist culture.[5] It is no wonder that to al-Husri compulsory education and universal conscription were the two most important mechanisms for the cohesion of the nation.[6]

For his work in Iraq, therefore, al-Husri had to shift pedagogical gears. By 1923 when he published the first primary school curriculum, al-Husri's earlier concern for minorities, for language differences, and for practical education was replaced by the overriding emphasis on Arab unity and nationalist education. When he was later criticized for not providing practical education—education for a better life—al-Husri replied that first the fallahin (peasants) must receive a new national consciousness, then improved methods in agriculture.[7]

The Ministry of Education, 1921–1941

Date	Minister of Education	Director General of Education	Inspector General of Education	Director General of Public Instruction
1921–1922	Muhammad-al Shahrastani	Sati' al-Husri (1921–1927)		
1922	Tawfiq al-Khalidi			
1922–1923	'Abd al-Husayn al-Chalabi			
1923–1924	Shaykh Muhammad Hassan Abu al-Muhassin			
1924	Ja'far al-'Askari			
1924–1925	Shaykh Muhammad Ridha al-Shabibi			
1925	al-Chalabi Hikmat Sulayman			
1925–1926	al-Chalabi			
1926–1927	al-Sayyid 'Abd al-Mahdi			
1927	Muhammad Amin Zaki Yasin al-Hashimi			
1928–1929	Tawfiq al-Suwaydi			
1929	Khalid Sulayman al-Chalabi (1929–1932)			
1931		Sami Shawkat (1931–1933)	Sati'al-Husri (3 months)	
1932–1933	Abbas Mahdi			
1933–1934	Salih Jabr	Muhammad Fadhil al-Jamali		
1934	Jalal Baban	(1934)		
1934–1935	al-Chalabi			
1935–1936	al-Shabibi	Fahmi Muddaris Sadiq al-Bassam Taha al-Hashimi	al-Jamali	Sati'al-Husri
1936–1937	Yusuf Ibrahim Ja'far Mamandi			
1937–1938	al-Shabibi	al-Jamali		al-Jamali
1939	Salih Jabr (1939–1940)	Sawkat		(1937–1942)
1940	Shawkat	al-Jamali		
1940–1941	al-Bassam	Shawkat (1940–1942)		
1941	Dr. Muhammad Hassan Salman			

Al-Husri's curriculum for Iraq, like the Ottoman course of study before it, followed the French academic primary school curriculum of the last quarter of the 19th century, with its emphasis on language and national history to the exclusion of practical subjects.[8] Now based on Arabic instead of Turkish, the curriculum concentrated on classical Arabic grammar and reading, using the standard phonetic method rather than the whole word method the progressives would want to introduce,[9] so as to achieve national and regional unity through the use of a standard Arabic to the exclusion of local dialects.[10] It was a narrow academic course of study, mandatory for urban and rural student alike, which required memorization of facts from compulsory textbooks for success in the state-administered examinations and allowed the teacher no leeway for inspiration or local concerns. In short, as his critics were to observe, the curriculum, which in essence remained in effect throughout the monarchy, was adademic, and al-Husri's purpose was exactly the same as that of the nineteenth-century German and French nationalists—to use the schools to inculcate the nationalist spirit.

It was said that the Prussian schoolmaster and not the army won the Franco-Prusssian War of 1870. The battle, which achieved German unification under Prussian hegemony and which later inspired Iraqi pan-Arabs who dreamt of Arab unity under Iraqi aegis, resulted in part from basic education reform geared to the regeneration of a proud German society which had been humiliated by Napoleon at the Battle of Jena (1806). Reacting to the catastrophe the Prussians suffered at the hands of Napoleon I, Johann Gottlieb Fichte, in his *Addresses to the German Nation*, proposed a different kind of remedy for the unification of the fragmented German people, namely, nationalist education which would inculcate "wholehearted, devoted love of fatherland."[12] Designed to mold German national characteristics which would express German genius, education should emphasize moral and patriotic instruction. The teacher was to "lead the youth into knowledge of the history of our rulers and our people . . . and to fill the minds and hearts of the pupils with love for their king and respect for the laws and institutions of the Fatherland."[13] The new policy centralized Prussian schools and required compulsory primary school attendance. Secondary schools were elitist and higher education educated those who were to rule. Teaching methods required little initiative; all that was needed was discipline and a minimum of textbook reading references. The teacher was the source of knowledge.

After 1870 education reform struck France. Legislated by the civilian Third Republic, successor to the Empire of Napoleon III, the educational reforms of 1882, like their German counterpart, required compulsory primary education. The French instituted moral and civic instruction to replace religion, and emphasized national subjects: French history and geography, the French language and literature, civics, the singing of nationalist songs, and physical education consisting of military drill. The purpose of the civics course was to "socialize the students in terms of French nationalism and republican politics."[14]

History emphasized French genius and French civilization—its gift to the world—including France's "unselfish colonial undertakings."[15] It stressed military prowess illustrated in primary school by biographies of French heros, most of whom were generals, and by the virtual exclusion of local history and general European history and geography except for fortuitous propinquity. Children read emotionally patriotic stories of French heroism ("The Torn Flag") and of German barbarism.[15] They yearned for revenge and the return of Alsace-Lorraine. Military drill became physical education and private pre-induction military societies were encouraged to prepare students for compulsory military conscription. Textbooks, although by different authors and publishers, were virtually identical in content. Teachers did not deviate from the texts and required frequent long memorization from them in this thoroughly centralized education system. The result, Carleton J. H. Hayes concluded in his classic study of French education, was to make the French citizen know and love his country, to unify and strengthen France so that she was able to withstand the German onslaught of 1914.[16]

The French curriculum was al-Husri's model and he followed it closely, even incorporating its ideas and instructions to teachers in his own course of study. Including instruction in Arabic, the second element in al-Husri's nationalist philosophy—the first being history, the national subjects accounted for about half the hours the Iraqi child spent in primary school.[17] Intermediate and secondary school curricula were not completed until the mid-1930s, but throughout the interwar period, despite the plethora of subjects, the student, nevertheless, spent almost 15 percent of his time studying history, geography, and civics.[18] There was no compulsory education law in Iraq so al-Husri took into account the strong attrition rate as the students progressed via state-administered examinations at every level,[19] and designed his program to inculcate nationalism in primary school and reinforce it in the upper grades. Thus, like the French curriculum, national subjects were presented in simplified narrative in the early grades with more detail added as the student proceeded.

This approach provided more continuity with Ottoman education as it appeared in Iraq during the second half of the nineteenth century than with the short British interlude which followed World War I. Liberalization and access to secular education, two of the Ottoman reforms of the Tanzimat period, had given the provincial Iraqis opportunities for bureaucratic and military careers in the Ottoman Empire. More schools helped to increase literacy from one-half percent in 1850 to 5-10 percent fifty years later.[20]

The Young Turks, whose regime followed the 1908 coup in Anatolia, accelerated the educational program while implementing their policy of Turkification of the non-Turkish population via the schools. They mandated Turkish as the language of instruction, taught Sunni doctrine in religion classes, and emphasized Turkish history and culture to the exclusion of Arab in order to prepare the students to be loyal military and civil servants of the empire.

Increasing the numbers of primary schools in Iraq, the Turks also set up more secondary schools in the major cities, and opened a teacher-training school and a law college in Baghdad. By 1914 native Iraqis outnumbered Turks in government employ, and a native intelligensia existed alongside the Turkophiles. But the statistics are misleading, because not all schools had all grades and many were short-lived. Furthermore, the Shi'i did not send their sons to government schools for fear of Sunni indoctrination. Thus, Turkish academic education really did not penetrate the fabric of Iraqi life.[21]

Most of the teachers and civil servants fled as the British pushed north from Basra in 1917, creating a new problem for the occupation forces.[22] In Mesopotamia, as in Egypt before, the need was for a loyal, efficient, inexpensive, local bureaucracy to relieve the overburdened troops in the field and the taxpayer at home. British policy in Mesopotamia, as Sir Pecy Cox described it—"administration with an Arab façade"[23]—was self-serving and utilitarian as it affected education. The British did authorize Arabic to be the language of instruction in the schools; but, in essence, British policy centered around establishing elementary schools supplemented by denominational schools which they fostered and subsidized in order to train minor functionaries for the civil service.[24] From 1917 to 1920 the British restricted funding for education and closed secondary schools, limiting Iraqi access to higher education.[25] They did open one secondary school in Baghdad in 1920 in response to popular demand.[26] They claimed, however, that the 400 secondary school students in the four schools were too many for the country to absorb, fearing, the British maintained, that only office seekers would want a higher education, but their true concern was that the graduates would serve as a potential source of anti-British agitation.[27]

Al-Husri spent the 1920s first in battling the British over policy and then in conflict with functionaries within his own ministry over methods and political control. The British concept of administration was antithetical to his goal of establishing a system of national schools, primary and secondary, accompanied by a gradual elimination of denominational schools whose very presence connoted foreign and therefore

undesirable influence. Under al-Husri, primary schools and student enrollment doubled and secondary schools quadrupled,
their student population growing from 238 boys in 1921, to
1,863 in 1930.[28] And to compensate for the lack of higher education and local teaching talent, al-Husri began to send student
missions abroad and to recruit Arab teachers.

The British lost control of Iraqi education by 1923
when the last order in the Ministry of Education was given by a
British official.[29] To be sure, there were British advisors there as
in every department, but they were not supported by their superiors, and, although they made suggestions, al-Husri did as he
pleased. Jerome Farrell (1920-1922) resigned in 1922 over conflict with al-Husri.[30] Farrell wanted to institute the British system
in Iraq—i.e., character building via cold showers and team
sports. Believing that the "moral degeneration of the Iraqi people was due to vices of all kinds," he pressed for the introduction of physical education and boyscouts in the schools.[31] Al-
Husri, of course, worked for an Iraqi system, maintaining that
each country should have its own system of education linked to
historical conditions. Farrell's successor, Lionel Smith
(1923-1932), resigned more than once because of disagreement
with al-Husri but returned to work with him. He and the British
in general had a high regard for al-Husri's work and integrity, as
the Colonial Report for 1927 tells us when reporting al-Husri's
resignation during that year:

> His [Hursi's] unremitting efforts to secure efficiency and a high
> standard in teachers and pupils naturally aroused opposition and
> it is a deplorable fact that his retirement was largely the result of
> his failure to obtain even the moral support of those who at heart
> approved his policy and appreciated his value. No other Iraqi
> combines his enthusiasm, his experience and knowledge of edu-
> cation systems, and his fearlessness.[32]

Not all of the Iraqis agreed.

We are told that al-Husri never fit in as an Iraqi. He
was accused of not knowing Iraq's problems. He spent his residence in Iraq as a cold intellectual without many close friends.

He was too Western, too secular in a country that was the backwater province of the Ottoman Empire, and his strong personality alienated colleagues and subordinates. William Cleveland, al-Husri's biographer, describes al-Husri as descending upon teachers, school directors, religious instructors, and British advisors with rapid-fire critical questions, blunt comments, and uncompromising recommendations for reform.[33] He was a professional whose goals were difficult to achieve in an unsympathetic environment and he could not suffer the stupidity of his detractors. Talib Mushtaq, who worked for him from 1921 to 1931, identified al-Husri's enemies as the incompetent, the religious fanatics, and the greedy.[34]

There was constant turmoil in the Ministry of Education throughout the 1920s. Sloan, the American representative in Baghdad, reported in 1932 the impressions of Edward Knight, one of the members of the Monroe Commission invited to study Iraqi education. Knight informed him that every official in the Ministry of Education seemed to be a member of one of the numerous cliques which had been formed and that these cliques appeared to be constantly engaged in intrigues to gain power, to create positions for their friends, or to oust their enemies.[35] There were intermittent altercations among the British advisors, the Ministers of Education, recent graduates of American educational institutions, and al-Husri, culminating in frequent resignations—his and theirs.[36] In 1927 al-Husri resigned as Director General of Education, claiming that his critics' self-interest ran contrary to reform. The prolonged controversy paralyzed administration and embarrassed al-Husri's supporters. In 1931, al-Husri resigned his position of Inspector General of Education after three months because he could not work with the Director General, Sami Shawkat, a man al-Husri had recommended for the job.[37] Finally, in 1936 he left the administration for good after disagreements with Mohammad Fadhil al-Jamali and his associate Matta Akrawi.

Jamali was al-Husri's chief antagonist. An Iraqi Shi'i, Jamali—unlike the token Shi'i ministers of education who had little or no effect on policy, virtually rubber-stamping all proposals placed before them[38]—was never Minister of Education, but he did hold powerful administrative posts. Whether as Director General of Education or Inspector General, after 1934, he, like al-Husri, controlled policy, the curriculum, textbooks, examinations, and student missions to foreign countries, and he brought Shi'is to positions of power within the educational system.

Born in al-Kadhimayn in 1903 to an important Shi'i family, Jamali received a combination of religious and secular instruction.[39] After a period of theological study in al-Najaf, Jamali returned to Baghdad to attend the newly opened Elementary Teachers' Training College and was later sent to Beirut, as one of the first six Iraqis to attend the American University of Beirut (AUB) on government scholarship. By the time he received his B.A. in 1927, Jamali had become an Arab nationalist, influenced by the Palestinian members, and an admirer of Mustafa Kemal (Atatürk) and his social revolution. These ideas were later to be combined with the strong impact of his American experience.

Summary of Sati' al-Husri's Career in Iraq, 1921–1941

1921-1927: Director General of Education
1927-1937: Professor at the Higher Teachers Training College
1931-1935: Dean of Law College
1934-1941: Director of Antiquities

Jamali spent the years 1929-1932 in the United States studying at Teachers College, Columbia University, where he specialized in teacher education, but he wrote his doctoral dissertation on bedouin education at the request of his advisor[40] and spent one semester at the University of Chicago studying psychology and anthropology. Professor Paul Monroe was his thesis advisor at Columbia and Jamali later accompanied him to Iraq when the Iraqi government invited Monroe to study and report on Iraqi education.

John Dewey, the founder of American progessive education, exercised a profound impact on Jamali's pedagogical approach, and as late as 1969, Jamali wrote of his continuous admiration for the experiental approach to education with its lack of discipline, its respect for pure scientific inquiry and constant questioning, its emphasis on practical education for a better life, and its promotion of the democratic philosophy in education—the development of individual potential[41]—an approach quite the opposite of the European academic philosophy. These views were augmented by Jamali's impressions of Europe and Turkey after his travels in 1938 and 1939.

On his return from Germany, England, and France, where he spent time touring educational facilities and studying the teaching methods and school systems of each country. Jamali gave three lectures which were later published by the Ministry of Education.[42] Although British intelligence reports liked to stress Jamali's advocacy of Nazi education, he was also impressed by the British public school which prepared leaders for the nation.[43] He had opposed Faysal and al-Husri's interest in a special school for tribal leaders and sons of notables and pashas, as well as the British proposal for a national "public school" on the model of Eton or Harrow when these proposals were advocated in the early 1930s.[44] By 1939, however, Jamali was convinced that such a school, under Iraqi control, which would bring the top students each year from every province, would create an intellectual elite capable of ruling Iraq as the British public school graduates governed the Empire. Although the British opposed Iraqi control, Sadiq al-Bassam, the Minister of Education, approved the plan, and the school operated until 1948, teaching a standard English curriculum, history of the Arabs, and emphasized sports in order to prepare its graduates for English and American universities, and AUB.

In Germany, Jamali was interested in mass rather than elitist education. He lauded the Nazis for the work-service concept (Arbeitsdienst), the pedagogical skills of their teachers, and the concept of the Hitler Youth, all of which he helped to incorporate in the Iraqi curriculum. The democratic concept that all boys between the ages of eighteen and twenty spend six months at manual labor in the country appealed to Jamali, who always advocated practical, technical education, and work with the hands. This he deemed important for a people who eschewed even the concept of manual work and considered the function of education to be to obtain a white collar job in government service. He was impressed that the Nazi teachers, who were strong nationalists, also went to summer camp for rustic rejuvenation and were "not content merely to stuff their students' heads with facts but were concerned with substance and character," requiring students of all classes to participate in the roughness of life. And he further maintained that the discipline and military training instilled in young Germans by the Hitler Youth would be healthy for the Iraqis.[45] Jamali later added Mustafa Kemal's use of the Turkish military in education and Turkish eclecticism in borrowing methods from all countries without sacrificing Turkish culture to his methodological framework.

The demagogic propagandist for Jamali's increasingly militaristic educational philosophy was the third member of the triumvirate, Sami Shawkat. A physician not a pedagogue, with little interest in Iraqi education beyond instilling the militarist spirit in the schools, Shawkat had been trained in Istanbul, served on the Turkish side during World War I, and had joined Faysal as an avowed Arab nationalist after the fall of Damascus. He spent the 1920s working for the Iraqi Ministry of Health and writing articles for the press under the names "Amr ibn al-As"— the seventh-century Muslim conqueror of Syria and Palestine— and "Hajjaj"—the infamous eighth-century Umayyad governor of rebellious Iraq.[46]

A firm believer in pan-Arabism and totalitarianism, Shawkat admired Nazi Germany and in the 1930s used his positions in government as Director General of Education and Minister of Social Affairs to promote militarism. He not only continued to publish, but lectured students on the "Profession of Death," telling them that the most important thing for them to learn was how to kill and how to die.[47] "I hereafter shall permit no one to make any propaganda for peace and shall oppose anyone who advocates peace," he wrote for *al-Bilad* in 1939. "We want war. We should shed our blood for the sake of Arabism and the Arabs. We should die for our national cause. We should be impregnated with military spirit."[48]

Shawkat appealed to students to abandon their easy comfortable life and urged them to follow the life of the Arabs in the early Islamic period, maintaining that the army was the best school for the creation of character and that military organization would make the individual brave, nationalistic, open, frank, and proud.[49] To these ends, he helped institute military instruction in the schools created an Iraqi paramilitary student organization modeled on the Hitler Youth, included German as the third language in the secondary schools, and sent student missions to Germany. He also used the schools and the nationalist Muthanna Club to spread Axis propaganda.

Jamali's eclectic approach to life conflicted with al-Husri's in method, not substance. He agreed with al-Husri's concept of Arab nationalism but added a mystical concept of the divinely created and guided Arab nation in which Iraq, which had the necessary material and human potential, was the country most qualified for leadership. Cultural and geographical unity were crucial, and Jamali, like al-Husri, advocated a standard curriculum, textbooks, and syllabi for all of the Arab countries. On the role of the individual in this cosmic design, he was ambivalent, however. On the one hand, Jamali advocated discipline, national service, and obedience to the king as the symbol of rule. On the other hand, he later wrote, the individual must find his place within but "not crushed by the Divine design"; "he must not [be] dissolved in the stormy stream of nationalism." This later concern for the individual advocated in the 1950s, during his swing back and forth from right to left as Na'im 'Attiyah, in her study of education in the Arab world, characterizes Jamali's philosophy, was closer to his Dewey-inspired concept of progressive education. It was here that Jamali came into direct conflict with al-Husri.[50]

From 1932 until 1942 Jamali and Shawkat held administrative posts almost continuously and lectured at the Teachers Training College and the Muthanna Club. Jamali had three major pedagogical goals, and with all of them he collided with al-Husri. Jamali was concerned with the equalization of educational opportunity, education for life rather than book learning, and the modernization of education to turn out whole individuals. On the surface the conflict was pedagogical, but it had personal and political overtones.

Jamali headed the anti-al-Husri movement which began early in the 1920s and culminated in al-Husri's virtual retirement from active participation in the education administration in 1936. From then until his exile from Iraq in 1941, al-Husri held the single post of Director of Antiquities.

The assault began soon after al-Husri's curriculum was adopted. In 1923 a Shi'i educator, Muhammad Abs al-Husayn, published *Sirr Táakhar al-Ma'arif* (Secret of Why Education Is Backward), a book that raised questions about the efficacy of al-Husri's curriculum. Soon after, students returning from study in the United States—first 'Abd 'Allah al-Hajj, who became assistant to Rustam Haydar in the palace, and later Matta Akrawi, who worked with Jamali—spoke to the king, criticizing al-Husri's policies. Then, Jamali, while studying in the United States, visited the Winnetka, Illinois, school system and invited its superintendant of schools, Carleton Washburn, to visit Iraq. Washburn and al-Husri tangled during the 1931 visit as the American was vociferous in his comments. The next year the political pedagogical explosion erupted in public when the Monroe Commission was invited by the Iraqi Government to visit Iraq and study its system of education.

It is not entirely clear who actually instigated the 1932 visit to Iraq by an American team headed by Paul Monroe, William C. Bagley, and Edward Knight of Teachers College, Columbia University, but Matta Akrawi. Al-Husri suspected Jamali, who had studied at Columbia and who later accompanied the mission.[51] Jamali wrote the section on bedouin education for the commission's report after the Iraqi cabinet decided to officially invite Monroe despite al-Husri's objection.

The commission's report, which the Iraqi government published in 1931, caused a stir in Iraq and comment in Europe.[52] Consisting of 170 pages, it contained a summary of recommendations for the improvement of Iraqi education and a thorough evaluation of Iraqi economic and social conditions. It reflected current American pedagogical thinking with its emphasis on the practical and its disdain for the "Latin" academic system, and was, consequently, controversial.

In short, the Monroe Commission recommended decentralization, practical education, and the inculcation of democratic ideals. It suggested the complete reorganization of administration, replacing the directors general and inspectors general with an advisory council representing the rural areas, minorities, and girls' education, whose members could advocate local needs for a flexible curriculum and thus free students from the constraints of the academic system. With its concentration on rural and tribal areas, the report advocated special emphasis on agriculture, health, handicrafts, teacher preparation including practical in-service training, attention to education for girls, and peripatetic schools for the bedouin. But secondary education, except for support for a national school (Faysal's idea), was deemphasized in comparison with a dramatic push for mass elementary education and the instillation of democratic ideals and positive patriotism, themes Monroe stressed for a country which had parliamentary insitutions.

There were inherent contradictions. On the one hand, the commission understood the need for centralization given Iraq's diverse ethnic, religious, and social components, but it condemned the existing centralization as dangerous, censuring state intervention in education. It supported Faysal's idea of an elitist secondary school but opposed the general expansion of secondary education in Iraq as too expensive and dangerous, sentiments which harked back to British policy. And while it claimed that the secondary school students were apathetic, without any *esprit de corps,* recommending team sports and boy scouts to ameliorate the condition, it soundly criticized the unhealthy nationalism, extremism, xenophobia, and militarism it found in the schools.

Al-Husri's reaction was immediate and culminated in thirteen letters addressed directly to Monroe published in

Baghdad newspapers and later compiled in his *Naqd Taqrir Lajnat Monroe* (Criticism of the Monroe Commission). He attacked the basic justification for a foreign evaluation of Iraqi education. "Is a commission composed of American specialists of benefit to Iraq?" he asked and then proceeded to denounce foreign intrusion into Iraqi affairs. There are two areas of education, he claimed: national goals and the means to achieve these goals. First, foreigners have no right to interfere; but they may contribute their expertise to assist in the achievement of the national program. Thus, while acknowledging the need for practical courses in agriculture and health, al-Husri argued that these areas had to be subordinated to the national aim: the creation and inculcation of a nationalist ideology. While al-Husri could accept suggestions for individual self-improvement, he could not tolerate any interference with the national objective.[53]

The letters, which are not coherent expositions of particular points, are explicitly critical of Monroe's stand on higher education, cultural versus practical education, national spirit and the related question of minorities, many of these areas ones that al-Husri had so successfully opposed in the earlier British policy. Al-Husri denounced Monroe's opposition to the development of Iraqi secondary education and the creation of a national university. He labeled Monroe elitist for his support for an elite secondary school and colonialist for blaming all ills in society on excited students. Where is the proof, al-Husri asked, for the assertion that too many secondary school graduates would be unhealthy for the country?[54] If Monroe had really studied the situation in the Middle East, al-Husri noted, he would have realized that there are two kinds of politics in that area of the world: imperialist rule, which implants its influence and administration in the country, and a government wanted by the nationalists for the good of the country, one that is concerned with the augmentation and reinforcement of educated nationalists. Where is the proof that Turkey and Iran, which are independent, have political problems due to an overabundance of secondary school graduates? Stressing the fact that Iraq had had no more than 700 secondary school graduates since the creation of the state, al-Husri likened Monroe's prescription for Iraq to the medical advice given by a doctor to an anemic patient dying of malnutrition—to stop eating.[55]

Al-Husri noted areas in the curriculum devoted to practical subjects—health and natural science—and recognized the need for special attention for farmers and girls.[56] But since Iraq's social problems, which had been under study for some time, could not be solved overnight, everyone required a basic cultural—nationalist—education, especially those students selected to study abroad because of the lack of higher education facilities in Iraq.

Similarly, al-Husri could not condone special consideration for minorities in a system geared to nationalist indoctrination. Thus, he opposed opening teacher-training colleges in Mosul and Hillah where the majority of the students might be Christian or Shi'i, fearing a consolidation of communal spirit; and he opposed subsidies for minority schools—Christian and Jewish—because he would have no control over them.[57] Minorities, who have played privileged roles in the past beyond their natural rights because of their ties to Western powers and whose schools have been treated with excessive generosity by the British, had to decide, he believed, whether these schools were public or private. If they were public, then in the national interest, they would have to be under the Ministry of Education which should approve their teachers.[58]

On the question of patriotism, al-Husri vehemently attacked Monroe, for this issue was the key to his curriculum. Unlike Monroe who condemned the anti-government attitude in the schools, the militarism and xenophobia as unhealthy patriotism, al-Husri considered political ferment healthy in a society assiduously engaged in developing a national identity; and he continued by emphasizing the importance of teaching Arab and pre-Islamic history to the schools. They were not taught to the detriment of specifically Iraqi history, he maintained, for if Monroe had studied the curriculum, he would have observed the recommendations for field trips to national monuments and archaeological sites suitably placed in the course of study. Then, as a parting shot, al-Husri accused Monroe of visiting Iraq like a tourist, of not speaking at length to students in the cities, and trekking out to the Euphrates provinces when the students were on vacation.[59]

Other opponents to the mission claimed that the government had no right to underwrite an expensive mission which insisted on the practical aspects of Western education to the detriment of Arab culture, and advised not following all of the recommendations. Al-'Iraq, the semi-official mouthpiece of the government, countered that the Monroe Commission volunteered its services, that Iraq was a country in a state of transition and must depend on advice on education in order to materially improve Iraqi life, and that the suggestions were not mandatory.[60]

Edward Knight, a member of the commission, was pessimistic about any implementation of the recommendations because not only did the government not wish to allocate funds, but it seemed to him that nobody was interested in the expansion of the educational system except those who expected to profit by it.[61]

By 1933–1934 Jamali had become actively involved in the ministry and began to implement some of the guidelines specifically in the areas of decentralization and practical education, issues which concerned politics more than pedagogy. Tied to the organization of administration, for example, was the problem of equal opportunity of education and the perception of a government anti-Shi'i policy. Al-Husri, Faysal, and the Sharifians were Sunni Muslims ruling from Baghdad a country where most of the population was Shi'i and rural. Although the purpose of centralized education was to be a means toward creating a cohesive national unity, al-Husri's centralized administration controlled from Baghdad with directors of education in the major cities of Baghdad, Basra and Mosul was criticized as being anti-Shi'i. Al-Husri's inability to work with the Shi'i ministers of education, while stemming from tension over spheres of authority, resulted in 1932 in a Shi'i proclamation which complained that the Shi'i portfolio (Minister of Education) carried "little, if any, power or prestige."[62] Al-Husri, quite understandably, always attempted to circumvent the authority of the political appointees who had little or no experience.

Jamali, on the other hand, was criticized for his "Shi'i policy." In 1933–1934, after he was appointed to the ministry, Jamali established additional directors of education in the provinces including the heavily Shi'i Euphrates provinces. Whenever he could, Jamali favored sending elementary school graduates from disadvantaged areas to teacher-training programs and on to missions abroad while al-Husri admitted only *bona fide* high school graduates into the programs. Although Jamali claims that he never had an overt Shi'i policy, he nonetheless established a secondary school in Najaf when he was Director General of Education and staffed it with AUB graduates and Christians in order to give the Shi'is a better quality education. He also tended to appoint Shi'i and AUB graduates to teaching posts and to administrative jobs in the Ministry of Education.[63]

The culmination of this pro- and anti-Monroe struggle occurred in Yasin al-Hashimi's government (1935–1936). Nuri al-Sa'id and the king supported Jamali, and Yasin al-Hashimi and his brother, Taha al-Hashimi, Chief of Staff of the Army, were al-Husri partisans. Thus, when Yasin came to power in 1935, there was pressure to remove Jamali as Director General. He was duly transferred to a newly created less powerful post of Inspector General. The new government requested al-Husri's return to the Ministry (he was Dean of the Law College at the time), but al-Husri demurred, finally assuming the dual role of Director of Public Instruction and Director of Antiquities.[64] At the same time the office of Director General of Education changed hands and Sadiq al-Bassam assumed the post. Jamali's appointment to the ministry had originally caused a stir because of his youth and progressive ideas, and his transfer resulted in an uproar—first from those who opposed the Monroe report and then from those who supported the changes Jamali had begun to institute.[65] While originally requesting assistance from al-Husri to remove Jamali outright, al-Bassam later became a Jamali partisan. Yasin opposed Jamali because of the implications of Shi'i advancement via implemented Monroe reforms. It is not clear exactly why, but after altercations over a textbook with Jamali and frequent run-ins with al-Bassam, al-Husri decided to resign.[66] With his resignation, Jamali controlled education in Iraq.

In essence, the Monroe Commission and its Iraqi supporters emphasized method, which translated into the pedagogical clash between Jamali and al-Husri. It represented the struggle of youth against the established status quo, of the postwar American and Beirut educated versus the old Ottoman generation. It reflected the cultural competition for superiority in the Middle East of the established academic tradition and the newly emerging theories of practical education diffused throughout the area of American University of Beirut graduates and graduates of American universities. But it did not involve any disagreement over Arab nationalism. For while Jamali implemented some of the practical aspects of the Monroe report, when he emerged in control of education, he also accelerated al-Husri's policy of nationalist indoctrination in the schools leaving much of al-Husri's work intact.

The Curriculum

Jamali retained al-Husri's curriculum, slightly modifying subject placement in particular grades and increasing the nationalist content in the history courses. Syrian and Palestinian Arabs had been teaching in Iraq since the 1920s; but Jamali began actively recruiting them and placing them in administrative positions, appointing them as history teachers, and commissioning their history textbooks for use in Iraqi schools. In Iraq, the pan-Arabs emphasized pan-Arab political issues rather than Iraqi local concerns. And after military instruction had been instituted in the schools, Shawkat and Jamali, impressed with the German original, accelerated the training in the schools of an Iraqi paramilitary movement, the "Futuwwah," which ultimately participated in the Rashid 'Ali revolt.

History, followed by instruction in civics and physi-

cal education in the form of military drill, was the most important tool used to inculcate national awareness in the younger
generation. "History for history's sake," Shawkat preached to a
meeting of history teachers in Baghdad, "has no place in our
present society; it is a matter for the specialist and for those who
devote themselves to learning alone. The histories which are
written with this aim in view are buried and nobody reads
them."[67]

On the contrary, the teacher's task was to guide history. To al-Husri, the teacher was both a sculptor, molding the
facts and events to a nationalist form, and an artist "producing a
finished picture by the use of shading, emphasis, and omis-
sion."[68] Shawkat extended the instructions: he enjoined teachers not to present any history but that of the Arabs in a positive
light and admonished them against teaching anything critical of
the Arabs, vehemently taking to task the renowned historian Ibn
Khaldun: "I believe," he said, "that the Arab masses which are
instinct with deep national feeling and sentiments of pride and
glory, must desecrate the tomb of Ibn Khaldun for his saying
'The Arabs are a people who cannot unite, and a people without political capacity,' and just for his blaspheming in such a
manner."[69]

The goal of history, the teachers were instructed, was
to present the "history of the fatherland, and the past of the
nation" in order to strengthen the national patriotic consciousness."[70] They were directed to pay particular concern to the
conduct of heroes, to the translation of "glorious historical ex-
ploits through bravery, courage, determination, endurance, and
noble deeds." The "study of history is glorious, filled with life,
great and exciting tales, sentiments to awaken national pride,
free from complexities, not loaded with names, dates, and facts
which oppress the memory in such a manner as to restrict the
understanding of the course of history."[71]

Heroes chosen to introduce the history of the Arabs
to the third or fourth grades were adapted to politics. The stories
about them were to emphasize the virtuous and pious charac-
ters of the personalities and their service to the nation. In the

syllabi for the 1920s, for example, there were twenty-eight names on the list of heroes, including six women. In 1936 the number was increased to forty and included such modern personalities as King Ghazi, King Faysal, King Husayn (of the Hejaz), 'Abd al-Krim, al-Mukhtar, 'Abd al-Qadir, and Muhammad 'Ali—these last, all recent Middle Eastern rulers or Muslim rebels against the Europeans from both the Fertile Crescent and North Africa. The list continued with Salah al-Din and then turned back into history to the most important of the 'Abbasid Caliphs, al-Ma'mun, al-Rashid, and al-Mansur; the conqueror of Spain, Tariq b. Ziyad; the Umayyad Caliph, 'Umar b. 'Abd al-'Azziz; Muslim conquerors and governors of Iraq, al-Hajjaj bin Yusuf; Muhammad bin al-Qasim al-Thaqafi, 'Umr bin Yasir, al-Muthanna ben Harithah al-Shaybani, Abu Muhjin al-Thaqafi, Sa'ad bin Abi Waqqas, Khalid bin al-Walid; Husayn and the Four Righteous Caliphs, 'Ali bin Abi Talib, 'Uthman bin 'Afan, Umr bin al-Khattab, Abu Bakr al-Sadiq. The Prophet Muhammad, "God bless him and grant him salvation," completed the list of Muslims who were followed back in time by such pre-Islamic heroes as the Jewish poet al-Samwa'il; the Arabs Hatim al-Ta'iy, 'Antarah bin Shaddad, Umr bin Kulthum, Umr bin Muadikrb al-Zubaydi, Imr al-Qays al-Kindi, Sayf Din Thi Yazin, and the women: Khadijah, 'Aishah, Fatimah, al-Khinsa, Bilqis, and Zenobia.[72]

From 1936 to 1940, however, a change occurred. In the 1940 elementary school syllabus, the heroes became "Arab heroes," the list shrank to thirty-two names, and non-Arabs and the modern Muslim rebels of Egypt, Algeria, and Morocco were replaced by Arab conquerors of Syria and Palestine, the Syrian Umayyad Marwan, and the founder of the Spanish Umayyads, 'Abd al-Rahman al-Dakhil, as follows:

Sayf bin Thi Yazin, 'Antarah bin Shaddad, Hatim al-Ta'iy, Zenobia, Sayyidna Muhammad bin 'Abdallah, Khadijah, Abu Bakr al-Sadiq, 'Umar bin al-Khattab, 'Uthman ibn 'Affan, 'Ali bin Abi Talib, Khalid bin al-Walid, al-Muthanna bin Haritha, Abu 'Abayda bin al-Jarrah, 'Amr bin al-'As, Sa'ad bin Abi Waqqas, al-Khinsa, 'Abdalmalik bin Abd al-aziz, 'Abd al Rahman al-Dakhil,

Abu Ja'far al-Mansur, Harun al-Rashid, Zubaydah, al-Ma'mun, Salah al-Din al-Ayyubi, 'Umar al-Mukhtar, al-Malik Husayn bin 'Ali, Faysal al-Awal, Ghazi al-Awal, Faysal al-Thani.[73]

The change in the description of Muhammad, who in 1936 was referred to only as the Prophet Muhammad, is the most striking of all. In 1940, conforming to Akram Zu'aytir's text, *Ta'rikhuna bi Uslub Qisasi* (Our History in Story Form), which teachers were advised to use for reference, Muhammad was identified on the list of personalities as Sayyidna Muhammad bin 'Abdallah, and in their instructions, teachers were told to stress to the students the greatness of the Prophet Muhammad, the "Commander (Za'im), emphasizing the historical Muhammad, the "leader of this nation and the source of its power in the past, in the present, and in the future."[74]

The shift in emphasis in the curriculum reflected the pan-Arab views of the authors of the new textbooks. One pan-Arab historian, Muhamad 'Izzat Darwazah, did not teach in Iraq, but his books *Durus al-Ta'rikh al-'Arabi* (Studies of Arab History) and *al-Watan al-'Arab* (The Arab Nation) were used as teaching aids. These works, some of the earliest secular histories of the Arabs, illustrated Darwazah's Arab nationalist approach to politics; for he had been active in the Arab revolt in Damascus (1919–1920), was a leading member of the Istiqlal in Palestine, and was an organizer of the Palestine revolt 1936–1939, spending the last two years of it in Syria.[75]

Sati' al-Husri had hired Darwish al-Miqdadi, a Palestinian graduate of the American University in Beirut, in 1924–1925 along with Anis al-Nasuli, whose purportedly anti-Shi'i, pro-Syrian history of the Umayyads, *al-Dawlah al-Umawiyyah fi al-Sham* (The Umayyad State in Syria) resulted in his expulsion from his teaching post at the Baghdad Secondary School in 1927.[76] Al-Miqdadi, who had been a leader of the pro-al-Nasuli demonstration which followed, was also fired from his post and later, along with al-Nasuli, reinstated. He received Iraqi citizenship in 1928. Al-Miqdadi taught at the Higher Teachers College throughout most of his sojourn in Iraq until he was exiled in 1941 and his text, *Ta'rikh al-Ummah al-'Arabiyyah* (History of the Arab Nation), was reissued continuously and used in Iraqi schools throughout the 1930s. Al-Miqdadi accompanied Iraqi student missions to Germany in the 1930s. While there, the British report, he organized an Arab youth movement along Nazi lines, escorting its members on a grand tour of European capitals in order to rally Arab youth to the Nazi cause. In Iraq, he revived the Palestine Defense Committee and was active in the Muthanna Club and other pan-Arab organizations. The British considered him to be a pro-German agitator.[75]

British views of Akram Zu'aytir, a member of the Palestinian Istiqlal and leader of the Arab revolt in Palestine, were similar. From Nablus, Zu'aytir was invited to Iraq in 1937 by Sami Shawkat where the Palestinian nationalist hired him to write textbooks and other pedagogical materials. In 1939 the French refused Zu'aytir a visa to Syria, where he wished to publish a textbook, because of a particularly anti-British speech he delivered during the special memorial ceremony for Ghazi.[76]

Zu'aytir's *Ta'rikhuna bi-Uslub Qisasi,* which he co-authored with al-Miqdadi, was used in the early grades, and his touch seems evident in the primary school curriculum guide for 1940. History was taught, according to an observer, "in the spirit of narrow-minded declamatory and xenophobe nationalism concealing from the student everything which may arouse critical spirit, including even some of the more important events of Arab and Muslim history."[77]

The "core of historical studies" was the history of Iraq and of the Arab nation; and the "idea of unity of the Arab nation and of the Arabism of Iraq" was to be brought out clearly from the beginning.[78] This al-Husri ordained and his successors implemented. By 1940 the instructions to teachers took on a more nationalistic hyperbole and enjoined them to describe the "history of our glorious nation replete with more magnificent tales of valor, courage and heroism, and filled with high moral and social example." Youths were told to strengthen themselves by studying the past in order to be able to recover the nation's splendor, to assist it in occupying an exalted place among the living powerful nations, and dedicate themselves to this high ideal, "strengthening themselves for the struggle (jihad) in order to achieve it."[79]

The study of the past was the key, and the Arabs adopted a view of history common in the 1930s. Borrowed from the German "Volk" historians, the theory of a primeval ancestor nation transmitting civilization to the rest of the world during its meanderings from an original homeland to its present abode had been Turkified by the Ottomans at the turn of the century. Atatürk, after the Ottoman Empire had ceased to exist, modified it to promote the original concept that the waves of "Aryan" Turks such as the Sumerians and the Hittites, who migrated westward throughout antiquity carrying with them the arts of civilization, originated in Central Asia, "the cradle of civilization" and very early made Anatolia their home. Using this approach to rebuild shattered Turkish pride at the loss of their Empire, to emphasize Turkey's European-ness, and to discourage pan-Turanism and Ottoman irredentism by reinforcing Turkish attachment to Anatolia, Atatürk used the schools to inculcate Turkish nationalism.[80]

Similarly, the pan-Arabs extolled both the historic role of the pre-Islamic Arabs and the geographic unity of the territory which was to be the modern Arab nation. Its boundaries were the Taurus Mountains and Kurdistan, Iran, the Arabian Sea, the Indian Ocean, the Gulf of Suez, and the Mediterranean Sea—or, the Arabian Peninsula and the Fertile Crescent. Palestine and Syria were integral parts of this area, but Egypt and North Africa were not included. The Semites were the progenitors of the modern Arabs.

According to the Winckler-Caetani "Semitic wave theory," as it was sometimes called, the Fertile Crescent, from which the British, the French, and the Zionists had torn greater Syria which included Palestine, had been identified as Arab since ancient times. From the "cradle of the Semites," Arabia, waves of Arabs migrated to Iraq, settled, and then proceeded westward from the "cradle of civilization," forming the peoples and the empires that created and transmitted ancient civilization.[81] Shawkat expressed the idea in a speech to teachers in 1939:

> In reality, however, the history of our illustrious Arab nation extends over thousands of years, and goes back to the time when the peoples of Europe lived in forests and over marshes, in caves and in the interstices of the rock; at that time our own ancestors used to set up banks, sculpt statues, and lay down canons and codes of law; they invented then the first principles of medicine, geometry, astronomy, the alphabet, and the numerals.[82]

Different authors claimed different Semites: Shawkat included the Chaldeans, Assyrians, Africans, Pharoahs, and the Cartheginians in his list, while Zu'aytir added Babylonians, the Phoenicians, and the Canaanites, omitting Egypt and Africa from the Arab nation. Darwazah included the Hebrews, although in his story of Solomon and Bilqis (Sheba), the wise king is from Palestine.[83] But there is no disagreement that the Arabs, whose pre-Islamic states of Hira, Palmyra, Yemen, and Mecca, for example, played significant historic roles, were the greatest of the Semites, bringing to the world Islam and the Arabic language.

The history of the Arabs was one of military conquest from Spain to China followed by foreign subjugation and decline. The lesson to be learned was strength, independence, and unity. While the Arabs were united, they "conquered the world," established an empire, and transmitted civilization to the Europeans. This period, including the Abbasids in the East and al-Andalus in the West, emphasizing Arab splendor and culture during the European Dark Ages, occupied the bulk of al-Miqdadi's *Ta'rikh al-Ummah al-'Arabiyyah* (History of the Arab Nation), which attributed the fall of the Umayyads to tribal dissension. Then, it continued, the Turks, the Mongols, and the Ottomans—here listed as just another in a series of Turkish invaders—capitalized on Arab weakness and disunity, subjugating the Arabs during the period of "negligence": from the fall of the

Abbasids to the Arab "awakening" in the 19th century. After World War I, the West divided the spoils.

In the sixth grade, after a review of Arab history and Islam from the Abbasids to the Crusaders (according to the 1936 syllabus) and extended through the Ottomans in the 1940 course of study, European history was introduced—the European Renaissance and a survey of modern inventions—and political history covered France, the Revolution and the Republic; the United States, its independence and expansion; and Germany, independence, unity and expansion. The curriculum turned to a study of foreign penetration in the East, especially in the Arab world and Japan, and ended with a survey of independence movements in the East, the Iraqi and the Arab Renaissance.

In 1940, the syllabus was even more explicit. After covering Italian independence, unity, and expansion and German unity (independence was deleted) and expansion, Japan is similarly introduced; "Japan—its awakening and acquisition of Western civilization," the curriculum concluded with the following:

6. How foreigners came to rule some Arab countries and how these areas struggle against colonialism
7. The Arab Renaissance, its affairs, personalities, situation of the Arab countries in general and Iraq in particular at the present time; Arab unity
8. The Iraqi Renaissance as part of the Arab Renaissance; its affairs, its personalities
9. The Arab nation—its great virtues; its service to human civilizations; the Arab nationalist answer today[84]

Darwazah reminded his readers at the end of his *Durus al-Ta'rikh al-'Arabi* (Lessons of Arab History) that even though the Arabs trail the West in science and power, the student must study history not only to avoid dangers but to take advantage of what is useful.[85] One could study European history with this in mind, therefore, for here important models could be found in the story of English constitutional development, Italian and German unity, and Japanese "awakening and greatness."[86] Talib Mushtaq's *Durus al-Ta'rikh* (Lessons of History), used in the mid-1930s, described how Germany under the Prussian leadership of Bismarck and Wilhelm I and with the aid of German intellectuals who planted the seeds of nationalism based on German unity, was able to defeat her greatest enemy, France.[87]

Iraqi secondary-school students took the lessons to heart. 'Ali al-Tantawi, a Syrian teaching in Iraq, mentions that Iraqi schoolboys wished Iraq to become a Piedmont or a Prussia and unite the Arab world.[88] Their candidate for leader, a student tells us, was Yasin al-Hashimi, whom they adored, hoping that he would seize power, dismiss the English, and make himself a benevolent dictator like Mustafa Kemal. They even wrote to politicians and, to their surprise, received long answers.[89]

The Japanese victory over Russia in 1905, the most important war before World War I, according to Talib Mushtaq, shattered Western invincibility, and proved that an "awakened Eastern state could defeat a Western tyrant" and free itself from subjugation. Then, at the end of a work carefully free from overt anti-British sentiment, going so far as to discuss British colonialism in India, New Zealand, and Australia, while conveniently omitting the British presence in the Arab world—except to say that the British had to impose peace on Egypt in 1882—Mushtaq tells his students to awake from sleep in order to achieve the goal: "We students must," he wrote, "strive with all our strength to obtain independence for the Arab countries and their freedom from the hands of the greedy usurpers."[90]

British unease began after the shock of the Bakr Sidqi military coup in 1936. The wife of the judicial advisor (Mrs. Drower), "who has quite an exceptional knowledge of Arabic and Iraqis," suggested an examination of schoolbooks because she was concerned with the "violent anti-imperialist and anti-British tone of the Iraqi schools textbooks." She had been present in Iraqi schools, a British dispatch reports, "when children were rehearsed in a sort of catechism of hate against the West in which all of the blame for the infirmities of the Iraqi state were put upon Great Britain and no word said of the Alliance."

George Rendel, head of the Eastern Department of the London Foreign Office, requested a report from Ambassador Clark-Kerr, but it seems to have taken imminent war to spark action.[91]

The British complained to the Iraqis in 1939. They were upset that the Iraqis were not grateful to them for creating the Iraqi state. "Young people," Sir Basil Newton wrote to Lord Halifax in July, "were taught that Iraq had gained her freedom in a triumphant struggle against British oppression and that only British imperialism now stood in the way of the rapid progress and development of the new Iraqi state. Nothing was said," he continued

> of the fact that it was Great Britain that had created Iraq out of three obscure Ottoman provinces of the Ottoman Empire, given her national cohesion and set her up in the short space of ten years as an independent state member of the League of Nations. Nor was it ever made clear to the youth of the country that, but for the alliance with Great Britain, the liberty and independence newly gained by Iraq without help might prove short-lived. The very existence of Iraq depended on Anglo-Iraqi friendship and cooperation, and yet the youth of the country (who would be its rulers in a few years) were being taught to believe that the essence of patriotism was enmity towards the one country which assured their independence.[92]

In his textbook, *Ta'rikh al-Ummah al-'Arabiyyah,* for use in the second year intermediate schools, Darwish al-Miqdadi, as did Darwazah in his *Durus al-Ta'rikh,*[93] underlined the view that it was Iraqi boldness and bravery and their infliction of heavy British casualties in the 1920 revolt which proved to the British that Iraq had to be independent:

> The British officials continued to employ harsh measures. They expelled some of the shaykhs and imprisoned others. The revolt broke out and the tribes began to destroy the railroad. They stood up before the enemy and they captured armored cars and armored trains. At Rumaythah . . . the rebels were victorious over their enemies who greatly outnumbered them and there is no doubt that the English incurred heavy losses in people and material.

Because of the Iraqi revolt in which the Iraqis defied the English, the English occupiers realized that it is impossible for Iraq to remain ruled by the foreigner and that it is impossible for the foreigner to subdue the people of Iraq. A meeting was held in Baghdad and the Iraqi officers returned from Syria after the fall of the Arab state. And they began to ask for independence in order that King Faysal might assume the throne. The Cairo Conference was organized and Churchill, the British minister, was present for the settlement of the Iraqi issue. An agreement was concluded for the announcement of a general pardon and the establishment of a national government. And King Faysal came to Iraq and he was crowned king on 23 August 1921.

. . .

And Iraq will continue to progress on the ladder of progress and strength until the day of its goal dawns.[94]

This view was reinforced in the classroom, a student reported to the British. Because of the widespread anti-British views of his teachers, the student wrote, he graduated from secondary school with the views that the British

are cowards who cried during the battles like children, and they won the war only through their money and mean diplomacy. Any Iraqi can beat ten Englishmen in any kind of fighting, through his bravery and physical strength, and Iraqis actually proved it in the "Revolution" of 1920. In that revolution many Arabs captured British cannons and artillery when they were armed only with clubs. As for capturing machine-gun nests, that was an easy job which the Arabs could do with sticks only.[95]

To be sure, the textbooks were written from an Arab point of view, but they were not anti-British diatribes. On the contrary, many of them seemed innocuous, containing interspersed "suspect" sentences or paragraphs or even omitted facts which, when they did get around to analyzing the texts, the British, who had not been actively involved in education, could find offensive. For example, al-Miqdadi's *Ta'rikh al-Ummah al-'Arabiyyah* taught Iraqis that Sir Percy Cox, Sir Harold Wilson, "and the occupiers had contempt for the people of the country and did not respect their traditions."[96] Zu'aytir included a similar phrase in his *Ta'rikhuna bi-Uslub Qisasi* where in a story about Solomon and Bilqis, he discussed the neighboring kings and inserted: "So it is today with regard to the imperialists who corrupt the character of those they rule and criticize them."[97] Darwazah's *Durus al-Ta'rikh al-'Arabi,* an Arab nationalist history like George Antonious' *The Arab Awakening,* was an ongoing tale of Muslim rebels against the powers and biographies of Syrian martyrs in the nationalist struggle against the French.

What the British could not understand was why these textbooks were in use when they were not even written by Iraqis, but were contributed by Palestinians. "The *tariqa* that is being given to them (the Iraqis) is not the Iraqi *tariqa,*" bemoaned C. J. Edmonds, "it is a tariqa based on their own grievances in their own countries and is not the teaching which the founders of Iraq would convey if they were doing the actual teaching. Iraq may sympathize with some of those grievances but that does not mean that it should surrender the sacred duty of forming the minds of the coming generation to others." "It is intolerable," he concluded, "that aggrieved persons from the outside, who have no knowledge of the real history of Iraq . . . should seek to destroy this unity in pursuit of secondary aims of a local character."[98]

Zu'aytir, for example, in his *Ta'rikhuna bi-Uslub Qisasi,* which covered the history of the pre-Islamic Arabs through the four "Righteous Caliphs," frequently interjected remarks about Palestine. Palestine was part of southern Syria. The Arabs claimed Palestine as an indispensible part of the Arab territory, the "jugular (neck)" of the Arab land. It was the place of the Prophet's journey to heaven and from where the conquest of Syria was launched. After the conquest, Palestine in all of its parts became Arab, he concluded, and "it is impossible for it to lose its Arabism as long as there are Arabs in the world."[99]

Al-Miqdadi's *Ta'rikh al-Ummah al-'Arabiyyah* continued the story. It stated that the British government in Palestine was pro-Zionist, allowing Jewish immigration, granting the Zionists privileges and posts, and allowing them weapons, while denying the Arabs arms.

Palestine is a natural part of Syria; there is no partition between the two. When the Allies put Palestine under British mandate, Palestine befell a calamitous misfortune because the Allies promised Palestine to the Jews for a national homeland under the terms of the Balfour promise which was published on 2 November 1917. Since 1917 Jewish immigration to Palestine has continued even though there are enough people. The British government allied themselves with the Zionists, granting them favors and benefits, appointing them to important posts, giving them weapons while preventing the Arabs from carrying them, paying their workers excessive wages while prohibiting Arab workers from working or if they did work, then paying the Arabs a smaller amount of pay.[100]

Darwazah ended his *Durus al-Ta'rikh al-'Arabi* with the assertion that the "Arabs refuse to accept all conditions which do not guarantee their independence and sovereignty over their own country."[101] And al-Miqdadi added the refrain: "And still the Arabs of Palestine are struggling to end the idea of a Jewish national home and to achieve freedom and independence within Arab unity."[102]

During the 1930s, the Ministry of Education not only mandated the use of these prescribed texts, even by private and denominational schools in order to advance national unity, but slowly controlled what teachers taught. The government constantly sent circulars admonishing schools against subversive and divisive political activity which would tend to provoke ethnic and regional differences.[103] Shawkat ordered the schools to stop using books "harmful and prejudicial to patriotic and national spirit," authorizing inspectors to inform the ministry of suspicious materials.[104] These directives resulted in the passage of the Public Education Law in 1940 which, when under discussion, was to legislate that no Iraqi child could attend a foreign primary school, but, when passed, required only that Iraqi teachers approved by the Ministry of Education teach national subjects: Arabic, history, geography, and civics.[105] In addition to standardized textbooks, the government appointed the teachers who, in effect, became political agents. The English teacher in the Baghdad secondary school tells us that teachers had to teach history to order, to file reports of students' loyalty to the regime, and to adjust grades on the basis of a student's background and politics.[106]

Teachers encouraged students to give eloquent anti-British speeches, especially on national holidays such as Renaissance Day, which commemorated the Arab revolt. Although the revolt was against the Ottomans, the British were the target of the rhetoric, which extolled the virtues of all leaders who had opposed the Anglo-Iraqi treaty. Sponsors of the treaty with Britain such as Nuri al-Sa'id and Ja'far al-'Askari were condemned as traitors and British spies.[107]

The British had warned of the danger of a politicized student body and foreseen the consequences of lenient punishment meted out to student demonstrators. In 1927 teachers of the Teachers Training College and the Baghdad secondary school, Talib Mushtaq among them, led students in an organized demonstration at the Ministry of Education against the expulsion of Syrian history teacher Anis al-Nasuli and the retraction of his pro-Syrian history of the Umayyads. The Shi'is were offended by the secularism of the text and by al-Nasuli's objection to their custom of self-flagellation during Muharram and his dedication to the descendants of the Umayyads—the Syrians—and demanded his speedy retirement. Although the police dispersed the demonstrators, who agitated for freedom of teaching, freedom of publication, and freedom of thought, the student leaders were expelled from school as were their mentors, Palestinian teachers Darwish al-Miqdadi and 'Abdallah al-Mashnuq.[108] When tensions subsided, all were reinstated, a situation that caused the British to comment that

> political and religious agitators have learnt thereby that schools can be stirred up, even on the most childish of pretexts, into action which may well result in a breach of the peace. The Ministry of Education must apparently reconcile itself to the fact that in a crisis it cannot trust either the commonsense or the loyalty of teachers. And public opinion seems to accept it as axiomatic that no student should be regarded as responsible for

his actions . . . No one seems to reflect what a disastrous effect such an assumption is bound to have on the training of young citizens.[109]

The following year the students, again guided by Talib Mushtaq and other teachers in collusion with politicians Yasin al-Hashimi and Rashid 'Ali, demonstrated against the visit of Sir Alfred Mond, a British industrialist and Zionist who had come to Iraq to investigate the use of fertilizer in Iraqi agriculture. Mushtaq called these demonstrations anti-Zionist in which he encouraged his students to participate after school hours.[110] A student on the scene claimed that the students did not know what Zionism was and demonstrated because they were called upon to do so. And Peter Sluglett, in his study of the mandate period, concluded that Sir Alfred's visit coincided nicely with upcoming elections and that the Opposition politicians were manipulating the students.[111]

In 1930 when the revised treaty with Britain was signed, the students protested once again. There were demonstrations led by Yasin al-Hashimi and Rashid 'Ali against British policy in Iraq, and the students, it is reported, were

"so much encouraged that we believed ourselves to have reached the gates of London. In all these the British seemed to us like powerless spectators, and we started to believe that our teachers had been right when they told us that Great Britain was too old to rule and that she was merely a falling Empire. Our belief was that we were able to "have shaken London," if we wanted, and the British were quite afraid of us, we brave Iraqis."[112]

After independence the demonstrations added pan-Arab political concerns. That is not to say that students neglected their own grievances. Fifty students went on strike in 1931 "alleging that the problems given to them by their mathematics teacher were much too difficult," and in 1937 and 1938 students left *en masse* when they felt that the final examination in mathematics was too difficult, demanding and receiving revised exams from the Ministry of Education.[113]

Generally, however, the 1930s saw increasing interest in British and French policy in Palestine and Syria. "Several times a year," an English teacher reported to the British, "there were demonstrations about the British in Palestine, or the French in Syria, or against the Jews, or the Iranians.[114] Once, the Syrian teacher 'Ali al-Tantawi reports in his memoirs, when the government desired a demonstration against the French presence in Syria, he and his colleagues from the Central Secondary School were informed and detailed to other schools to organize the students.[115]

Students were encouraged to collect funds for the martyrs of Palestine, to form support clubs for the Palestine Arabs, and they took to the streets during the Palestine Arab revolt of 1936–1939.[116] In November 1938 medical and secondary school students demonstrated and rioted in an anti-British spree of window smashing, looting, and stone throwing which brought about official disciplinary measures in government schools. The Ministry of Education decided to close any class from which a majority of students took part in demonstrations and to expel the students.[117]

But once the Iraqi paramilitary youth movement, the "Futuwwah," was officially instituted in the schools as it was the following year, there were government-sponsored and sanctioned student military parades and demonstrations. The movement provided the opportunity for the students to act out what the schools had been preaching; namely, that the youth represented the nationalist ideal, the heroic qualities of the Arab, and they were to restore past glory.

Evocative of the medieval *futuwah,* a social organization which the 'Abbasid Caliph al-Nasir li-Din Allah had tried to use to unite society around a rejuvenated caliphate, the Iraqi Futuwwah was the culmination of a decade of increasing militarization of the schools. Physical education and singing, both in the curriculum, were, in effect, military drill and the singing of patriotic songs. After independence Faysal moved to install military education directly in the schools. From 1932 until 1936 a cooperative program between the ministries of education and defense was drawn up and implemented, whereby army officers would teach marksmanship and horsemanship, and teachers would teach military terms and a simplified history of war for three hours a week. In addition, both ministeries undertook jointly to sponsor and run a voluntary military summer camp for secondary school students, secondary school teachers, students of the teachers college and professional educators—a kind of Iraqi *Arbeitsdienst*.[118]

The object of the program was "to train the students for hard living, to overcome difficulties, in qualities of manhood, devoting [sic], military exercises, shooting and qualities of obedience and love of discipline.[119] By 1936 military training was made an official subject in the Teachers Training College, technical schools, and all government intermediate and secondary schools. It was compulsory and any student absent from training faced expulsion and induction into the Iraqi army as a private soldier. The course was considered as important as science, and its emphasis was such as to occasion the American representative in Baghdad to remark that "lately the Minister of Education has displayed more enthusiasm for military training than for any other line of education."[120]

The Iraqi boy scouts had been organized since the mandate and were considered to be a positive socializing agent by al-Husri and the educators,[121] but membership was not compulsory and Iraqi representation in the British-sponsored movement was not large, in part because of the Christian origins of the movement. By 1938 there was a question of Iraqi affiliation with the international movement because the British had to compete with the German invitation to Iraq to send a delegation of Iraqi "scouts" to Nuremberg.[122]

There were rumors, but no proof, that Germany subsidized the Iraqi Futuwwah movement. In any event, the Germans certainly encouraged the idea of a paramilitary youth movement. In 1937 at the instigation, it seems, of the German envoy, Fritz Grobba, the Hitler Youth leader Baldur von Schirach and eight of his staff stopped over in Baghdad on their way home from Tehran. Von Schirach took tea with King Ghazi and invited a delegation of students receiving military training, not the scouts, to attend the Nuremberg Rally in 1938.[123] The delegation, composed mainly of physical education teachers and students, traveled to Germany and were encouraged by the Syrians, whom they visited on the way, to solicit German support in the fight against Zionism. The delegation was hosted by the Hitler Youth on the fourteen-day trip, was received by Hitler, and returned to Iraq as enthusiastic Nazi supporters.[124]

With the establishment of Nuri al-Sa'id's government on December 25, 1938, there was a stong impetus to establish a movement similar to the Hitler Youth in Iraq in addition to the already enforced military training. At the conclusion of a parade of students taking military training at the end of Janury 1939, the new Minister of Education, Salih Jabr, spoke to the students from a platform surrounded by microphones and with "other trappings so familiar to similar meetings in Germany and Italy" and called upon the youth of Iraq to unite and make sacrifices for the Arab nation. Students were again called out on parade in March on the birthday anniversary of Ghazi.[125]

But it was Sami Shawkat who, once he took office as Director General of Education in 1939, formalized the movement and created the uniforms, ranks, and badges.[126] Regulations were broadened and students were required to be in uniform at all times, "in order to recognize with ease students of government schools wherever they may go and sow in them the spirit of militarism."[127] Now combined with the scouts, which organized elementary school students, the Futuwwah consisted of units of "rovers" and *fityan* from the intermediate and secondary schools. If the students did not pass the military course, they risked failure in the entire year's work.[128]

Shawkat, the "Protector of Chivalry," and Jamali were Generals Number One and Two—resplendent in uniforms adorned with gold braid, crossed sword and pen. They led the movement along with Major Fadhil al-Janabi, who had accompanied the students to Germany and was on loan from the Iraqi army as military advisor to the Ministry of Education. Teachers were assigned rank and appropriate insignia according to their pay and were required, after enough material was secured, to

wear their uniforms during military training and formal meetings.[129] By law in 1940 Iraqi and foreign teachers had to be in
uniform during school hours or be considered on leave without
pay.[130] The Minister of Education appeared suitably attired at
meetings of the Chamber of Deputies.[131]

In 1939 Jamali and Shawkat chose a summer resort in
northern Iraq for Futuwwah summer training, one month's stay
for students to be mandatory. That summer over 500 teachers
attended, most of them instructors in physical education. Detachments of the army and the Kirkuk Futuwwah saw them off.
On their return, they were feted by an army band which accompanied them in formation from the railroad station, and the
Minister of Education expressed his satisfaction with their performance of military training.[132]

The British thought that, in theory, the movement
was healthy for Iraq: "it should be physically and socially beneficial because it provides for discipline on the square (the British
teachers all say that lack of discipline is one of the worst difficulties in the classes)," they wrote in 1939.[133] And al-Husri generally supported the Futuwwah, like the scouts, as a socializing
agent; in a lecture to the Muthanna Club in 1941, he attributed
the fall of France earlier in that year to political and moral division, factionalism, and individualism.[134]

But he was disgusted with Shawkat's fanaticism, with
his flamboyance, and with the uniforms and badges. "The best
fools," he quotes one of Shawkat's detractors, "are proficient in
the profession of death"[135] and, noting that Sami Shawkat was a
physician, other critics added that the "art of death can only be
perfected by an ignorant doctor."[136] Paul Knabenshue, the
American minister in Baghdad, was more specific. He criticized
the excesses of Shawkat's speeches and their influence on the
students, claiming that the excessive nationalist feelings had
influenced the students to the extreme anti-British excesses on
the day of King Ghazi's death and had stirred up the students of
Mosul. The demonstration which resulted had led to the death
of the British Consul, Monck-Mason.[137]

For Shawkat had been extolling the virtues of the

army and military life for half a decade, extolling Mussolini and his Black Shirts and calling for power, discipline, and sacrifice. In his "Profession of Death" he told Iraqi youth that in order to achieve power they had to know how to die. Nothing was so holy as "to spill one's blood for the sake of one's country" and to "tear one's enemy limb from limb and pour out his blood."[138] Shawkat had personally staged and led parades and demonstrations in which he appeared on horseback and in full regalia.[139] This increasing militarism in the schools was a natural corollary to the growing role of the army in Iraqi politics.

V. The Army

An Iraqi army was a nationalist requirement not only for internal peacekeeping but for the transmission of pan-Arab ideology. During the interwar years, the army became an instrument for the propagation of nationalism in two ways. First, by advocating universal military conscription, the Sharifians hoped to make the army a school for the nation, an extension of the educational system. Second, the officer corps entered politics. Certainly one might say that the army had been in politics since 1921 as the Sharifians were former military officers. But the officers, who, in 1936, began the series of military coups which ended in 1941 with the military in control of the government, were career military men, ex-Ottoman officers who had never entered civilian life, and the new generation of Iraqi army officers. This chapter, therefore, will survey the development of the Iraqi army and the conscription issue, and will analyze the role of the officers in Iraqi politics.

Responsible for Iraq's defense under the terms of the mandate, Britain acceded to Faysal's demand for a national army. Certainly during the early years, the not yet demobilized British and Indian battalions, the armored car companies, the auxiliary force of British loyal primarily Assyrian tribesmen, and the two detachments of the Royal Air Force sufficed to defend British interests—Iraq, itself, its oilfields, and the lines of communication of the Empire—from external foe and internal rebel and secessionist. Throughout the 1920s British Royal Air Force (RAF) bombing missions, Churchill's innovation in cheap and effective internal peacekeeping, along with Assyrian support, kept the Kurds and the various Arab tribesmen in line. But a national army kept small and dependent upon Britain, used primarily for internal policing and border holding, was an excellent expedient.[1] Advised, trained, and organized by the British and financed by at least 25 percent of Iraq's annual revenue as stipulated by the Military Agreement of 1924, the army would relieve the British taxpayer (a common concern always uppermost in the minds of British policymakers);[2] it would substitute Iraqi defense responsibility for British and at the same time fulfill requirements for eventual Iraqi independence and entry into the League of Nations.

From the Iraqi side, the army was to be both a symbol of the regime's legitimacy and a mechanism for creating internal cohesion and loyalty.[3] The British, Nuri al-Sa'id and Ja'far al-'Askari viewed a national army as a solution to the immediate loyalty problem of the more than 640 returning ex-Ottoman army officers, only 190 of whom had supported Faysal.[4] The Sharifian officers, to be sure, received the politically powerful positions; others were encouraged to join the army and were required to take refresher courses under British tutelage. Many were dissatisfied and threatened to go and work for the French in Syria or with Mustafa Kemal. Some taught school and others, such as Yasin al-Hashimi, accepted jobs and financial perquisites in the provincial bureaucracy, and later entered the political opposition.[5]

Recruits were scarce in the beginning, despite a palace-sponsored newspaper campaign advocating the strengthening of the armed forces. Faysal even tried to instill nationalist spirit in the country by assigning nationalist names to different units.[6] But it was not until the British decided in 1922 to make the pay of the Iraqi soldier equal to that of the Assyrian levy that enlistment began to exceed demand—requiring maximum monthly quotas—and the army slowly grew from some 3,500 men in 1921 to just under 12,000 at independence.[7] By the mid-1920s there was no lack of enlistees even from Shi'i areas where the tribesmen seemed to prefer army discipline to shaykhly authority. In 1927 the first class of the new Royal Military College graduated and cadets were studying in England and India. The next year the Staff College opened. Military standards generally improved because of the policy of placing certain units directly under British officers and a newly instituted pro-

gram of general education for the rank and file taught by selected instructors who had taken the course in civilian schools.
Even the British seemed pleased, remarking as early as 1926 that
the army was a "valuable means of fostering a true national
spirit," providing a "degree of homogeneity," a common language, and a "common obedience to the central government."[8]

Nevertheless, the nationalists constantly opposed
the British policy of restricting the size of the army, and as late as
1933 Faysal feared that the army could not contain simultaneous
insurrections on two fronts. The government had at its disposal
15,000 guns; but there were more than 100,000 rifles in private
hands.[9] For this reason as well as the ideological commitment to
the use of the army to inculcate Iraqi patriotism, Faysal, as had
his first Minister of Defense, Ja'far al-'Askari as early as 1922,
advocated universal military conscription.

For the Sharifians, Phebe Marr in her biography of
Yasin al-Hashimi informs us, military conscription had become
close to a dogma if not an ideology, to be used not only to
strengthen the army but also to achieve national cohesion. Derived from their own military experiences, these ex-Ottoman
officers preferred the "cheaper method of induction and indoctrination" to the "longer and more arduous task of political development." During the parliamentary debate on the issue in
1927, Ja'far al-'Askari, for example, took conscription past military defense:

> We will . . . open the door of participation in the defense of the
> country before all classes of the nation. There is no doubt that an
> army in which all these classes participate, will be more inclu-
> sive of the racial qualities and national virtues with which the
> Iraqi nation is graced than an army built on any other basis.

And Yasin al-Hashimi, while advocating induction as cheaper
than a volunteer army, extended conscription to everyone. In
theory, he claimed, conscription should not be limited to those
under twenty for military service but applied equally to all citizens for the exploitation of natural and industrial resources.[10]

Even Sati' al-Husri considered military service in the

cause of nationalism to be more important than education, for elementary education was only preparation for service to the state. In a speech to the teachers, he declared that the passage of the conscription law in 1934 was the most important event in the Arab east. Conscription would place individuals from different backgrounds in common service to the state. The barracks would have more influence than the school, he maintained, for the moral education taught to children dissipates after adolescence. Iraqi youth would now socialize with comrades from diverse backgrounds for years rather than hours, and military service would accustom recruits to altruism and equalization, rather than individualism, and to discipline and the preparation for the sacrifice of "blood and soul for the people and the nation".[11]

It was the Sharifians in the main who supported the first attempt at passage of a conscription bill which occupied the legislature from 1926 to 1928. Both the British and the Shi'is opposed the measure with varying degrees of intensity. While the British gave their moral support to the idea, supporting conscription as a cost-effective method for building up the army, they nevertheless warned that unless the government could generate overwhelming support for it, conscription would not pass. They pointed to the Turkish experience in Iraq, and showed that the Turks had not been able to enforce mass induction outside of the towns during the war. The British also refused the use of British forces to bring the writ of Baghdad to the tribes.[12]

But Iraq's Shi'i tribes had contributed their own paramilitary forces to the Turks in Ottoman times—some 16,000 tribesmen during peace and double their number in wartime. Toward the end of the nineteenth century, however, after the reforms of the Tanzimat began to take hold, and when military service became secularized and no longer a Muslim preserve, Shi'i interests ran to local concerns and tribesmen tended to purchase military exemption rather than serve under discriminatory Sunni officers. The Yazidis and others reacted to conscription during World War I with armed resistance or mass desertion and willing capture. The Shi'is, therefore, saw national conscription to be renewed domination by the Sunni effendi and increasing control by the Baghdad central authority. It was also a convenient opportunity for tribal shaykhs to send rivals off to the army in retaliation for old grievances. If it were ever to be adopted, Sir Kinahan Cornwallis—the British advisor to the Ministry of Interior—observed, military induction should not be enforced south of Baghdad.[13]

Nevertheless, some Shi'i saw the issue as useful for political leverage, offering their support for conscription in exchange for increased Shi'i participation in the government and civil service. They revived the dormant al-Nahda party and renewed advocacy for Shi'i interests. Unfortunately for the nationalists, however, the debates over conscription in 1927 coincided with a number of events interpreted as anti-Shi'i. These were the al-Nasuli affair and the general turmoil over control within the Ministry of Education (see chapter 4), which coincided with the sensed anti-Shi'i provocation at the mosque in Kadhimayn on the tenth day of Muharram,[14] in addition to Iraqi-British negotiations over the treaty and Iraq's desire for early independence. Throughout the next year opposition increased and the matter was mentioned more infrequently in Faysal's speeches from the throne and in parliamentary debate. By 1929, with all attention turned to the issue of the treaty, interest gradually dissipated.

Five years later, overwhelming popular demand for conscription brought immediate legislation. The bill was revived in 1933 by Rashid 'Ali's government and it passed easily, carried by the wave of frenzied support for the army after the Assyrian affair during the summer. The army had been used in peacekeeping missions before. It had performed adequately, but it was generally backed by the RAF which received the credit. But when the Iraqi forces tried to smoke out the Kurdish forces of Shaykh Barzan in 1931, their noses were bloodied.[15] Nevertheless, Faysal continued his campaign to create support for the Iraqi military immediately after independence by introducing compulsory military education in the schools under the combined direction of the ministries of education and defense.[16] There were private campaigns to encourage people to donate funds in order to augment military equipment and supplies. Thus, during the impending Assyrian crisis from May to June 1933, the Ministry of Education solicited funds from students and teachers to buy a tank; the Ministry of Defense asked its employees to donate two-days salary to a fund to buy a plane; and nationalists in southern Syria, desiring to express their appreciation for the Iraqi military, proposed to purchase and donate to the army an airplane or a tank to be named "Southern Syria."[17]

The Assyrian crisis, which erupted in the summer of 1933 and threatened the internal stability of the newly independent state, provided the Iraqi army with its first major opportunity against a formidable and thoroughly unpopular foe. It is not the point here, however, to dwell upon the events that terminated in the "Assyrian tragedy" on August 11, 1933, the systematic Iraqi massacre of the male inhabitants of the Assyrian village of Sumayl. The moral issues and the foreign revulsion at Iraq's treatment of minorities have been studied elsewhere.[18] What is significant in this discussion of the army and nationalism is the popular reaction to the "Iraqi victory," which resulted in the immediate passage of conscription and catapulted the army into politics, making it the focus of national unity.

In short, the British imported the Assyrian Christians during World War I where they fought with the British, and they continued to serve as British auxiliary troops after the war. Many settled, under British protection, in the north. With Iraqi independence, their new spiritual-temporal leader, the Mar Sham'un, a British-educated young man in his twenties, decided to claim Assyrian autonomy within Iraq, again looking to Britain for support. While he pressed his case before the League of Nations in 1932, his followers planned to resign *en masse* from the levies and to concentrate in the north, creating a *de facto* Assyrian enclave. In June 1933, the Patriarch was invited to Baghdad for negotiations with Hikmat Sulayman's government and was detained there after he refused to relinquish temporal authority. In August, more than one thousand Assyrians who had been refused asylum in Syria crossed the border to return to their villages in Iraq. The French had notified the Iraqis that the Assyrians were not armed; but while the Iraqi soldiers were disarming those whose arms had been returned, shots were fired resulting in thirty Iraqi deaths and some Assyrian casualties. Anti-Assyrian and anti-British xenophobia, apparent throughout the crisis, accelerated. Reports circulated of Assyrian mutilation of Iraqi soldiers. In Baghdad, the government panicked, fearing disaster as the Assyrians presented a formidable fighting force that could provoke a general uprising in the north. The government unleashed Kurdish irregulars who killed some one hundred inhabitants of two Assyrian villages.[19] Then, on August 11, a machine gun company under the command of Bakr Sidqi's aide, marched into Sumayl and systematically massacred the entire male population.

From the nationalists' point of view, the Assyrians were British proxies, to be used by their masters to destroy the new state whose independence the British had consistently opposed.[20] The British had brought the alien and swaggering anti-Arab Assyrians, who had their Christian sympathizers in London, to Iraq. They allowed their auxiliary troops to retain their arms and granted them special duty and privileges: guarding military air installations and receiving higher pay than the Iraqi recruit. Under British protection, the Assyrians did not become Iraqi citizens after independence but settled in a separate enclave in the north, preparing to destroy Iraq's internal cohesion by becoming independent and by inciting others to follow their example. And, as a final insult to their host country, they disparaged Iraq's reputation abroad, drawing international criticism over Iraq's treatment of minorities. It does not seem unusual, therefore, that the Iraqis saw the Assyrian campaign as a strike against Britain and so enthusiastically chanted: "Ghazi shook London and made it cry."[21]

Immediately, there was demand for a conscription bill. Throughout the crisis, beginning in late spring 1933, public feeling against the Assyrians was at "fever heat," American representative Paul Knabenshue wrote to Washington. Tribesmen offered to serve in the army, although their motives were questionable, running more to loot than to politics. In August the government *Ikha* party of Mosul demanded that the central government "ruthlessly" stamp out the rebellion, that it eliminate all foreign influence in Iraqi affairs, and that the government take immediate steps to enact a law for compulsory military service. The next week forty-nine Kurdish tribal chieftains joined in a pro-conscription telegram to the government, expressing thanks for punishing the "Assyrian insurgents," stating that "a nation can be proud of itself only through its power, and since evidence of this power is the army," they requested compulsory military service.[22] Rashid ʿAli presented the bill to parliament. His government fell before it was legislated and Jamil Midfaʿi's government passed conscription in January 1934.

That is not to say that all opposition disintegrated. The tribes still considered induction to be an attempt by Baghdad to weaken tribal organization, and the Shiʿi marsh Arabs, who had heretofore been recruited as mercenaries, bemoaned their lost livelihood.[23] Moneys already allocated for the Gharraf project, the dam to be built at al-Kut to irrigate Shiʿi areas, were to be transferred for the implementation of conscription.[24] By 1935 so many effendis were leaving the country to evade the draft that the government increased passport control and sponsored demonstrations enjoining all eligible young men to join the army.[25] Conscription was uneven at best: it could be applied only to areas where the Iraqi census had been taken, breadwinners were exempt, and anyone could purchase exemption.[26] Nevertheless, by 1936 the army had doubled in size to 23,000 men, and the air force grew from a few planes to three squadrons.[27]

The army, and especially the officer corps, emerged from the Assyrian campaign as the new national symbol led by their new hero, the new king: Faysal's son Ghazi. For by the end of August 1933, Faysal was dead, his support completely eclipsed by the popular adulation of Ghazi. Ghazi had vociferously backed the army and the commander of the north, Bakr Sidqi, who was thought to have given the orders for the massacre. Faysal was seen as a British puppet, thoroughly dominated by London—for had he not signed the hated treaty? On the contrary, Khaldun Husry points out, Faysal was a strong monarch who even in the end did not bow to British pressure: he did not remove Bakr Sidqi from his command, and it was he who sent the strong force to the north to deal with the Assyrians.[28] Nevertheless, at the review of the returning heroes in Mosul, a few days before Faysal's death, enthusiasm for Ghazi was especially great, but his father's name was never mentioned. Ghazi solemnly decorated Bakr Sidqi, the victorious general.[29]

For Ghazi represented the new Iraqi, the younger generation which grew up during the 1920s, now actively expressing its animosity toward the British and their Iraqi supporters and its support for Arab nationalism represented by the army. The American dispatches provide us with a graphic illustration. In February 1932, the Royal Theatre in Baghdad showed a British film, "Tell England," which depicted scenes of Gallipoli during the war. From the first night, the Arab section of the audience applauded loudly every scene in which a British soldier was killed or wounded. Each night the audience grew larger, the crowds of Iraqis pushing to get in increased, and the pandemonium in the theater reached such a pitch during those scenes that the mayor of Baghdad finally refused the theater permission to show the film, fearing a clash between the Iraqis and the privates of the RAF.[30] These Iraqis were the young men who idolized Ghazi, carrying his photograph with them; some even had it in their wallets more than twenty years later.[31]

Like his father, Ghazi had spent part of his youth with the bedouin, but he disliked desert life.[32] Faysal's personal physician, Sir Harry C. Sinderson Pasha, suggested that a British public school education would straighten the boy out, but Ghazi performed poorly in his studies at Harrow and wished only to have an automobile.[33] Back in Iraq, Ghazi was happiest taking classes in the military college, where he excelled in horsemanship. He liked drinking, motorcycles, planes, motion picture equipment, practical jokes, and, especially, fast cars.[34]

As king, he disliked touring the country and was ill at ease in the company of tribal skaykhs, so he neglected them. He wore dark glasses during his rare public appearances and frequently complained of heart trouble and other ailments, summoning his physician to the palace in the middle of the night. At times he attempted to play his hand in politics, but the Ottoman-trained army officers of his father's generation who held the power in Iraq were not his personal friends.[35]

In fact, the king disliked Yasin al-Hashimi, especially when the Prime Minister tried to curb Ghazi's private life in the wake of the king's sister's marriage scandal during the summer of 1936. After the news broke in Baghdad that Ghazi's sister had eloped with a Greek waiter, there were discussions to consider replacing him with Amir Zayd.[36] Ghazi remained; but the Prime Minister tried to limit the king to suitable companions and behavior. When Yasin's government was overthrown a few months later, therefore, it was thought that the king was privy to the coup.[37]

Ghazi never got along with Nuri either. More than once, Nuri and the British discussed replacing Ghazi with another Hashimite.[38] And, in 1939, the British ambassador tells us, Nuri had the king's mail censored. Ghazi received so much "provocative fan mail" after his radio broadcasts, notes Peterson, that it served to further "unbalance the king."[39] When Ghazi died soon after, Nuri was accused of complicity in his death (see chapter 2).[40]

The British thought Ghazi totally irresponsible, showing no aptitude for his heavy responsibilities. They accused him of conspiracy in the Bakr Sidqi coup and later were especially exercised over the king's broadcasts from his private radio station in the palace—it was said to be a gift from the Germans.[41] For two months in 1939, Ghazi continuously advocated the annexation of Kuwait by Iraq. He read letters violently attacking the British-sponsored Shaykh of Kuwait and his family, calling his regime feudal, and suggested that the Kuwaitis look to Iraq for leadership. The British ambassador spoke to the king. There was a lull in the broadcasts; then they began again.[42]

Faysal had been apprehensive about Ghazi's character and ability,[43] but the young Iraqis enjoyed the king's pluck and his confrontation with the British. Iraqi youth listened to him entranced. And although Ghazi's speeches contributed to an abortive revolt in Kuwait in which several persons were killed, Ghazi summoned the Shaykh of Kuwait to Iraq in order to apologize to him, thus making the venerable shaykh appear inferior to the young king.[44]

Ghazi's accession to the throne of Iraq signaled a shift in the role of the army. Idolized for its successes against the Assyrians in 1933, the army was now to be used by the politicians to suppress tribal revolts which were incited from Baghdad. The tribal revolts of 1935–1936 which ultimately brought Yasin al-Hashimi to power were a case in point. Yasin al-Hashimi, Rashid 'Ali al-Kaylani, and Hikmat Sulayman, using their Ikha party to represent Shi'i grievances, conspired with Shi'i shaykhs of the Middle Euphrates area and tribal shaykhs of the north to revolt against the central government. 'Ali Jawdat, prime minister at the time, considered suppressing the revolts by force, but Hikmat Sulayman convinced his friend, General Bakr Sidqi, commander of the forces in the north, not to lend active support to the government. Unable to cope with the revolt, 'Ali Jawdat resigned.

The Ikha leaders refused to take office, leaving the government to Jamil al-Midfa'i. Al-Midfa'i ordered Chief of Staff Taha al-Hashimi (Yasin's brother) to send reinforcements against the tribes, but Taha reported that the army was too weak. Al-Midfa'i also considered arresting the Ikha conspirators, but his cabinet fell thirteen days after taking power. In March 1935 Yasin al-Hashimi became prime minister.

Once in power, Yasin ordered the tribes to lay down their arms. The Ikha's original allies sided with the government but a shaykh of the Banu Izrayj, while originally inspired by the Baghdad politicians to revolt, now opposed an Ikha government in power. He was involved in a land settlement claim and feared that this government would not settle it in his favor. He started a revolt at Rumaythah on the railway line between Baghdad and Basra. This time, when Yasin called upon Bakr Sidqi to quell the revolt, the general suppressed it, ruthlessly.

By 1936, therefore, the army already had some experience in politics. It began to see itself filling the political void created by the death of Faysal and the succession by a weak king. It became not only the focus of popular adulation, but an instrument in the increasing militarization of society. As the years went by, the military as a profession became more popular than teaching.[45] The government encouraged public participation in augmenting military equipment and more than once solicited contributions from government employees toward the purchase of planes.[46] When, in 1935, Yasin al-Hashimi and other ex-Ottoman officers proposed to apply to the Ministry of Interior for the organization of an ex-servicemen's association, Knabenshue remarked that it was just "another example of the efforts being made to inculcate a military spirit throughout the country." The society was to include former officers who fought on both sides during World War I, and its purpose was to "disseminate the spirit of militarism in the country's youth by means of lectures and publications."[47]

Toward the end of the 1930s, the officers became the center of political in-fighting, with Rashid 'Ali and Nuri al'Sa'id plying them with wine, food, and whiskey, each vying for their political support.[48] Corruption was rampant. Both Tawfiq al-Suwaydi—disdainful of the young military upstarts—and Taha al-Hashimi, their beloved commander who deplored the spread of the civilian graft epidemic in his army, tell us how the politicians competed for support and describe the overriding importance paid to the perquisites of power, prestige, and privilege: rank, salary, cheap housing, servants, and medical treatment in Europe.[49]

Certainly the politicians tried to keep the army out of daily decision-making, but Ghazi continuously asked for the officers' advice, creating a feeling of military indispensability in political life. The officers interfered in nonmilitary matters. Thus, for example, they insisted on Baghdad—for strategic reasons—as the location for an oil refinery which should have been built outside of the capital, relieving the city of pollution. And they opposed—again for security—the proposed rail connections between Iraq and Kermanshah and between Iraq and Turkey, which would have included Iraq as a direct link between Iran and Europe.[50]

The Army in Politics

The army began to involve itself actively in politics beginning in October 1936 when General Bakr Sidqi, conspiring with Hikmat Sulayman, overthrew the government of Yasin al-Hashimi. In a sense the series of military coups which Bakr Sidqi began in 1936 can be seen as a series of political intrigues, a continuation of the personal politics which characterized the first few years of Iraqi independence, substituting the army for tribal revolt as the vehicle to power. And, on the surface, this is a valid description of the eight changes of government that occurred from 1936 on and ended with the second British occupation of Iraq in June 1941. But this superficial political in-fighting masked an undercurrent of internecine ideological struggle within the officer corps itself, which represented, over the long view, an attempt to chart Iraq's relations with the rest of the Arab world. A short description, therefore, of these political coups will provide a framework for the subsequent analysis of the ideological struggle within the officer corps.[51]

The Bakr Sidqi coup which overthrew the most stable government Iraq had seen since independence—that of Yasin al-Hashimi—was a case of political pique. Both Hikmat Sulayman, omitted from Yasin's government in 1935, and Bakr Sidqi, a Kurd who had achieved acclaim for his role in suppressing the Assyrian and tribal revolts, but who saw no opportunity for promotion in an army controlled by Yasin's brother, Taha al-Hashimi, combined forces to overthrow the regime. They represented two political extremes: the social reform Ahali group which Hikmat joined and the army.[52] Hikmat headed the government and Bakr, preferring to exercise influence from behind the scenes, became Chief of Staff. Another officer, 'Abd al-Latif Nuri, became Minister of Defense.

A group of pan-Arab army officers, among them Husayn Fawzi, Amin al-'Umari, Fahmi Sa'id, Kamil Shabib, Mahmud Salman, Salah-al-Din al-Sabbagh, and 'Aziz Yamulki conspired and had Bakr Sidqi assassinated at the Mosul airport in August 1937. The commander of the Mosul forces, Amin al-'Umari, issued a manifesto declaring that his forces would no longer support the cabinet. Hikmat resigned a few days later, replaced by Jamil al-Midfaʻi, a neutral in the Bakr/Hikmat vs. Yasin/Nuri/Rashid ʻAli struggle, and was persuaded, as he was again in 1941, to hold the line until the politics could be sorted out. He became prime minister because he would "lower the curtain" on the events of the recent past, that is to say, grant amnesty to both sides: to Bakr Sidqi's assassins who had killed the general because he had ordered the death of the popular Jaʻfar al-ʻAskari soon after taking power, and to Hikmat Sulayman, the surviving leader of the Bakr government.[53]

Revenge, however, was one issue around which the pro-Yasin forces rallied in order to overthrow al-Midfaʻi. In 1937, while in exile, Yasin died of a heart attack, most likely brought on by the coup.[54] Nuri and Rashid ʻAli, however, continued to intrigue a return to power and, as the British would not help them, they turned to the pan-Arab officers, telling them that since they helped put al-Midfaʻi in office, he owed them his support. Al-Midfaʻi was inadvertently of service to the conspirators. He tried to curb the power of the pan-Arab officers and so provoked them to action. They wanted to avenge the death of Yasin al-Hashimi whom they admired because of his support of Palestine and they wanted to promote pan-Arabism. But they were restrained by al-Midfaʻi's appointment of Sabih Najib as Minister of Defense. Here was an attempt to curb further any power of the young officers as Najib wanted the army back in the barracks and the junior officers out of politics. He began to promote former Bakr supporters over the pan-Arab officers and their supporters. Fearing for their own fortunes, the Four Colonels—Salah al-Din al-Sabbagh, Fahmi Saʻid, Kamil Shabib, and Mahmud Salman—turned to the good offices of Taha al-Hashimi and to the politicians Nuri al-Saʻid and Rashid ʻAli, who were only too eager to use the new army as their route back to Baghdad. In December 1938 the officers insisted on al-Midfaʻi's resignation. Amin al-ʻUmari and Husayn Fawzi did not participate. ʻAziz Yamulki broke the news secretly to the Prime Minister at a public gathering and al-Midfaʻi yielded in order to avoid civil war. The politicians who had left in 1936 now returned to power.

Nuri spent his first year or so as prime minister plotting to avenge old grievances while trying to control the army officers who brought him to power. Taha al-Hashimi took the defense portfolio and Rashid 'Ali became the power behind the throne, the Chief of the Royal Diwan. Disappointed with this position, however, Rashid 'Ali spent the time drawing the officers away from Nuri. Undeterred, Nuri soon found the opportunity to imprison political enemies and to emerge in control of all factions because of a plot against King Ghazi in March 1939, Ghazi's death a month later, and the assassination of the Minister of Finance, Nuri's friend Rustam Haydar, in January 1940.

The plot, uncovered by Iraqi Intelligence (the alleged perpetrator was said to have confessed the plans to Amir 'Abd al-Ilah, Ghazi's cousin, who told the police) was to murder the chief politicians at a banquet at the home of 'Abd al-Ilah. He was then to assume power. But it was found to be spurious, at best, by the Court of Inquiry.[55] In spite of the findings, Hikmat Sulayman was convicted to avenge the death of Ja'far al-'Askari, Nuri's brother-in-law.[56] This left only the king to stand in Nuri's way. Consequently, Ghazi's death a month later, while probably an accident, was seen by the nationalists as a British-Nuri conspiracy, especially because of Ghazi's anti-British sentiments. In the struggle over the appointment of a regent for Faysal II, Nuri and the Four Colonels supported the malleable twenty-six year old 'Abd al-Ilah over Amir Zayd, the choice of the Midfa'i group: Jamil al-Midfa'i and the officers Amin al-'Umari and Husayn Fawzi. Finally, Rustam Haydar's assassin, whose motives were personal, was found to have spoken to Sabih Najib at a party before the event. Najib, enemy of the pan-Arab officers, was convicted as an accessory and as a pro-Nazi sympathizer.[57]

Thus, by February 1940, Nuri had finished with his enemies list, gained an ally in the pro-British regent, and decided to at once resign and then to return to power taking the defense portfolio in a Rashid 'Ali government. The Four Colonels, at this time, resisted a government under Rashid 'Ali, preferring their protector, Nuri, instead. But the al-Midfa'i faction—Chief of Staff Husayn Fawzi, 'Aziz Yamulki, and Amin al-'Umari, wanted to remove both Nuri and Taha. Fawzi's ultimatum to the

Regent was thwarted when the Four Colonels threatened civil war. 'Abd al-Ilah sided with the colonels, Nuri was back in power, and he immediately retired Husayn Fawzi, Amin al-'Umari, and 'Aziz Yamulki, all of whom had originally brought him back from Egypt. The Prime Minister proceeded to promote friends of the Four Colonels in their places. Amin Zaki became Chief of Staff and Kamil Shabib replaced Amin al-'Umari as Commander of the First Division. The Four Colonels, led by Salah al-Din al-Sabbagh, now virtually controlled the country.

Two months later, in April 1940, Nuri was gone, replaced by Rashid 'Ali, after Taha tried to soften al-Sabbagh's influence; he transferred the Colonel from the General Staff to Commander of the Third Division away from Baghdad. The Colonels called in the Mufti of Jerusalem by then residing in Baghdad, to mediate among Taha, Nuri, and Rashid 'Ali, and on March 31 Nuri resigned. Nuri retained Foreign Affairs, however, and the Colonels still sided with him on issues of policy. But Nuri and the British were unhappy with Rashid 'Ali and in January 1941, Nuri tried to oust the Prime Minister. Now the Colonels sided with Rashid 'Ali and, although he had their support, the Prime Minister realized that most of the people opposed him, so he asked the regent to call for new elections. 'Abd al-Ilah had meanwhile taken a trip to Diwaniyyah, where he had the support of the commander of the division, deliberately leaving the order for new elections unsigned. Al-Sabbagh urged the regent to name Taha prime minister and, although 'Abd al-Ilah preferred Speaker of the Senate Muhammad al-Sadr, he acquiesced.

Taha's tenure lasted two months. At the end of March 1941, in another attempt to weaken the Colonels, Taha ordered Kamil Shabib out of Baghdad. Shabib refused. Chief of Staff Amin Zaki and the Commander of the Armored Forces Fahmi Sa'id had a "chat" with Taha, and he resigned. The army attempted to seize the regent but failed. Amin Zaki declared that 'Abd al-Ilah, having fled, had failed in his duties as regent and thus forfeited his position. He ordered Rashid 'Ali to form a government of National Defense, appointed a new regent, and the events known as the Rashid 'Ali coup began.

The Four Colonels, who now controlled the country, were the transitional generation. Like Nuri al-Sa'id, 'Ali Jawdat al-Ayyubi, and Ja'far al-'Askari, they were products of the Ottoman military system. They, too, came from lower-middle-class backgrounds and used the military for an education and as a career. But they came to Istanbul late, joined the Arab nationalist clubs just before the war, and fought on the Turkish side, eventually finding their ways to Syria and Faysal. They returned to Iraq under British occupation, became career officers in the British-controlled army, and opposed the treaty.

Unlike the previous generation, however, they were neither pro-British nor Turkophiles, nor local Iraqi nationalists. They had not gone through the ideological conflict of Ottomanism versus Arabism. On the contrary, they were pan-Arabs, fighting for Iraqi independence from Britain and for the liberation of Syria and Palestine from French and British control. Thus, to them, working with the British was treason, not pragmatism. Salah al-Din al-Sabbagh, who emerged as the leader of the pan-Arab army officers, was from Mosul and had attended an elite school in Beirut before his education at the Ottoman Military College. He took post-graduate courses in England. He was a member of the Arab nationalist societies before the war, but became active politically only later in Iraq over the issues of Palestine and arms for the Iraqi army. In a last letter to his family before his death, al-Sabbagh summed up his position: "Had I been an Iraqi nationalist, I would have become more endeared by the English than Nuri al-Sa'id and 'Abd al-Ilah, but it is my sacrifice for beloved Palestine and Syria which led to the condition I am in now."[58]

Al-Sabbagh's circle in turn influenced the junior officers who, by 1940, were described as pro-German and anti-British. This was the generation educated in Iraqi schools via Sati' al-Husri's curriculum, where they received a pan-Arab education. They learned how to put their nationalism to work in the Military College.

Opened in 1924, the Military College admitted secondary and law school graduates, and those of other recognized suitable institutions, but in the mid 1930s entrance requirements were lowered.[59] There was a separate class for sons of tribal shaykhs "suited to their standard of knowledge," many of whom later became anti-British, thus showing, to the British mind, a distinct lack of gratitude for the extra trouble it took to get them into the school.[60] Other entrance requirements were a lack of anti-social behavior, good health, and Iraqi citizenship, although some Syrians and Palestinians were admitted.[61]

The school was set up along British lines and staffed by British and Iraqi officers. English technical manuals were translated into Arabic.[62] Like their European counterparts, the cadets studied continental military campaigns, especially those of Napoleon and the Prussian army, and, as in most military schools, the development of the German General Staff. The Germany of Frederick the Great and Bismarck was the model, and although it was not assigned reading, many cadets did read von Clausewitz's *On War*. Some books on the French Revolution translated in Egypt reached them, but by far the most influential were works about the unification of Germany and Italy, the book *The Awakening of Japan,* and most especially, lectures on modern Turkey by Tawfiq Husayn.[63]

It was during Tawfiq Husayn's tenure at the Military College Mahmud al-Durrah who attended his classes tells us, that the army began the process of politicization. Appointed lecturer in military history at the college by Taha al-Hashimi who knew him from Istanbul, Tawfiq Husayn—a product of the Ottoman military system—had remained in the Turkish army until his return to Iraq in the early 1930s. His enthusiastic lectures, which emphasized nationalism, influenced the post-1930 generation of Iraqi officers. In them, he advocated that Iraq be like Turkey and Iran, that the military intervene in politics. His hero was Atatürk and, al-Durrah describes, his lectures inspired more than one officer to envision himself in the role of the Turkish leader. By 1934 Tawfiq Husayn had more than seventy officers, including al-Sabbagh, in his circle, and his encouragement of the military to enter politics directly influenced those who followed Bakr Sidqi.[64]

Other ex-Ottoman officers taught in Iraq. Taha al-

Hashimi, a graduate of the Baghdad military *rüşdiye* and *idadi* programs, attended the Istanbul *Harbiye* and Staff College. Although he served in the Ottoman army where he reached the rank of Lieutenant Colonel, he was better known as a teacher because of his predilection for military studies, history, and geography. Taha was Ghazi's tutor. He served as Director General of Education in 1935 and began the student missions to Germany. Most of his career in Iraq, however, was as Commander in Chief of the Iraqi army where he was eventually promoted to General. Taha also taught in the military college and wrote textbooks. He entered politics after the death of his brother, Yasin al-Hashimi, but was considered a weak replacement. From 1939 to 1941 he was the intermediary between the Colonels, Nuri, and the Jerusalem Mufti, believing that the army's role was to fill the political void.

Bakr Sidqi taught mountain warfare in class and politics to a group at his home, and Fawzi al-Qawuqji, who resigned his commission in the Iraqi army to lead the guerillas during the Palestine revolt in 1936, also taught in Iraq.

But by the mid-1930s, al-Sabbagh had broken away from Tawfiq Husayn to form his own more pan-Arab group which, by 1939, successfully challenged the "Iraqi-firsters" for leadership within the officer corps. More and more entering cadets were from Arab Sunni backgrounds. Although originally the military college was open to all ethnic and communal groups, fewer non-Sunnis attended as their colleagues continuously gauged their feelings of *'Urubah* (Arabness). And while the totalitarian political regimes of the 1930s certainly impressed the officers, they had no interest in social or economic reform.[65] Their cause was Arabism. "I do not believe in the democracy of the English nor in the Nazism of the Germans nor in the Bolshevism of the Russians," al-Sabbagh wrote. "I am an Arab Muslim. I do not want anything as a substitute in the way of pretensions and philosophies. . ."[66] To that end, al-Sabbagh joined the pan-Arab clubs, was one of those who trained the Futuwwah units,[67] and worked for his major goals—the rearming of Iraq and the independence of Palestine from British control.

Bearing in mind the background and goals of these

officers who were to assume power in Iraq, the shifting alliances and frequent changes in government assume a significance beyond personal politics. Bakr Sidqi was brought down by the pan-Arab nationalists. There was general criticism of Bakr's private life, which increased to disgust over his debauched and immoral behavior, his lack of religion, and his personal inclination toward dictatorship and his delusions of grandeur[68]—there had even been talk of erecting a statue of the general in Baghdad. Bakr and his followers, who were inexperienced young men, along with Hikmat, frequented the nightspots and Bakr's influence declined as his excessive behavior in the Baghdad cabarets and nightclubs increased and as his ruthless suppression of the opposition, which was said to have resulted in several deaths, drove many into exile. The people of Mosul resented Bakr's attempt on the lives of two of Mosul's political leaders; and the shayks feared the implementation of land reform advocated by the Ahali members of the coalition cabinet which could depreciate their wealth and influence.[69]

These Arab nationalists avenged Bakr's injudicious order soon after the coup to execute the popular founder of the Iraqi army, Ja'far al-'Askari. They retaliated against Bakr's promotion of Kurds and non-Arabs in the army over the Arab nationalists to the point where, according to al-Sabbagh, his group represented only 10 percent of the officer corps,[70] despite the fact that Bakr, as Chief of Staff, gave most of his attention to the army—to its expansion, refurbishment, and supply with modern arms. He opened the military college to an additional 150 cadets a year, and he requested that Britain accept more trainees at the British Staff College at Camberley.[71] Nevertheless, the pan-Arabs challenged his Kurdish policy: he was thought to be planning the establishment of a Kurdish state and to be consulting with Germany for its defense.[72] Al-Sabbagh called Bakr a Kurd first, and Bakr and Hikmat, both of Turkish descent, were seen to be conspiring to shift Iraqi orientation to Turkey and Iran to the neglect of Arab nationalists.[73] The pan-Arabs conveniently forgot that Bakr had been an Arab nationalist during World War I.

Arab nationalists and members of the opposition in

exile barraged Baghdad with accusations of the regime's lack of interest in Arab nationalism,[74] this despite Hikmat's repeated support for Ghazi's continued participation in the mediation of the Arab strike in Palestine. He allowed the military leader of the Palestinian Arabs, Fawzi al-Qawuqji, domicile in Iraq; he supported renewed activities of the Palestine Defense Committee; and Hikmat appealed to Britain to commute the death sentences passed on two Palestinian Arabs.[75] Then he approached the German ambassador to Iraq, Dr. Fritz Grobba, requesting German assistance to frustrate the Royal Commission plans for Palestine and a German financial grant to Iraq to free her from Britain so that Iraq could then help Palestine.[76] Nevertheless, the nationalists conspired first to remove Hikmat and then his successor, Jamil al-Midfa'i, from power, returning the pro-British Nuri al-Sa'id to Iraq.

In late 1939, however, after Nuri had consolidated his position—Ghazi had died and the officers involved with the Bakr Sidqi coup removed from power—the sudden possibility of war impinged upon local politics, and the nationalists were forced to question openly their relations with Britain and their compliance with the treaty. Iraq conditioned its role in the war on Britain's Palestine policy.

Grobba had repeatedly pressed the Iraqis about their stand on the possibility of war between Britain and Germany. Al-Midfa'i responded that Iraq would try to remain neutral and would refrain from taking any anti-German measures. But Tawfiq al-Suwaydi, his Foreign Minister, and later Nuri, whose government had to make the decision, were determined that Iraq would abide by its commitments even if it meant antagonizing the army, which hated the British and had become, in al-Suwaydi's view, Nazi "from top to bottom." If, however, Germany were to control the Persian Gulf, Iraq's policy would certainly be pragmatic as Nuri's later diplomatic feelers to the Germans were to prove.[77]

Therefore, in September 1939, when the British asked Iraq to break diplomatic relations with Germany, the officers acquiesced. But they refused to let Nuri declare war on

Germany as he desired and opposed his request to send Iraqi divisions to the Balkans to fight with the Allies. If Iraqi soldiers were to be sent anywhere, declared General Husayn Fawzi, it should be to Palestine.

> "Supposing" he said, "The two Iraqi divisions would be sent to the Balkans, and that on the way through Aleppo an Arab would stop one of the Iraqi soldiers inquiring: 'O brother, where are you going?' 'To the Balkans, to fight Germany,' he will answer. 'Allah, Allah,' the Arab will protest, 'What about Syria and Palestine, O brother?' "[78]

By the time Italy entered the war in June 1940 the situation had changed. Now, in a Rashid 'Ali government, the officers were not eager to accede to British requests. The stunning Axis victories in Denmark, Norway, and the Low Countries, accompanied by the Axis propaganda barrage, convinced the nationalists that the Axis might win the war. Suddenly, the Allies awoke to the fact that there was a potential Fifth Column in Iraq, that Grobba's propaganda and the World War I link with Germany had achieved results (see chapter 2). "It was widely acknowledged that most of the junior officers in the Iraqi army are pro-German and anti-British," Paul Knabenshue wrote in May 1940.[79] He asked Rashid 'Ali to take steps to allay the fear that Britain would lose the war and the Prime Minister agreed, authorizing editorials warning against the spread of false rumors and cautioning the public against the work of German agents. The Minister of Defense called meetings with army officers to warn them that an Allied defeat in northern France did not mean ultimate defeat.[80] Nevertheless, the politicians and the officers became convinced that the future of pan-Arabism lay with the Axis.

The summer of 1940 marked the beginnings of a shift in Iraqi foreign policy. Iraq began to use the Palestine issue as a condition for her treaty compliance, and when Britain provided no satisfaction, Iraq turned to Germany, which had unofficially aided Iraq since 1935.[81]

Soon after independence, when it was perceived that

Britain was reneging on her obligation to supply the Iraqi army with modern arms, the government turned to Dr. Grobba. Bakr Sidqi requested that his friend, the German ambassador, with whom he was in almost daily contact, intercede with the Reich to equip the Iraqi army.[82] In March 1937, Grobba notified Berlin that Iraq was interested in purchasing artillery, anti-aircraft guns, machine guns, trucks, and fighter aircraft and that Britain had agreed, in spite of the treaty, that Iraq could purchase arms which Britain could not supply.[83] Bakr also requested that Colonel Heins, a former member of the German General Staff, come to Baghdad in the guise of a representative of an industrial firm to work out a plan for the defense of Kurdistan in the event of an Iraqi-British war. However, as was to occur repeatedly in Iraqi-German negotiations, while Grobba had prepared the local ground well (see chapter 2), Berlin demurred, this time explaining that the German War Ministry could not meet Iraqi requests due to German rearmament problems and the fear of rising British opposition to the deal.[84]

An agreement was signed eventually, in December 1939 (after Bakr's death), as a result of Rheinmetall-Borsig consultations with the British to sell the Iraqis arms. Throughout the negotiations, the British thought the Iraqis to be "hysterical" over the issue. The British told the Iraqis repeatedly, when Taha al-Hashimi brought up the issue with King Edward VIII during his visit to London, and later when Bakr Sidqi repeated requests, that Britain was in the throes of her own rearmament problems and could not supply Iraq with modern arms. The nationalists were convinced that Britain did not wish to see a strong Iraq for fear that Iraq would intervene militarily in Palestine as she had become the most vociferous opponent of the Peel Partition plan.[85] Nevertheless, representatives of Krupp and of the Rheinmetall-Borsig, including a former army officer Otto Wolff, who came to instruct the Iraqis in the use of heavy guns, negotiated an arms deal for some £20 million which Iraq could pay off over fifteen years in cash or raw materials. The arms were due to arrive beginning in 1939.[86] There were other smaller contract negotiations as well.

More problems arose with Italian negotiations for planes. The British Embassy in Baghdad was upset that Britain would not sell Iraq planes. As the Iraqis could be pacified with older models, the British could probably find something suitable in England; and Ambassador Clark-Kerr did not think it suitable for Iraq to turn to Italy. London eventually permitted sales from Italy, but refused to allow Italian personnel on Iraqi soil.[87]

In 1939 Germany was ready unhesitatingly to sell Iraq arms, this time not via the Foreign Ministry but through the army, most probably through representatives of German Intelligence, the Abwehr. Al-Sabbagh mentions that a Major Steffan, the representative of a German arms factory appeared in Baghdad, showed al-Sabbagh samples of German ware, and promised quick delivery and good terms. Al-Sabbagh consulted with Taha; the Minister of Defense agreed; and despite Nuri's opposition, the deal was consummated.[88]

Once the war broke out, however, all German personnel left Iraq or were interned, and overt connections with Germany ceased. Covert negotiation continued via the Italian Legation, and once the Jerusalem Mufti, al-Hajj Amin al-Husayni, arrived in Baghdad in October 1939, negotiations continued, accelerated, and resulted in Iraq's break with England and offer to fight with Germany in 1941.

The Mufti came to Baghdad from Syria where he had been in exile as the leader of the Palestine Arab revolt. He came at the invitation of the pan-Arabs and was not, as the British at one time claimed, an undetected refugee, surreptitiously crossing the frontier.[89] The British ambassador was worried; the American representative feared that the Palestinian leader would use Iraq as his base of operations.[90] But Major C. J. Edmonds was positive: he thought, as did Nuri, that not only could the Prime Minister immobilize al-Husayni and use him to refute German propaganda, but that once the Iraqis saw the Mufti, his influence would wane, since they would realize that he was not "a nebulous deity as they had formerly visualized."[91] The Mufti promised not to engage in politics while in Iraq.

He had a dominating personality. Tawfiq al-Suwaydi,

who opposed him, nevertheless acknowledged his unquestioned loyalty to the Arab nation.[92] The British called the Mufti an "arch mischief-maker," with an aggressive character, "watery pale-blue eyes," and a "cunning expression." They saw him as the leader of a gang of gunmen and as an associate of communist agents constantly proclaiming that the end justifies the means.[93]

Nevertheless, the Mufti had friends in Baghdad, some of whom he knew from Istanbul; for the Mufti, too, had passed through the Ottoman Military College and served together with one of the Four Colonels, Mahmud Salman, in Smyrna during the war.[94] He knew Taha al-Hashimi from his work as the prime mover of the Iraqi Palestine Defense Society and had been acquainted with Rashid 'Ali since the early 1930s.[95] The Mufti's link with the Iraqi officers was Yunis al-Sab'awi.

To Hanna Batatu, al-Sab'awi represented the Rashid 'Ali movement more than its namesake. Born in Mosul, a graduate of the Baghdad Law College, al-Sab'awi had known al-Sabbagh since 1929 when they formed a pan-Arab military group. In 1936 they organized an arms and ammunition smuggling operation out of Iraq's military depots to the Arab fighters in Palestine with the help of Iraqi and Palestinian Communist contacts. After the Bakr Sidqi coup, al-Sab'awi followed Yasin al-Hashimi (who had secretly authorized the arms smuggling) to Syria; then he worked in Palestine. When he returned to Iraq, al-Sab'awi along with Naji al-Suwaydi (brother of Tawfiq al-Suwaydi), Taha al-Hashimi, Sa'id al-Hajj Thabit (President of the Palestine Defense Society), Rashid 'Ali, and Naji Shawkat joined forces with the Mufti.[96]

Al-Sabbagh was impressed with the Mufti before their first meeting, al-Husayni's reputation having preceded him to Baghdad. He noted with pride the Mufti's military service and their common hatred of the British, and he accepted him as a worthy successor to Faysal I and Ghazi as leader of the pan-Arab movement, the Regent, 'Abd al-Ilah, being pro-British. Their first encounter at the Mufti's home in Baghdad left them mutual admirers and friends, even though initially their views of the international situation did not entirely coincide.[97]

Soon after his arrival, the Jerusalem Mufti was received in state by the Iraqi politicians who welcomed and feted him and voted him an immediate subvention of ID 18,000 to be followed by other grants throughout his stay in Iraq: ID 1,000 monthly from hidden funds of the Iraqi secret service, 2 percent of the salary of every Iraqi government official including the military and the police, grants of ID 12,000 between 1939 and mid-1940 for the relief of distress in Palestine, and special sums donated by the Palestine Defense Society, the Red Crescent, and other public donations. He received gifts from Egypt, from King 'Abd al-'Aziz Al Sa'ud, payments of some ID 60,000 from the Germans and some ID 40,000 from the Italians, who also promised £20,000 in gold monthly if the Mufti initiated another Palestine revolt.[98]

He was the guest of honor at state functions and, with his 5,000 to 6,000 followers, the Mufti installed a mini-government in Baghdad where he settled and began to renew contact with old friends and make new ones in the Iraqi army and police force, with doctors, lawyers, and teachers. By 1941 his influence was such that he could place Palestinians in the Iraqi bureaucracy, adding more teachers and other professionals to those Palestinians already working in Iraq.[99] It was said that he controlled hirings, firings, and promotions in Iraqi government departments, that he could have passports issued on demand to his followers, and that he could authorize the importation of personal effects such as automobiles into Iraq duty free. He controlled newspapers and propaganda mechanisms, some mutually with German influence and money, which were not interfered with.[100] He created clubs and societies throughout the country.[101] He was in contact with the Italian Legation which relayed his messages to Germany—Dr. Grobba having left before his arrival—and al-Hajj Amin sent regular dispatches to the Iraqi radio announcer Yunis al-Bahri, who used the information in them in his propaganda broadcasts to Iraq from Berlin.[102]

The Mufti translated a nebulous pan-Arab ideology into a political program of action and by 1940 was in control of the pan-Arab movement.[103] As the situation in Europe worsened for the Allies, al-Hajj Amin al-Husayni advocated that Iraq stick to the letter of her treaty with Britain and wished Iraq not to enter the war, lest she be exhausted in Britain's war and unable to play her role as the liberator of the Arab lands. If, however, Russia, Japan, and Italy were to fight on Germany's side, the Iraqis would then proclaim a revolt in Palestine against the British. It would be led by Fawzi al-Qawuqji.[104] He was the Mufti's military advisor in the "Arab Committee" the Mufti had formed in Baghdad soon after his arrival. It included Syrian political refugees Jamil Mardam and Shukri al-Quwwatli and members of the Iraqi pan-Arab movement, all of whom were in some of the governments after 1939: Naji Shawkat, Naji al-Suwaydi, Taha al-Hashimi, and the Four Colonels.[105] Once the Mufti was called upon to intervene in the choice of an Iraqi government, as he was in February 1940 when he was asked to mediate between the Four Colonels and Rashid 'Ali in order that the latter assume leadership, the Mufti controlled Iraqi policy via al-Sabbagh's group.[106]

Thus, when Italy declared war in June 1940, and Nuri wished Iraq to declare war on Italy, the Colonels backed Rashid 'Ali's advocacy of absolute neutrality. Now Iraq began to negotiate its declaration of war against Italy for concessions in British policy in Palestine, namely, for the immediate implementation of the White Paper, and for arms in sufficient quantities. During the summer, therefore, there ensued a double set of diplomatic maneuvers.[107] While Nuri visited Turkey early in July in order to ascertain that ally's (Sa'dabad Pact 1937) stand on the war, Naji Shawkat, the Minister of Justice, accompanied him but visited von Papen, transmitting a letter from the Mufti to Hitler in which the Mufti pledged his admiration and Arab support for the Axis in exchange for German diplomatic recognition and material support for the pan-Arab cause. While Nuri met with British Colonel Newcombe, a comrade-in-arms from World War I sent to Baghdad to discuss the international situation and Palestine with the Iraqis, and then with General Wavell in Cairo to present a plan for Palestine, the Mufti sent his secretary 'Uthman Haddad first to Turkey and then to Berlin to discuss Arab-Axis collaboration.[108] When in August the British rejected Nuri's proposals, deciding not to take any action in Palestine until after the war, and Churchill authorized Jewish self-defense in Palestine, which the Iraqis interpreted as a shift in policy, Nuri also sent diplomatic feelers to the Germans.[109]

The question arises, however, as to whether or not Nuri was playing a double game. Was he privy to the Mufti-German negotiations while he was Foreign Minister in Rashid 'Ali's government? Majid Khadduri maintains that the Mufti and his group did not trust pro-British Nuri, never discussed plans with him, and totally rebuffed his proferred cooperation. But Jon Kimche, relying on German documents found in Tillmann's recent work on Germany's Middle East policy, concludes that Nuri lied to Majid Khadduri, who asked him this question, specifically, in an interview, and that he knew all along what transpired; for Nuri was a consummate politician and very little escaped him.[110]

By the autumn of 1940, Nuri was again working with the regent and the British, who by the end of the year tried to remove Rashid 'Ali from power, hoping to duplicate their recent coup in Egypt. They suspected the Prime Minister's implication in the German declaration of friendship for the Arab cause which the Germans finally published in October 1940, only after Italian defeats in Libya induced them to become more active in the Middle East and to ignore Italy's professed influence in the area.[111] The British complained that the declaration had not been suppressed when it appeared in the Iraqi press. They complained further that Iraq had resumed telegraphic communications with Germany and Italy, had not broken off diplomatic relations with Italy, was not suppressing anti-British propaganda in the press, and did not deny the rumors of imminent resumption of relations with Germany. In essence, the British charged, Iraq did not act like an ally in its failure to lead public opinion to a pro-British position.[112]

The Iraqi press, except for the pro-British *al-'Iraq*, continued to emphasize German successes. It did not condemn the German bombing of London, even though at one point it expressed admiration and surprise for the way the British people withstood the bombing, nor did the newspapers report British raids on Germany. There was general respect for the German military machine.[113] The nationalist press praised the cabinet's support for neutrality, while calling Iraqi youth to the colors:

> It [the cabinet] put before the eyes of the nation the duty of preserving Iraq from the evils of war and from everything which might prejudice its sovereignty, which is built on the skulls of innocent martyred sons and on their blood shed on many battlefields. The independence which the nation has obtained by blood and defended by blood also. The only way to maintain security and defense is through the performance of military service.[114]

The standards for the officer corps were lowered to increase the number of officers; in 1940 all secondary school graduates had to register for training as reserve officers.[115]

The British had much less leverage in Iraq than in Egypt, and their new ambassador, Sir Basil Newton, who had replaced Sir Maurice Peterson in mid-1939, found it very difficult to deal with Rashid 'Ali.

But Rashid 'Ali's subsequent resignation did not change policy. The Colonels placed their ally, General Taha al-Hashimi, in power; but Taha saw his role as mediator between the army and Nuri and the Mufti. While negotiations with Germany continued, Taha sent Tawfiq al-Suwaydi to Cairo to discuss arms for Iraq with Anthony Eden. Al-Suwaydi claims that had the army really wished for reconciliation with the British, it was possible;[116] but once Taha attempted to transfer one of the Colonels, Kamil Shabib, from Baghdad and the Regent supported the move, the army took formal control of the government, forcing Taha's resignation and Rashid 'Ali's return as a spokesman for the Colonels.

At this juncture all of the preparations coalesced. The officers in *de facto* control of the government were now in a position to implement the goals of pan-Arabism.

VI. The Rashid 'Ali Coup

Rashid 'Ali al-Kaylani was not a soldier.[1] He was a locally trained provincial—compared to those who had studied in Istanbul—lawyer, a descendant of the twelfth-century Muslim philosopher and mystic, 'Abd al-Qadir al-Gaylani, whose tomb was a Baghdad shrine. Rashid 'Ali's father, by marrying beneath his station, had invoked the ire of the Naqib of Baghdad, Sayyid 'Abd al-Rahman al-Kaylani who administered the shrine. The Naqib deprived the family of any financial allowances it was entitled to and Rashid 'Ali grew up in poverty. He attended the Baghdad Law College, established in 1908, and served in administrative positions and in political office while still young. In 1933, he combined talents with Yasin al-Hashimi to form a government and then served in Yasin's cabinet in 1935. After the Bakr Sidqi coup, Rashid 'Ali changed military cliques with the political tide until 1939 when Nuri appointed him Royal Secretary in order to control him. He was, at the time, conspiring with the Four Colonels to replace Nuri. The Colonels backed Rashid 'Ali and made him prime minister after Nuri resigned early in 1940.

Rashid 'Ali was a nationalist and a political pragmatist.[2] He was, said Freya Stark, "a hard worker, a persuasive speaker, a passionate nationalist, ambitious and reckless, and apt in the heat of argument to give undertakings sincere at the moment but impossible later to fulfill."[3] Sir Maurice Peterson, the British ambassador, considered him an evil influence, reputed for "intrigues and venality"[4] and Tawfiq al-Suwaydi thought him "unbalanced." But Salah al-Din al-Sabbagh found Rashid 'Ali to be courageous and daring, a fitting spokesman for the nationalist movement.[5] Throughout his political career, Rashid 'Ali picked the winning side until he was forced by personal pique to turn to the Colonels and to the Axis.

British connivance with the regent to have him replaced at the end of 1940 most probably was a factor in his support of the Colonels' coup against Taha al-Hashimi[6] and most
certainly pushed him to Italy and Germany. At the end of November, Rashid 'Ali appealed to the Italians to trasmit propaganda
broadcasts denouncing Britain's attempt to remove him. He requested more arms, this time to be used specifically for an Iraqi
uprising against the British.[7] The Italians refused, reasoning that
the broadcasts would not be in Rashid 'Ali's best interests.

He was present at the secret meeting held at the
Mufti's house on Zahawi Street in Baghdad, recorded by al-
Sabbagh and dated by Hirszowicz as February 28, 1941, where
the conspirators, using code names (the names of their grand-
fathers), headed by Amin al-Husayni and including Yunis al-
Sab'awi, Naji Shawkat, and three of the Four Colonels—al-Sabbagh, Fahmi Sa'id, and Mahmud Salman—swore on the Qur'an
to give no more concessions to Britain, to refuse to break diplomatic relations with Italy, to expel the most pro-British politicians from the country, and to depose Taha al-Hashimi if he did
not agree with these policies.[8] Taha was deposed and the Colonels returned Rashid 'Ali to a position that he coveted but in a
role not entirely to his liking.

The coup d'état which discarded Taha had no legal
backing. The conspirators under the National Defense Government, especially Rashid 'Ali, insisted on the legal fiction of replacing the regent, 'Abd al-Ilah, his flight having connoted
dereliction of duty, with Sherif Sharaf, a distant royal relative,
who could then appoint a prime minister whose cabinet could
operate legally. The Muthanna Club and the Futuwwah praised
the fact that "a strong government free from lingering commitments, hotly patriotic and backed by the Army, had at last been
established."[9] Italy and Japan offered congratulations. Iraq resumed relations with Germany but the regime was not recognized by Britain, the United States, Egypt, or Iraq's ally, Turkey.
Throughout April 1941, Rashid 'Ali negotiated for British recognition, which he desperately wanted, until he was overruled by
the officers who were in control.

The war, however, conspired to elevate the local Iraqi putsch to international levels. With German advances in the Balkans—the occupation of Bulgaria and the invasion of Greece—and Rommel's advance across North Africa, Churchill decided that Britain had to "make sure of Basra"[10] both as a port and as a future air base for American planes. The treaty issue, which involved breaking diplomatic relations with Italy and the landing of British troops on Iraqi soil, emerged in April with drastic consequences.

Did the British push the Iraqis to war? Were they going to reoccupy the country? If so, then, as the nationalists maintain, Rashid 'Ali's subsequent action—the ulitmatum and the Thirty Day war with Britain which followed—was a direct nationalist response to British provocation, not a foolhardy exercise by political opportunists bent on leading the country into a quixotic adventure. If, however, Iraq was negotiating with the Axis powers and intended to join them in the war against Britain, Iraq's strategic and economic importance required a direct British response.

Both positions are correct. Iraq was playing both sides, attempting to maintain neutrality in a war which did not concern it, while veering ever so slightly toward support of Germany. While Rashid 'Ali negotiated with the British for recognition in April, promising adherence to the letter of the treaty and diplomatic status quo, he also requested support from the Axis, while his backers, the Jerusalem Mufti and the Four Colonels, certain by this time that Germany would win the war, were feverishly contacting the Germans for military and material support. In October 1940, they had received an Axis declaration supporting pan-Arab goals in the Fertile Crescent, but now they required arms and money. Throughout the crisis, Rashid 'Ali sincerely wanted British recognition of his regime; but he was not in charge. He was the façade for the officers and the Mufti who did not want any compromise. The British, meanwhile, had cracked the Italian intelligence code—the Mufti used the Italians in Baghdad as a conduit to the Germans—and were fully informed about the Iraq-Axis negotiations. Thus, despite the wishes of the British diplomats on the scene, and General Wavell's protestations of lack of manpower, Churchill overruled everyone and decided to press the Iraqis.

The daily developments of the diplomatic drama have been fully covered elsewhere from the vantage point of American, British, German, and Iraqi diplomacy.[11] Nevertheless, we must survey briefly the events leading to May 1941.

The British, sensing trouble with Taha's cabinet in February 1941, decided to change amabassadors to Iraq. Recalling Sir Basil Newton who had been there for just about a year, they appointed Sir Kinahan Cornwallis. Cornwallis had served as British advisor to the Iraqi ministry of interior for fourteen years until he was ousted by Rashid 'Ali in 1935. He knew the local scene well, and, as some would have it,[12] was opposed, for personal motives, to Rashid 'Ali, who had meanwhile replaced Taha. In mid-April, however, the British ambassador changed his mind and supported Rashid 'Ali because of the overwhelming popular support for the government. If force is to be used against Rashid 'Ali, Cornwallis told the Foreign Office on April 9, "we shall have to take careful precautions to ensure that our action is not resented by the people."[13] Throughout April, Cornwallis would plead for "breathing space" while Churchill pressed for action.

While Churchill had the Foreign Office notify the ambassador that British troops—Indian troops diverted from their original destination in the Far East—were on their way to Basra for transshipment to British lines in Palestine, Cornwallis both objected to his government's pressure on Iraq and dangled British recognition of the Iraqi regime before Rashid 'Ali in return for permitting the troops to land at Basra in accordance with the Anglo-Iraqi alliance. On April 17, Rashid 'Ali agreed. Two days later, after the first contingent of British troops had landed, he recanted his agreement, replacing it with conditions which he knew would be unacceptable to the British: moving the troops as quickly as possible from Basra to Rutbah in the west, giving Iraq advance notice of the landing of additional troops, limiting these troops so that the total number of British troops in Iraq at any one time did not exceed one mixed brigade, and preventing any additional force from landing until all those that had already arrived left Iraq.

The pro-German officers, Tawfiq al-Suwaydi tells us, accused the Prime Minister of treason to the nationalist cause for his initial agreement with the British. Salah al-Din al-Sabbagh and Yunis al-Sab'awi told Rashid 'Ali that the army opposed the understanding with the British, that it was a British tactic to stall for time until measures could be taken against the regime. A war with Britain was necessary, Yunis al-Sab'awi maintained, if not immediately then within a matter of days or weeks.[14]

There is evidence to support the nationalists' analysis. Britain had drawn up a contingency operation to occupy Basra—the TROUT plan—in March 1940 when the Soviet threat to the British shield for India seemed real, according to the rumors reaching the British of the Nazi-Soviet deliberations at the Brenner Pass.[15] Churchill initiated its implementation during the summer of 1940 by requesting that Iraq permit troops to land at Basra when Rashid 'Ali's pro-German regime seemed menacing. The TROUT plan and the Newcombe diplomatic mission were the first efforts to thwart Rashid 'Ali's perceived pro-Axis intentions. They were followed by the British/Nuri/Regent attempt to remove him from power, and by plans for a possible assasination of the Mufti.[16] TROUT was shelved until April 1941, when Churchill decided that quick decisive action was required to keep Iraq in line.

For their part, the officers and the Mufti were awaiting a positive response to their appeals to Italy and Germany of January 1941 for aid for the pan-Arab cause. Al-Sabbagh asked the Italians for immediate supply—400 light machine guns and ammunition, 50 light tanks, 10 anti-aircraft batteries, explosives, anti-tank weapons, and 10,000 gas masks—[17] and the Mufti followed on January 20 with a long letter addressed directly to Hitler. The Mufti began by expressing the sympathy of the Arab peoples for Germany and the Axis cause and pledged Arab support if the Axis powers provided moral and material backing.[18] The moral support had come in the October declaration, but the weapons the Mufti required from the Italians in September—10,000 rifles, 100 machine guns, ammunition, and grenade throwers to be used to blow up the Jerusalem to al-Qantara railway—did not.

With the letter the Mufti sent his personal secretary, ʿUthman Kemal Haddad, to Ankara, Rome, and Berlin on an odyssey that ended with a German response dated April 8 but received in Baghdad a week later during the crisis with Britain. In the interval, the Italians stalled—ever suspicious of Iraqi military capabilities—and the Germans deliberated and discussed: the Foreign Ministry and the military each proposed a more active German Arab policy.[19] Haddad was given a radio to take back to Baghdad in order to communicate with Berlin directly, and funds were made available to the Mufti. But there were no arms. Haddad was told that Germany was not averse to Iraq's pursuing arms negotiations with Japan, delivery from the Far East being a more certain possibility than from Europe.[20]

In March, the *Abwehr* (Military Intelligence) decided to establish an intelligence network in Baghdad that would cover the entire Middle East because the Germans wished to promote sabotage against British installations in Palestine and Transjordan. But von Ribbentrop, who wanted his Foreign Ministry to establish its own intelligence center in the area, delayed the implementation of Admiral Canaris' *Abwehr* proposals until April 9 after Rashid ʿAli's coup. Meanwhile he sent Grobba back to the Middle East and Grobba suggested that General Hellmuth Felmy be dispatched to the scene to assess the military situation.

Similarly, the Germans dallied over the question of arms. Rashid ʿAli told the Germans on March 25 that if he had arms, he would resist the British. He told the Italians, who relayed the message to the Germans, that he believed the British were preparing to occupy Iraq and he needed arms immediately. But it was not until April 10 that Hitler approved arms shipments to Iraq, and it was only then that the Germans began to discuss seriously the logistical problems.[21]

Thus, while Rashid ʿAli seemed initially open to compromise when Cornwallis presented him with the British request to land troops, he had been, in truth, overruled by the military and the Mufti who decided to appeal again to the Italians for aid. On April 18 Rashid 'Ali told the Italian ambassasor, Gabrielli, that the National Council for Defense of Iraq had met on April 17 and decided that Iraq would defend itself. The government, therefore, needed to know as soon as possible from the Axis governments

> first, whether the Iraq army could count on support from the air force of the Axis powers; the airfields of Iraq would of course be placed at the disposal of the Axis powers. Second, whether the Iraq army could count on receiving rifles and ammunition by air transports. . . . In any case he [Rashid 'Ali] requested that all the help which the Iraq government had requested even earlier be made available to it and that financial aid also be given.[22]

The Iraqis were now asking for direct military intervention.

But while the Germans were sympathetic, the Axis governments told Rashid 'Ali to wait, to "resist Great Britain with arms when the balance of forces offered chances of success,"[23] for the Axis were preparing to send arms, ammunition, and money after they had solved the logistical problems. Emboldened by the promises, however, the government presented the British with an ultimatum when Cornwallis informed Rashid 'Ali on April 28 that a second contingent of British troops was due to land. Meanwhile, the Prime Minister asked the Italians for extensive aid and requested that Axis aircraft bomb British naval units in the Persian Gulf and British bases at Habbaniyyah and Shu'aybah. He offered them air bases and the petrol stored in Iraq.[24] The German hope that the Iraqis would avoid a clash with the British, as they had no military plans whatsoever to assist them, collapsed as Rashid 'Ali, al-Sabbagh, and the Mufti, encouraged by British losses in Crete, Greece, and North Africa, plunged ahead.

On April 27 Rashid 'Ali repeated his demands to the British. On April 29 he rejected the British demand to land additional troops at Basra, but the troops disembarked anyway. The next day, Iraqi soldiers, stationed at the Rashid military

camp, were ordered to surround the British air base at Habbaniyyah. Rashid ʿAli ordered the British to stop all flights and
threatened to shoot down British planes. The British said they
considered this to be an unfriendly act; they evacuated women
and children from Baghdad and sent them to Habbaniyyah.
Meanwhile, Rashid ʿAli told Tawfiq al-Suwaydi that he really did
not wish a clash with Britain and that he would allow British
troops transit if the British would recognize him *de jure*. But it
was too late. Tawfiq al-Suwaydi told the Prime Minister that he
could not contact the British ambassador as the British Embassy
was under siege and that even if he were permitted to see Cornwallis, he would be a thought a spy. He warned Rashid ʿAli that
the government's policy was illegal according to Iraq's alliance
with Great Britain and advised the Prime Minister to leave the
government with trusted advisors, declaring that since the officers had become extremists, he could no longer work with
them. Rashid ʿAli considered the idea but feared personal repercussions if he followed that policy.[25]

At 5 AM on May 2, British planes based in Habbaniyyah bombed the Iraqi positions and the Iraqis returned fire.
"We were forced," Rashid ʿAli announced to the people the next
day

> to take defensive measures and the military operations which
> have begun are continuing with success to our army. The noble
> Iraqi nation is requested to remain quiet, proving its political
> maturity and confidence in the national forces. The people are
> requested never to attack foreigners amongst us, who will be
> regarded as our guests.[26]

The mood in Baghdad was jubilant. From 6:30 AM to
one o'clock daily, the radio broadcast martial music and news of
victories everywhere.[27] The government recruited the talents of
prominent citizens to denounce British aggression in Iraq: the
writer Fahmi al-Mudarris came out of retirement to denounce
the British in an article in *al-Bilad*, "Iraq's Choice Between Death
and Free Life." Mustafa al-Wakil, Vice-President of the Egyptian
Misr al-Fatat (Young Egypt), then teaching at the Baghdad Higher

Teachers' College, and Siddiq Shanshal, the Iraqi Director of Propaganda, "were probably the most violent in their anti-British broadcasts." On May 9 the Mufti declared a *jihad* and invited every "able-bodied Muslim to take part in the war against the 'greatest foe of Islam.' "[28]

There was Nazi propaganda throughout the day as well. British transmissions from Churchill and ʿAbd al-Ilah, who was already in exile, were jammed. The Germans transmitted for one hour and forty-five minutes in five segments daily and included readings from the Qurʾan, anti-British news and German military success, and literary and historical discussions of the glories of the Arab past "in order to strengthen their self-assurance."[29] There were music and teachings from the Qurʾan against foreign domination. The slant was nationalistic rather than religious, calling upon the Arabs to revolt against British domination, to follow the lead of Rashid ʿAli. The basic propaganda line was, wrote General Walter Warlimont in his analysis of German propaganda, directed to the Arab world:

> An Axis victory will bring to the countries of the Middle East liberation from the British yoke and therewith the right of self-determination. All who love freedom will therefore take their place in the ranks against England.[30]

On May 2, King Faysal II's birthday, Italian radio Bari broadcast congratulations, but expressed regret that the health of the king was entrusted to the British doctor, the same doctor who cared for his father and grandfather at the time of their deaths.[31]

Thus, it seemed appropriate that one of the requests made to the Germans was to send an expert in detecting "fifth column" infiltration to help the Iraqis root out the British sympathizers, this despite Rashid ʿAli's initial hospitable declaration. From May 8 on, the government frequently announced:

> We wish to inform the public that in their joy over the victory they are spending their ammunition in vain. We wish peace to prevail in every place, and after the victory over the British, revenge shall be taken on the internal enemy, and we shall hand him over to your hands for destruction.[32]

Baghdad citizens began the work themselves, at time frivolously, sometimes vengefully. A woman whose gold button inadvertently appeared through her black ʿaba was detained for signaling the British, as was a French violin teacher who was accused of carrying a wireless in his violin case.[33] A Jewish student holding an English book was accused of spying, and patients at the Meir Eliyahu hospital were accused of signaling to the British airplanes after British planes flew over Baghdad on May 6. A mob entered the hospital armed with "cudgels and knives," attacking patients and staff, and, although the police restored order, the hospital was closed.

There was a total blackout; but crime was down for the first two weeks of the war. Schools were closed and businesses paralyzed as banks were ordered not to pay any money. Collections were taken up for the army and the wounded. The government opened up a depot of the Red Crescent Society in the Jewish Shamash school and members of the Jewish community were appointed to operate the storehouse where merchandise was received and transmitted to the army.[34]

During the war members of the Futuwwah, "mostly hostile and over-enthusiastic," policed Baghdad.[35] Some detained an Englishman in an Iraqi jail for questioning and several broke into houses, beating the inhabitants whom they accused of signaling to the British on a hidden wireless.[36] Another group of youth, al-Kataʿib al-Shabab, founded by Yunis al-Sabʿawi on the Nazi prototype, demanded that the Jewish community hand over a school in the Jewish quarter for their use, as well as the cash register and the administration office.[37] Later, the police were to find detailed maps of the Jewish quarter in the safe and a list of al-Kataʿib members with aliases after their names.[38]

By the middle of the month, with the British advance, Baghdad had to be defended, and Mahmud al-Durrah, a staff officer, was recalled from Basra to organize civilian defense as the troops were occupied at the front. In his study of the war, al-Durrah recounts the unfailing spirit and loyalty of the Baghdadis—workers, students, and the Futuwwah—whom he mobilized for the defense of the city, as well as that of the religious students from outside the city, all of whom responded patriotically.[39]

From the balcony of the besieged British embassy, Freya Stark observed Baghdad at war and noted a shift in mood. "We could watch the passage of the troops in trucks camouflaged with palm fronds," she writes,

> and the return of the Red Crescent ambulances with wounded and judge of what was happening in the battle by the traffic on the bridge. Or we could see the crowds from the upper town, incited by speeches of the Mufti and their own radio, advancing with banners and drums and dancing figures silhouetted against the sky, towards our gates. They rarely came so far, and only once sent a few shots into our garden, for no rhetoric was able to stir this into a popular war.[40]

Shi'i tribes in the south did not support the rebels and Iraqi troops at Mosul and Kirkuk, while nominally supportive, did not move. Desertions increased as the war progressed, and sentiments of villagers and townsmen turned lukewarm.[41]

For the war had already been lost. The British, by taking the initiative at Habbaniyyah, despite their indefensible position and small numbers won the war in the air, destroying twenty-five out of forty Iraqi planes.[42] Withdrawing to Fallujah, the Iraqi army destroyed Euphrates dams, railway lines, and telegraph communications in an attempt to stop the British. But the tactics merely delayed them while reinforcements were marching eastward from Transjordan: HABFORCE under General George Clark which included contingents from Glubb's Arab Legion.[43] On May 19 Fallujah fell to the British; they reached Baghdad ten days later.

The Iraqis had been in constant contact with the Germans since before the outbreak of hostilities. Now, on May 6, they requested planes "to save the situation,"[44] increased aid, and a military mission to be sent to Baghdad. The German response was meager: German military intelligence trained twenty-four Iraqis in Germany, mostly students, in combat so that they could return to lead other untrained Arabs in battle. On

May 11 a German plane, sent as a morale booster in advance of German reinforcements, was shot down. The liaison officer, Major Axel von Blomberg, the son of the German general, was killed. Grobba, who had reached Baghdad by this time, was furious.[45] When Hitler finally issued a directive on May 23 authorizing a military mission, arms, and a liaison team for Iraq, it was too late. Nevertheless, the Germans continued to stall. Hesitating even at the desperate last moment, they did not believe that the Iraqis could seriously withstand the British.

Then there was the question of Syria. Not only was the Mufti not to stage a revolt against the Vichy French, but the Germans reluctantly approached the French about using Syria as a transit point for arms shipments to Iraq, land transportation being the only feasible means for getting the arms to Iraq. In the end, they used both land and air, and, after clearing their intentions with Vichy,[46] they began sending matériel. The arms began arriving in Mosul the beginning of June, after the war was over.

Again, Rashid 'Ali tried to negotiate. When Turkey offered to mediate at the beginning of the undeclared war, he wanted to accept; but al-Sabbagh threatened to kill him if he did. Al-Sabbagh claimed that they could hold out for three months if the arms arrived,[47] but he was one of the first to desert. On May 23, the French consul reported from Baghdad that the leadership had lost its nerve and the cabinet was preparing to flee. By May 29 the British were on the outskirts of Baghdad. That day the Four Colonels fled. Rashid 'Ali and the Mufti followed soon after, traveling first to Iran, then to Turkey,[48] and finally to Berlin, where they spent the rest of the war participating in the German war effort.

Recriminations abounded. Al-Sabbagh accused his colleagues of conducting the war badly. He deplored the low morale in the country, the disorder in the army, and the treachery of certain groups.[49] Mahmud al-Durrah, who had advised Rashid 'Ali to replace the military command while there was still time, thought al-Sabbagh to be overly ambitious and not equipped for the responsibility he had undertaken.[50] Haddad criticized the Iraqi military leadership and reported that al-Sab-bagh had three nervous breakdowns during the fighting.[51]

Inept leadership was also the British conclusion, in spite of the fact that the British had been the advisors to the Iraqi army for the previous twenty years.[52] The Four Colonels were better politicians than soldiers, wrote Glubb Pasha and Somerset de Chair, intelligence officer to HABFORCE.[53] They were over-confident and did not take advantage of their superior position and numbers to attack the British force at Habbaniyyah, thus quickly gaining the upper hand. Glubb maintained that Rashid 'Ali and the Four Colonels were not certain of the army's support, telling the troops sent to Habbaniyyah that they were going on training exercises.[54] The Iraqi soldiers were short of water and rations.[55] Then the petrol promised by the Germans for refueling their planes turned out to be for cars and not planes; the Germans had to bring along their own chemist to refine the gasoline.[56] After Fallujah, the German assessment was that the Iraqi army was in no position to put up a fight.

The Germans blamed themselves after accusing the Iraqis of taking on the British without waiting for German support.[57] German policy was unclear to the end. After deciding to supply the Iraqis, they sent too little to late. Germany delayed its decision to ignore Italian claims to the Middle East and to open the Eastern Mediterranean as a German area for cultivation.[58] But although Hitler had no interest in the Middle East until he decided to attack Russia instead of England in 1941, agents on the scene did supply the Foreign Ministry with information on local support. There was a dichotomy between the Foreign Ministry and the military as well as competition between the intelligence services. Consequently, reliable information never reached the top.[59] A German agent working with the Arabs later in the war told U.S. Intelligence that the minister to Baghdad was "a fool with grandiose visions of being a second Lawrence of Arabia, but one who forgot that a revolt required preparation."[60] The accusation was unfair, for Grobba as early as 1938 submitted a complete report to the Foreign Ministry urging the

Germans to take advantage of the pro-German sentiment in Iraq.[61] He had been cultivating support for his country since his arrival. It was he who recommended that on his return he be accompanied by Felmy, then a major, who would act as liaison officer between the Germans and the Iraqis.

Moderate Iraqis, whose views could be represented by Tawfiq al-Suwaydi, resented having their country embroiled in a disaster for the good of Palestine. In Iran, after the debacle, al-Suwaydi told the Mufti and Rashid ʿAli that a weak Iraq was nothing but a weak Palestine and in no one's best interests. Both the Mufti and Rashid ʿAli defended their actions. They had no intention of weakening Iraq, they said, but British maneuvers and British attempts to force Iraq to enter World War II compelled them to work with the extremists in order to avoid British pressure.[62]

The immediate effect of Britain's overwhelming defeat of the Iraqi forces, was the attack on the "internal enemy," a riot in Baghdad during Sunday and Monday, the first and second of June, in which 179 Jewish men, women, and children were killed and several hundred wounded.[63] Property damage was assessed in the millions of pounds sterling. The attack on the Jewish quarter of Baghdad occurred after Rashid ʿAli had left the city, but ʿAbd al-Ilah was already in the capital, and British troops were stationed outside of the city, forbidden to enter.

What is deplorable about the "farhud," as the pogrom is called, aside from the obvious horror of the events themselves, is the callous British reaction to them. The virtual lack of correspondence between the Embassy and London[64] can be contrasted to the international outcry against the Assyrians and the hundreds of pages of discussion by British committees concerned about every riot occurring in Palestine since 1920. Several questions, therefore, need to be discussed; namely, were the attacks premeditated, who perpetrated them, and why the disinterested British response?

The Iraqi government-appointed investigating committee, whose report was dated June 7, 1941, found that the following detrimental forces had dominated Iraqi life during the

previous decade: intensive Nazi propaganda, a politicized educational system and military, and the work of the Jerusalem
Mufti and Yunis al-Sab'awi.[65] It accused three of the four members of the Internal Security Committee, established after Rashid
'Ali's flight to safeguard the security of the civilian population, of
negligence. The Director General of Police, the Mutasarrif of
Baghdad, and the Commander of the First Division stationed in
Baghdad could have stopped the riots on the first day had some-
one given the order to fire on the mob. Although the committee
had prepared a plan for dealing with anticipated violence by
dividing the city into areas of responsibility, once the soldiers
and the police joined the Futuwwah, students, and individual
soldiers returning from the front in the murder and mayhem, no
one would assume any responsibility until the Regent felt compelled to authorize a curfew on June 2.[66] By that time the kill-
ings had given way to wanton looting by bedouin drawn to the
city—"a stream of people going empty-handed eastward, coming back laden with spoil."[67] By evening, after soldiers loyal to
the Regent had opened fire, the city quieted and the violence
virtually ceased.

There is evidence that there was some premeditation
involved in the attack on the Jewish community. It was not a
totally spontaneous outburst of frustration at the loss of the war
and the return of the British. Yunis al-Sab'awi, reputed to be the
most pro-Nazi member of Rashid 'Ali's group, remained behind
after the Prime Minister and the Four Colonels had fled and
proclaimed himself military governor of Baghdad and the south.
At ten o'clock in the morning of May 30, he summoned the
Chief Rabbi of Baghdad and told him to warn the Jewish community to prepare food for three days and not to leave their
houses. That afternoon, Arshad al-'Umari, head of the Committee for Internal Security, relieved al-Sab'awi of his post and informed the Chief Rabbi that the danger had passed, that he had
prevented al-Sab'awi from broadcasting an order to attack the
Jewish community.[68]

Mahmud al-Durrah and Elie Kedourie conclude that
the Jews were set upon because of their pro-British sympathies,

not because of Palestine,[69] while 'Abd al-Razzaq al-Hasani maintains that the "farhud" was a British plot. Throughout the war, Jews were accused of signaling the British and acting as a "fifth column." And when the Regent arrived in Baghdad on the morning of June 1, a Jewish delegation—along with Muslims and Christians—was present at the ceremonies. But Avraham Twena, whose diary of the events includes many interesting details, reports a meeting in May between Yunis al-Sab'awi and members of the Jewish community, who asked the Minister of Economics why he was inciting the Iraqis against the Jewish community, implying local Jewish complicity in the anti-British news reports concerning Palestine.[70] It is unlikely that, after five years of constant public interest in the question of Palestine, there was no fallout on the Jewish community.

Upon closer investigation, however, it seems that once the violence began, the "farhud" became a convenient mechanism used by the British and the Regent to deflect attention from their return.[71] It became a cog in the British policy to create the fiction that there really had not been a war; and that the Hashimites had returned by popular demand, not behind British bayonets. This was the thinking behind the negotiations over the armistice and the British decision not to allow British troops to stop the riots.

The terms of the armistice, requested by the Committee for Internal Security and drawn up by the British General Clark of HABFORCE and Air Marshal J. H. d'Albiac, were lenient. Majid Khadduri notes that Cornwallis had no authority to alter the text, but Elie Kedourie maintains that the British ambassador was consulted. To be sure, the British secured their rights to use all Iraqi facilities. But the Iraqi military was permitted to retain arms. The purpose of the agreement, which was not published in Iraq and which Cornwallis requested his government not to publicize, was "to afford his Highness the Regent every assistance in re-establishing legal government and assisting the Iraq nation to resume its normal and prosperous existence." Thus, according to the document, the British were not really protecting their rights, they were assisting the Iraqi government. Cornwallis asked London not to use the term "occupation."[72]

So, as Somerset de Chair, a witness on the scene, tells us:

> Baghdad was given up to the looters. All who dared defend their own belongings were killed; while eight miles to the west waited the eager British force which could have prevented all this. Ah, yes, but the prestige of our Regent would have suffered![73]

And the Regent was waiting for the arrival of Kurdish troops from the north; the loyalty of the soldiers in Baghdad was untrustworthy.

Jamil al-Midfaʿi was called upon to form a government. Like his "drop the curtain" policy of 1937, al-Midfaʿi wished to delay reprisals, his first mission being to calm the population and reestablish order. The treaty dispute was resolved and Iraq severed diplomatic relations with Italy. Nevertheless, with the establishment of martial law in June, it was obvious that the British had returned in force and that a "second occupation," as the nationalists call it, had begun. Although a strong British presence remained in Iraq only through the end of the war, the effects of the occupation were not forgotten.

British advisors accompanied the troops which were ultimately renamed PAIFORCE and consisted of two British divisions and an armored brigade, three Indian divisions and an armored brigade, and one Polish division. The force remained in strength, stationed throughout the country, until after the Battle of Stalingrad in 1943 when the Soviet Union no longer required British support on its southern flank. The advisors remained, most notably in the ministry of education and in the army.

These were the two areas judged the most vulnerable to the considerable Nazi propaganda, which continued to inundate the country throughout the war, broadcast by the Mufti and Rashid ʿAli from their new residences in Berlin. The government forbade citizens from listening to the transmissions, but the edict was unenforcable. Ultimately, the British and Americans, assessing that considerable pro-Nazi sentiment lingered, set in motion a counter-propaganda operation.[74] All pro-German and nationalist organizations and newspapers were closed.

The British resumed control of the ministry of education through their advisor, H. R. Hamley, who remained until 1944. Textbooks and curricula were altered: nationalist and militaristic material was deleted and replaced by an emphasis on social problems. No longer would the teacher be instructed to tell stories of the glorious battles of the Arab past, to praise the process and results of German unification, or to prepare the student for the *jihad* of the future. In the 1943 curriculum for the elementary schools, history teachers were instructed to emphasize how people lived, to give the events of the past personal meaning to the students: how did man dress, how was fire discovered, how did man discover writing, and how did he express his thoughts?

The list of heroes was also revised. Most of the Arab generals were eliminated as were the modern Arab rebels against the West. More attention was to be paid to Iraqi history (Mesopotamian antecedents) so the students in the fourth grade studied the lives of Sargon I, Hammurabi, Nebuchadnezzar, Alexander, and Zenobia in their pre-Islamic history. The life of Muhammad was covered as well as the period of the four Righteous Caliphs, the commanders Khalid b. al-Walid and al-Muthannah, the Umayyad caliphs, Mu'awiya and al-Walid, the governor of Iraq al-Hajjaj, and the founder of Andalus 'Abd al-Rahman al-Dakhil. After the Abbasid caliphs Harun and al-Ma'mun, the curriculum turned from Salah al-Din (Saladin) to the Ottoman governors of Iraq, Midhat Pasha and Nadhim Pasha, ending with King Faysal I. Throughout, the teacher was enjoined to emphasize what life was like in Babylonia, Nineveh, al-Hirah, Mecca and Medinah, in Umayyad Damascus and Abbasid Baghdad, this last being illustrated by stories from the *Thousand and One Nights*.

There was little European history to speak of. The emphasis on Arab history remained, but Iraqi history became more significant than before, with attention being paid to Iraq's Mesopotamian past, and the role of Iraq in the history of the area from prehistoric times to the present. In 1943 the students studied Arab participation in World War I, especially the Arab revolt under Sharif Husayn, the British occupation of Iraq, the reign of Faysal I, and an analysis of the Iraqi constitution. There was no mention of Germany, Italy, or Japan.[75]

This approach to education reflected the transition in political orientation undergone by the Iraqi intelligensia after World War II. As the nationalists were expelled and purged from government posts, the vacuum in education was filled by teachers trained in the West: pedagogues imbued with American progressive education and members of the political Left. "It may, therefore, be justifiably maintained," Hanna Batatu concludes, "that in the forties the principal vehicles of hostility to the existing social order were the teachers and the students, and the center of gravity of the Communist movement lay not in the factories or others workers' establishment but in the colleges and schools."[76] Just as the disaffected youth looked to the nationalists in the 1930s, in the 1940s they looked to the Communists.[77]

The army was purged and neglected to the point that in 1944 the British disapproved sending Iraqi troops to quell a revolt in Kurdistan. Officers who had participated in the events of May 1941 either fled, were retired, or were interned. After the defeat, soldiers deserted so that there were more than 20,000 deserters listed on the army rolls, men who were demoralized by the outcome of the war and by the flight of their heroes. Nuri, who was in power again in October 1941, some said, had deliberately weakened the army: its numbers were reduced, conscription was neglected, and older Ottoman-trained officers were brought out of retirement because they were considered safe. At the end of World War II, the regent, frightened at the prospect of a demobilized PAIFORCE leaving Iraq undefended, asked the British to retrain the army. The British advisor, General Renton, improved conditions, brought in modern equipment, and retrained the troops, retiring more than three hundred of the older officers. But Nuri's policy continued to rankle.[78]

Most significant, however, was the government's abuse of the almost total power it now had concentrated into fewer and fewer hands. Nuri and the regent were to be criticized for their vendetta—to pursue, try, and wreak vengeance on their political and personal enemies. While the al-Midfa'i government purged the higher echelons of the civil service and the army of all persons who participated in the Rashid 'Ali move ment, the regent was not satisfied. More than one hundred Syrian and Palestinian teachers were deported.[79] Those like Sati' al-Husri and Darwish al-Miqdadi who had received Iraqi citizenship were stripped of their citizenship and exiled. But friends of Nuri, such as Sami Shawkat, were not touched. Shawkat sat out the rest of the war in relative tranquility, emerging later in order to found a new Racial Renaissance Party.[80] Muhammad Fadhil al-Jamali, a target for expulsion, became Iraqi delegate to Washington at the end of the war, a chastened democrat.[81] But British pressure to remove lower echelons of people from office could not move al-Midfa'i. He resigned and to no one's surprise, Nuri became prime minister.

By October 1941, Nuri and 'Abd al-Ilah were fully in control. They appointed their strong supporters to the cabinet and began to pursue pro-Germans, "fifth column" suspects, and personal enemies. Those purged were interned in specially constructed internment camps at al-Fao, al-'Amara and at Salman. Although the number of internees varied from time to time, they totaled, by the end of the war, between 700 and 1,000 prisoners

Next, the government turned to the leaders of the Rashid 'Ali movement and tried them all in absentia. Rashid 'Ali, three of the Four Colonels, Yunis al-Sab'awi, 'Ali Mahmud al-Shaykh 'Ali, and General Amin Zaki were sentenced to death. Amin Zaki's sentence was later commuted to life imprisonment. The Iraqis requested extradition of the prisoners held in Turkey, Germany, and by the British in Rhodesia, the latter having been captured after their flight to Iran. The possibility of British complicity remains, but most agree that it was the regent who demanded the extradition, both to rid himself of all opposition, and to demonstrate that future opposition would not be tolerated. Nevertheless, the British cooperated, repatriating all Iraqi prisoners.

A second trial, at which the prisoners were able to defend themselves, was held in May 1942. On May 4, two of the

Four Colonels, Fahmi Sa'id and Mahmud Salman, and Yunis al-Sab'awi were sentenced to death and hanged the next day. Two years later, the British handed over Kamil Shabib. He, too, was sentenced to death and hanged. The last of the "four martyrs" was extradited to Iraq after the war.[82]

Salah al-Din al-Sabbagh has been revered by the nationalists not only because of his role in the Rashid 'Ali coup, but because he wrote his memoirs and recorded the thoughts and the decisions of the officers during the events. Al-Sabbagh fled to Iran, escaped British capture by dressing as a dervish and wandered to the Turkish border. He was captured in Turkey and interned there for the rest of the war, where he had the solitude to write his memoirs, which were published posthumously. After the war, the Iraqis demanded his return to Iraq and the Turks acquiesced, bringing al-Sabbagh to British-controlled Syria. He escaped again and resisted capture for a few days; but he was taken and transported back to Baghdad, the last of the conspirators.[83] He, too, was sentenced to death and was hanged at the gate of the Ministry of Defense, an event which the army would never forget. The officers who overthrew the monarchy in 1958 remembered 'Abd al-Ilah's over-zealousness in pursuing al-Sabbagh to the death.

VII. Conclusion

The legacy of these events has persisted to this day. The Free Officers who struck down the Hashimites and Nuri al-Sa'id in 1958 were determined to finish al-Sabbagh's work. 'Abd al-Karim Qasim and 'Abd al-Salam 'Arif, both of whom had been junior officers and had participated in the military actions against the British, referred to the war of 1941 as a glorious episode in the history of Iraq and of the army. It was no accident that 'Abd al-Ilah's corpse was hung near the gate of the Ministry of Defense. This symbolic act must have been encouraged by the army in vindication of its humiliation.[1]

Today the revolt is central to the Ba'th ideological teachings, a source of inspiration for Iraqi youth.[2] Although the president of Iraq, Saddam Husayn, was a child at the time, the 1941 war touched him personally. Because his father died a few months after his birth in 1937, Saddam Husayn was raised by his uncle, Khayr Allah Talfah, an officer who had participated in the war and whose career was ruined by the British occupation. Majid Khadduri, who interviewed Saddam, tells us that the suffering of the president's uncle humiliated him; his resentment of foreign influence and his later political activity was most probably a legacy of this period.

To Saddam Husayn, Salah al-Din al-Sabbagh was a great nationalist who tried to achieve pan-Arab objectives, but failed. Nevertheless, his teachings have inspired other nationalists. As Saddam told him, Majid Khadduri writes: "He [Saddam] was inspired by Colonel Sabbagh's memoirs to pursue the same nationalist goals which Colonel Sabbagh and his followers had advocated."[3]

Iraq's political situation during the interwar period, however, was not unique. Other developing countries such as Japan and Turkey found nonliberal European ideologies to be appropriate paradigms to emulate, because cultural nationalism and militarism were concepts compatible with their own cultural traditions. Even France, the great bastion of liberalism, underwent a nationalistic militaristic period during the pre-World War I years of the Third Republic.

What was unique about Iraq was that it was the only Arab country to become actively pro-German during this period. It rejected liberalism, in the sense of political reform and the promotion of individual liberty, for state-indoctrinated nationalism and militarism. But Iraq was not the only country to contemplate this shift in allegience. Egypt, which also had British liberal institutions superimposed on an autocratic tradition, contemplated a "Germanophile" switch, but was quickly brought into line by British tanks which surrounded King Faruq's palace in June 1940. This attempted political volte-face by the Egyptian government was accompanied by the gradual establishment of paramilitary groups as ancillary forces of the political parties. Syria, too, had its Iron Shirts, whose leader, Antun Sa'adah, saw a nationalist/militarist solution to Syria's identity crisis.

Iraq, however, was the only former mandate which was independent. While tied to the British by a treaty limiting its foreign policy options, Iraq, nonetheless, was able to create and implement a cultural identity that was inimical to British interests and values. And although the Egyptian Free Officers Movement of 1952 is touted as the model for the military's role in securing independence and leading the way toward "westernization," it was the Iraqi military which, more than a decade earlier, attempted what Khaldun al-Husry calls an Iraqi "Suez."[4] Because Iraq's "Suez" was unsuccessful, it is not given recognition.

One question remains, however. Why did Iraq reject the liberal model? Before World War I liberalism and democratic institutions were seen by the reformers, whom Albert Hourani discusses in his *Arabic Thought in the Liberal Age,* to be the anodyne to decline. Parliamentary democracy was the goal of the Young Ottomans and of the Egyptian and Syrian reformers studying in Paris.

In Iraq, however, liberalism was rejected for two reasons. First, Britain, which represented liberalism, had imposed liberal institutions on Iraq by its policy of government with an "Arab facade." All of the external trappings of a constitutional monarchy on the British model existed in Iraq after 1921. But Britain was the occupier. As such, Britain used nonliberal methods to maintain control. The British tampered with elections, deported the political opposition, played factions off against one another, and fostered reactionary elements of Iraqi society—the oligarchs against which the second wave of officers revolted in 1958. To the Iraqis, this so-called liberal process was a sham, a mechanism for control of power but not for the promotion of individual liberty. Thus, liberalism appeared to be hypocrisy.

Second, the officers who ruled Iraq after World War I were products of a nonliberal background that emphasized nationalism and militarism. Economics and social reform were not discussed in the military academies. Once the soldiers controlled the government apparatus, beginning with King Faysal's coronation in 1921, they began to implement reform. To these officers whose world view was conditioned by cultural nationalism and militarism, reform meant the inculcation of nationalism as a unifying focus of loyalty for their fractured society. The first generation—that which joined the Arab nationalist groups before World War I—created the ideology and implemented it. The second generation—that of the Four Colonels—acted out the ideology first by involving the military directly in politics and then by attempting to achieve the pan-Arab goals: total independence and unity of the Arab world. In order to achieve these ends, they turned to Germany and went to war with Britain.

Appendix I. The Hashimites

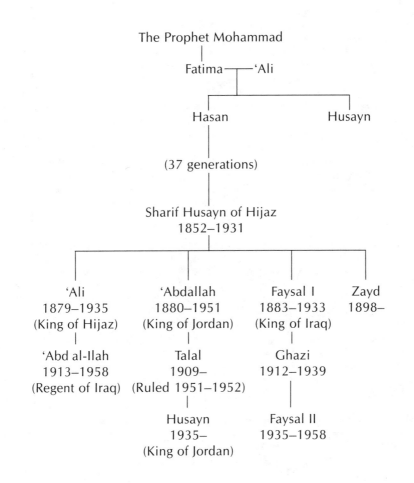

The Prophet Mohammad

Fatima——'Ali

Hasan   Husayn

(37 generations)

Sharif Husayn of Hijaz
1852–1931

'Ali
1879–1935
(King of Hijaz)

'Abdallah
1880–1951
(King of Jordan)

Faysal I
1883–1933
(King of Iraq)

Zayd
1898–

'Abd al-Ilah
1913–1958
(Regent of Iraq)

Talal
1909–
(Ruled 1951–1952)

Ghazi
1912–1939

Husayn
1935–
(King of Jordan)

Faysal II
1935–1958

Appendix II. Iraqi Cabinets 1921–1941

List includes army officers and major officeholders. Includes temporary appointments but does not specify dates of appointment.

2. September 12, 1921–August 19, 1922 (The first cabinet after Faysal's assumption of office)

'Abd al-Rahman al-Naqib	Prime Minister
Ja'far al-'Askari*	Minister of Defense
Naji al-Suwaydi	Minister of Justice
'Abd al-Muhsin al-Sa'dun*	Minister of Justice

3. September 30, 1922–November 16, 1922

'Abd al-Rahman al-Naqib	Prime Minister
'Abd al-Muhsin al-Sa'dun*	Minister of Interior
Ja'far al-'Askari*	Minister of Defense

4. November 20, 1922–November 15, 1923

'Abd al-Muhsin al-Sa'dun*	Prime Minister; Minister of Interior; Minister of Justice
Naji al-Suwaydi	Minister of Interior; Minister of Justice
Nuri al-Sa'id	Minister of Defense
Yasin al-Hashimi	Minister of Public Works and Communication

5. November 26, 1923–August 2, 1924

Ja'far al-'Askari*	Prime Minister; Minister of Education
'Ali Jawdat al-Ayyubi*	Minister of Interior
Nuri al-Sa'id*	Minister of Defense

6. August 2, 1924–June 21, 1925

Yasin al-Hashimi*	Prime Minister; Minister of Defense; Minister of Foreign Affairs
'Abd al-Muhsin al-Sa'dun	Minister of Interior
Rashid 'Ali al-Kaylani	Minister of Justice

7. June 26, 1925–November 1, 1926

'Abd al-Muhsin al-Sa'dun*	Prime Minister; Minister of Finance
Rashid 'Ali al-Kaylani	Minister of Interior
Hikmat Sulayman	Minister of Interior
Nuri al-Sa'id*	Minister of Defense

*Army officer.

8. November 21, 1926–January 8, 1928
   Ja'far al-'Askari*   Prime Minister; Minister of Foreign Affairs
   Rashid 'Ali al-Kaylani   Minister of Interior
   Nuri al-Sa'id*   Minister of Defense
   Yasin al-Hashimi*   Minister of Finance; Minister of Education

9. January 14, 1928–January 20, 1929
   'Abd al-Muhsin al-Sa'dun* Prime Minister; Minister of Interior; Minister of of Defense; Minister of Foreign Affairs
   Naji Shawkat   Minister of Interior
   Nuri al-Sa'id*   Minister of Defense
   Hikmat Sulayman   Minister of Justice
   Tawfiq al-Suwaydi   Minister of Education

10. April 28, 1929–August 25, 1929
    Tawfiq al-Suwaydi   Prime Minister; Minister of Foreign Affairs
    Muhammad Amin Zaki Minister of Defense
    'Abd al-Aziz al-Qassab Minister of Interior

11. September 19, 1929–November 13, 1929
    'Abd al-Muhsin al-Sa'dun Prime Minister; Minister of Foreign Affairs
    Naji al-Suwaydi   Minister of Interior
    Nuri al-Sa'id*   Minister of Defense
    Yasin al-Hashimi*   Minister of Finance
    Naji Shawkat   Minister of Justice

12. November 18, 1929–March 11, 1930
    Naji al-Suwaydi   Prime Minister; Minister of Foreign Affairs
    Naji Shawkat   Minister of Interior
    Nuri al-Sa'id*   Minister of Defense
    Yasin al-Hashimi*   Minister of Finance

13. March 23, 1930–October 19, 1931
    Nuri al-Sa'id*   Prime Minister; Minister of Foreign Affairs; Minister of Interior
    Jamil al-Midfa'i*   Prime Minister; Interior; Minister of Finance

*Army officer.

Ja'far al-'Askari*	Minister of Defense
'Ali Jaudat al-Ayyubi*	Minister of Finance
Rustam Haydar	Minister of Finance
Jamil al-Rawi*	Minister of Communications
Jamal Baban*	Minister of Justice

14. October 19, 1931–October 27, 1932

Nuri al-Sa'id*	Prime Minister; Minister of Foreign Affairs
Naji Shawkat	Minister of Interior
Ja'far al-'Askari*	Minister of Defense; Minister of Foreign Affairs
Rustam Haydar	Minister of Finance

15. November 3, 1932–March 18, 1933

Naji Shawkat	Prime Minister; Minister of Interior
Rashid al-Khujah*	Minister of Defense
Jalal Baban*	Minister of Public Works
Abd al-Qadir Rashid*	Minister of Foreign Affairs
Jamil al-Wadi*	Minister of Justice

16. March 20, 1933–October 28, 1933

Rashid 'Ali al-Kaylani	Prime Minister
Hikmat Sulayman	Minister of Finance
Jalal Baban*	Minister of Defense
Yasin al-Hashimi*	Minister of Finance
Rustam Haydar	Minister of Public Works
Nuri al-Sa'id*	Minister of Foreign Affairs

(Ghazi became king on September 8, 1933, after the death of King Faysal. The cabinet resigned and was reinstated without change.)

17. November 9, 1933–February 19, 1934

Jamal al-Midaf'i*	Prime Minister
Naji Shawkat	Minister of Interior
Nuri al-Sa'id*	Minister of Defense; Minister of Foreign Affairs
Rustam Haydar	Minister of Public Works

18. February 21, 1934–August 26, 1934

Jamil al-Midfa'i*	Prime Minister; Minister of Interior
Rashid al-Khuja*	Minister of Defense
Naji al-Suwaydi	Minister of Finance
Jalal Baban*	Minister of Education

*Army officer.

19. August 27, 1934–February 27, 1935
    'Ali Jawdat al-Ayyubi*   Prime Minister; Minister of Interior
    Jamil al-Midfa'i*   Minister of Defense
    Nuri al-Sa'id*   Minister of Foreign Affairs
20. March 4, 1935–March 17, 1935
    Jamil al-Midfa'i*   Prime Minister
    Abd al-Aziz al-Qassab   Minister of Interior
    Rashid al-Khuja*   Minister of Defense
    Nuri al-Sa'id*   Minister of Foreign Affairs
21. March 17, 1935–October 29, 1936
    Yasin al-Hashimi*   Prime Minister
    Rashid 'Ali al-Kaylani   Minister of Interior; Minister of
        Justice
    Ja'far al-'Askari*   Minister of Defense
    Nuri al-Sa'id*   Minister of Foreign Affairs
22. November 29, 1936–August 17, 1937
    Hikmat Sulayman   Prime Minister; Minister of Interior
    Mustafa al-'Umari*   Minister of Interior
    Gen. 'Abd al-Latif Nuri*   Minister of Defense
    'Ali Mahmud al-Shaykh
      'Ali   Minister of Defense; Minister of
        Justice
23. August 17, 1937–January 24, 1936
    Jamil al-Midfa'i*   Prime Minister; Minister of Defense;
        Minister of Interior
    Mustafa al-'Umari*   Minister of Interior; Minister of
        Justice
    Sabih Najib*   Minister of Defense
    Jalal Baban*   Minister of Public Works
    Tawfiq al-Suwaydi   Minister of Foreign Affairs
24. January 25, 1938–April 6, 1939
    Nuri al-Sa'id*   Prime Minister; Minister of Interior;
        Minister of Foreign Affairs
    Taha al-Hashimi*   Minister of Interior; Minister of
        Defense
    Naji Shawkat   Minister of Interior
    Rustam Haydar   Minister of Finance

*Army officer.

25. April 6, 1939–February 19, 1940

Nuri al-Sa'id*	Prime Minister; Minister of Interior; Minister of Foreign Affairs
Naji Shawkat	Minister of Interior
Taha al-Hashimi*	Minister of Defense
Rustam Haydar	Minister of Finance
Jalal Baban*	Minister of Public Works
'Ali Jawdat al-Ayyubi*	Minister of Foreign Affairs
Dr. Sami Shawkat	Minister of Social Affairs

26. February 22, 1940–March 31, 1940

Nuri al-Sa'id*	Prime Minister; Minister of Foreign Affairs
Taha al-Hashimi*	Minister of Defense
Dr. Sami Shawkat	Minister of Education

27. March 31, 1940–-January 31, 1941

Rashid 'Ali al-Kaylani	Prime Minister; Minister of Interior
Taha al-Hashimi*	Minister of Defense; Minister of Economics
Naji al-Suwaydi	Minister of Finance; Minister of Foreign Affairs
Naji Shawkat	Minister of Justice
'Ali Mahmud al-Shaykh 'Ali	Minister of Justice
Nuri al-Sa'id*	Minister of Foreign Affairs
Yunis al-Saba'wi	Minister of Economics

28. February 1, 1941–April 1, 1941

Taha al-Hashimi*	Prime Minister; Minister of Defense
Tawfiq al-Suwaydi	Minister of Foreign Affairs

29. April 12, 1941–June 1, 1941

Rashid 'Ali al-Kaylani	Prime Minister; Minister of Interior
Naji Shawkat	Minister of Defense
Naji al-Suwaydi	Minister of Finance
'Ali Mahmud al-Shaykh 'Ali	Minister of Justice
Yunis al-Saba'wi	Minister of Economics

*Army officer.

Appendix III. Biographical Sketches

Name	Background	Education Ottoman Military Academy (OMA)	World War I ex-Ottoman Col. Sharifian	Position in Iraq*
Ja'far al-'Askari	1885 Baghdad Sunni Arab	OMA	ex-Ottoman Col. Sharifian	Cabinet—12
'Ali Jawdat al-Ayyubi	1886 Mosul Sunni Arab	OMA	Ottoman officer Sharifian	Cabinet—5
Husayn Fawzi	1889 Baghdad Sunni Kurd	OMA	Ottoman officer	Officer (1937—Chief of Staff)
Taha al-Hashimi	1887 Baghdad Sunni Arab	OMA	Ottoman officer Sharifian	Cabinet—7 (1936—Chief of Staff)
Yasin al-Hashimi	1884 Baghdad Sunni Arab	OMA	Ottoman Major General, joined Faysal 1919	Cabinet—8
Mahmud Fadhil al-Janabi	Baghdad Sunni Arab	OMA	Ottoman officer	Officer Advisor to Futuwwah
Jamil al-Midfa'i	1880 Mosul Kurd/Arab Sunni	OMA	Ottoman officer Sharifian	Cabinet—8
Mawlud Mukhlis	1886 Mosul Sunni Arab	OMA	Ottoman officer Sharifian	Politician
Sabih Najib	1892	OMA	Ottoman officer Sharifian	Cabinet—1 Foreign service
'Abd al-Latif Nuri	1888 Baghdad Sunni Arab	OMA	Ottoman officer joined Faysal 1918	Officer Minister Defense—Bakr Sidqi
Ibrahim al-Rawi	Sunni Arab	OMA	Ottoman officer Sharifian	Officer Loyal to Abd al-Ilah February 1941

*Figures refer to number of cabinet posts held.

Name	Background	Education	World War I	Position in Iraq*
Salah al-Din al-Sabbagh	1899 Mosul Sunni Arab	OMA Iraqi Staff College	Ottoman Lt. Col. joined Faysal 1919	Officer One of four Colonels
'Abd al-Muhsin al-Sa'dun	1879 Basra	OMA		Cabinet—12
Fahmi Sa'id	1898 Sulaymaniyah Sunni Arab	OMA Iraqi Staff Col.	Ottoman officer joined Faysal after 1918	Officer One of four Colonels
Nuri al-Sa'id	1888 Baghdad Turk/Arab Sunni	OMA	Ottoman officer Sharifian	Cabinet—23
Mahmud Salman	1898 Baghdad Sunni Arab	OMA	Ottoman Lt. joined Faysal after 1918	Officer One of four Colonels
Kamil Shabib	1895 Baghdad Sunni Arab	OMA Iraqi Staff Col.	Ottoman Lt. joined Faysal after 1918	Officer One of four Colonels
Naji Shawkat	1891 Baghdad Sunni Arab	Law School—Istanbul	Sharifian	Cabinet—10
Sami Shawkat	1893 Baghdad Sunni Arab	Military Medical School—Istanbul	Ottoman officer joined Faysal after 1918	Cabinet—2
Bakr Sidqi	Sunni Kurd	OMA Turkish Staff Col.	Ottoman officer joined Faysal 1919	Officer Military coup—1936 Chief of Staff
Amin al-'Umari	1889 Mosul Sunni Arab	OMA Iraqi Staff Col.	Ottoman officer joined Faysal after 1918	Officer

Name	Birth	Sect/Ethnicity	Education	Affiliation	Posts*
'Aziz Mustafa Yamulki	1893 Sulaymaniya	Sunni Kurd	OMA	Ottoman army	Officer
Amin Zaki	1887 Baghdad	Sunni	OMA	Ottoman army	Officer
Sati' al-Husri	1882	Sunni Arab	Civil Service College—Istanbul	Joined Faysal 1919	Ministry of Education
Muhammad Fadhil al-Jamali	1902 Kadhimayh	Shi'i Arab	Columbia Univ. (USA)		Ministry of Education
Yunis al-Sab'awi	1906 Mosul	Sunni Arab	Baghdad Law College		Cabinet—2
Hikmat Sulayman	1885 Baghdad	Sunni Turk	Civil Service College—Istanbul		Cabinet—6
Naji al-Suwaydi	1882 Baghdad	Sunni Arab	Law School—Istanbul	Arab nationalist	Cabinet—8
Tawfiq al-Suwaydi	1891 Baghdad	Sunni Arab	Law School—Istanbul; Paris	Arab nationalist	Cabinet—6

*Figures refer to number of cabinet posts held.

SOURCES: Mohammad A. Tarbush, *The Role of the Military in Politics:; A Case Study of Iraq to 1941*, pp. 80–82;; Hanna Batatu, *The Old Social Classes and the Revolutionary Movements of Iraq: A Study of Iraq's Old Landed and Commercial Classes and of its Communists, Ba'thists, and Free Officers*, pp. 180–184; al-'Iraq. *al-Dalil al-'Iraqi al-Rasmi li-Sanah* 1936 (Baghdad, 1936); F.O. 406/78 "Report on the Leading Personalities of Iraq for the Year 1940."

Notes

Introduction

1. James S. Coleman, "Introduction," in James S. Coleman, ed., *Education and Political Development*.

2. See, for example, P. J. Vatikiotis, *The Egyptian Army in Politics: Pattern for New Nations?* M. Van Dusen, "Political Integration and Regionalism in Syria;" Frederick W. Frey, *The Turkish Political Elite*.

3. Toshio Nishi, *Unconditional Democracy: Education and Politics in Occupied Japan, 1945–1952*. See also the works by I. L. Kandel, "Nationalism and Education," pp. 27–46, and "Education and Social Change," *Journal of Social Philosophy* (October 1935) 1:23–35.

4. Hanna Batatu, *The old Social Classes and the Revolutionary Movements of Iraq: A Study of Iraq's Old Landed and Commercial Classes and of its Communists, Ba'thists, and Free Officers*. David Pool, "The Politics of Patronage: Elites and Social Structure in Iraq."

1. The Creation of a State

1. Robert Lacey, The Kingdom: Arabia and the House of Sa'ud, p. 160.

2. Faysal and his family are also known as *Hashimites*.

3. Lady Bell, ed., *The Letters of Gertrude Bell of Arabia* p. 610.

4. Quoted in David Pool, "The Politics of Patronage: Elites and Social Structure in Iraq," p. 88.

5. *Ibid.*, p. 28

6. Quoted from a confidential memo published in 'Abd al-Razzaq al-Hasani, *Ta'rikh al-Wizarat al-'Iraqiyyah*, 3:289. The translation is from Hanna Batatu, *The Old Social Classes and the Revolutionary Movements of Iraq: A Study of Iraq's Old Landed and Commercial Classes and of its Communists, Ba'thists, and Free Officers*, p. 28.

7. For thorough coverage of the social and economic background of Iraq under the monarchy, see the masterful work by Hanna Batatu cited above.

2. The Officers, Germany, and Nationalism

1. On the early period, see J. C. Hurewitz, *Middle East Politics: The Military Dimension*, pp. 28–40.

2. M. A. Griffiths, "The Reorganization of the Ottoman Army under Abdulhamid II, 1880–1897," pp. 44–45. See also Allan Mitchell, "French Military Reorganization," on French military organization after the Franco-Prussian War.

3. Talib Mushtaq, *Awraq Ayyami, 1900–1958*, p. 36. The translation is from David Pool, "From Elite to Class: The Transformation of Iraqi Leadership 1920–1939," pp. 333, 335.

4. *Ibid.*, p. 333.

5. Abdul Wahhab Abbas al-Qaysi, "The Impact of Modernization on Iraqi Society during the Ottoman Era," p. 67. The wealthier families sent their sons to the nonmilitary colleges such as law and medicine. Of the Iraqis, these were less than 8 percent of the number who received military degrees (Ayad al-Qazzaz, "The Changing Patterns of the Politics of the Iraqi Army," p. 5).

6. Arminius Vambery, "Personal Recollections of Abdul Hamid and His Court," p. 81.

7. Ernest E. Ramsaur, *The Young Turks: Prelude to the Revolution of 1908*, p. 140.

8. Mary Townsend, *The Rise and Fall of the German Colonial Empire, 1884–1918*, pp. 212–213.

9. Although E. M. Earle maintains that von Hatzfeld, the German ambassador took the initiative, I have followed Griffiths' account. Earle, writing in the 1920s, did not have access to the diplomatic papers Griffiths used. E. M. Earle, *Turkey, the Great Powers and the Bagdad Railway; A Study in Imperialism*, p. 38; Griffiths, "The Reorganization of the Ottoman Army," pp. 44–51.

10. Von der Goltz succeeded Kahler Pasha who died in 1885 (Griffiths, p. 66).

11. Townsend, *The Rise and Fall of the German Colonial Empire*, p. 209.

12. Earle, *Turkey, the Great Powers and the Bagdad Railway*, p. 40.

13. Fritz Fischer, *War of Illusions: German Policies from 1911 to 1914*, pp. 28–39.

14. Martin Kitchen, *The German Officer Corps 1890–1914*, p. 100.

15. Austin Harrison, *The Pan-Germanic Doctrine*, p. 193.

16. Fischer, *War of Illusions*, p. 42–43.

17. Paul Rohrbach, *German World Policies*, p. 229.

18. Harrison, *The Pan-Germanic Doctrine*, pp. 28–39.

19. Rohrbach, *German World Policies*, p. 226.

20. Fischer, *War of Illusions*, p. 333.

21. *Ibid.*, p. 335.

22. Ulrich Trumpener, *Germany and the Ottoman Empire, 1914–1918*; Frank G. Weber, *Eagles on the Crescent: Germany, Austria, and the Diplomacy of the Turkish Alliance 1914–1918*; W. O. Henderson, "German Economic Penetration in the Middle East, 1870–1914."

23. Townsend, *The Rise and Fall of the German Colonial Empire*, p. 209; Henderson, "German Economic Penetration in the Middle East," pp. 74–86; Evans Lewin, *The German Road to the East*, pp. 30–31.

24. There was a definite decision, according to Griffiths, to ignore the navy and to rely on land forces. The British did, however, provide naval advice throughout the period under discussion.

25. Earle, *Turkey, the Great Powers and the Bagdad Railway*.

26. Kemal H. Karpat, "The Transformation of the Ottoman State, 1789–1908."

27. Ahmad Emin (Yalman), *Turkey in the World War*, p. 33.

28. Griffiths, "The Reorganization of the Ottoman Army," pp. 57–61.

29. Phebe A. Marr, "Yasin al-Hashimi: The Rise and Fall of a Nationalist," pp. 71–72.

30. P. J. Vatikiotis, The Egyptian Army in Politics: Pattern for New Nations? M. Van Dusen, "Political Integration and Regionalism in Syria;" Frederick W. Frey, The Turkish Political Elite.

31. Al-Qazzaz, "The Changing Patterns of the Politics of the Iraqi Army," pp. 3–5; see also his "Power Elite in Iraq, 1920–1958," p. 279.

32. Mohammad A. Tarbush, The Role of the Military in Politics: A Study of Iraq to 1941, p. 78.

33. See Robert O. Paxton, Vichy France: Old Guard and the New Order 1940–1944, and Richard A. Preston and Sydney F. Wise, Men in Arms: A History of Warfare and Its Interrelationships with Western Society, for similar developments in France.

34. Kitchen, The German Officer Corps, pp. 26–27.

35. Colmar von der Goltz, The Nation in Arms: A Treatise on Modern Military Systems and the Conduct of War, p. 83; Kitchen, The German Officer Corps, p. 23.

36. Henry Morgenthau, Ambassador Morgenthau's Story p. 6.

37. F. W. Wile, Men Around the Kaiser, pp. 221–222.

38. Griffiths, "The Reorganization of the Ottoman Army," pp. 98–99.

39. Colonel Malleterre, "L'Armée Jeune-Turque."

40. Griffiths, "The Reorganization of the Ottoman Army," pp. 96–99.

41. Charles G. N. Le Brun-Renaud, La Turquie, puissance militaire, armée de terre et flotte (Paris, 1895), p. 88; cf. Glen Swanson, "Enver Pasha: The Formative Years," pp. 198–199, n. 13.

42. Griffiths, "The Reorganization of the Ottoman Army," p. 93.

43. Hans Kohn, Nationalism: Its Meaning and History, pp. 9–28.

44. Serif Mardin, The Genesis of Young Ottoman Thought: A Study in the Modernization of Turkish Political Ideas.

45. David Kushner, The Rise of Turkish Nationalism 1876–1908, p. 29.

46. Ibid., pp. 32–33.

47. Ibid., pp. 37–38.

48. Uriel Heyd, Foundation of Turkish Nationalism, pp. 164–170; Taha Parla, "The Social and Political Thought of Ziya Gökalp."

49. Griffiths, "The Reorganization of the Ottoman Army," p. 176.

50. Glen W. Swanson, "War, Technology, and Society in the Ottoman Empire from the Reign of Abdulhamid II to 1913; Mahmud Sevket and the German Military Mission," p. 381; cf. Bernard Vernier, La Politique Islamique de l'Allemagne, p. 11.

51. A. de Bilinski, "The Turkish Army," p. 407.

52. Sir Edwin Pears, A Life of Abdul Hamid, p. 108; see also "Public Opinion and Education," from annual report Istanbul 1907 in G. P. Gooch and H. Temperley, eds., British Documents on the Origins of the War, 1889–1914, 5:29–31.

53. De Bilinski, "The Turkish Army," p. 407.

54. Ramsaur, The Young Turks, p. 144; Ernest Jackh, The Rising Crescent: Turkey Yesterday, Today, and Tomorrow, p. 91.

55. Feroz Ahmad, The Young Turks, p. 48.

56. Dankwart A. Rustow, "The Military in Turkey," p. 360.

57. Ramsaur, The Young Turks, p. 118; Griffiths, "The Reorganization of the Ottoman Army," p. 175.

58. Ahmad, *The Young Turks*, p. 177.

59. Swanson, "War, Technology, and Society in the Ottoman Empire"; Ahmad, *The Young Turks*, p. 179.

60. Ahmed Djemal Pasha, *Memoirs of a Turkish Statesman 1913–1919*, pp. 65–68.

61. Ahmad, *The Young Turks*, p. 172.

62. Swanson, "Enver Pasha," pp. 198–199, n.13.

63. *Ibid.*, pp. 193–199; Ahmad, *The Young Turks*, pp. 168–169.

64. Harrison, *The Pan-Germanic Doctrine*, pp. 226–227; Rohrbach, *German World Policies*, pp. 229–231.

65. R. Davison, "Westernized Education in Ottoman Turkey," p. 295.

66. Frey, *The Turkish Political Elite*, p. 107.

67. *Ibid.*, p. 108. Frey cites Kemal Karpat.

68. H. E. Allen, *The Turkish Transformation*, p. 25.

69. Bassam Tibi, *Arab Nationalism: A Critical Inquiry*.

70. 'Ali Jawdat, *Dhikriyat 'Ali Jawdat, 1900–1958*, pp. 20–21.

71. Albert Hourani, *Arabic Thought in the Liberal Age, 1789–1939*; Sylvia G. Haim, *Arab Nationalsim*.

72. Al-Qaysi, "The Impact of Modernization on Iraqi Society," pp. 92–94.

73. For material on the Arab nationalist societies see: M. I. Darwazah, *Hawl al-Harakah al-'Arabiyyah al-Hadithah*; Ibrahim al-Rawi, *Min al-Thawrah al-'Arabiyyah al-Kubra ila al-'Iraq al-Hadith: Dhikriyat*, pp. 25–60.

74. Al-Qaysi, "The Impact of Modernization on Iraqi Society," p. 102.

75. *Ibid.*, pp. 102–103.

76. The Iraqis were: Nuri al-Sa'id, Taha al-Hashimi, Yasin al-Hashimi, Mawlud Mukhlis, Jamil al-Midfa'i, 'Ali Jawdat al-Ayyubi, 'Abdullah al-Dulaymi, Tahsin 'Ali, 'Abdul Ghafar al-Badri, 'Ali Rida al-Ghazali, Muhammad Hilmi al-Hajj Dhiyab, Hamid al-Shalehi, Rashid al-Khuja, and Muwaffaq Kamil. Darwazah, *Hawl al-Harakah al-'Arabiyyah al-Hadithah*, 1:32–33.

77. Taha al-Hashimi, *Mudhakkirat Taha al-Hashimi*, p. 255; al-Rawi, *Min al-Thawrah al-'Arabiyyah al-Kubra ila al-'Iraq al-Hadith*, pp. 52–53.

78. For biographical information on Sati' al-Husri, see William L. Cleveland, *The Making of an Arab Nationalist: Ottomanism and Arabism in the Life and Thought of Sati' al-Husri*.

79. *Ibid.*, p. 45.

80. Bassam Tibi, *Arab Nationalism*, pp. 93–94. Abu Khaldun Sati' al-Husri, *The Day of Maysalun*.

81. The analysis of Sati' al-Husri's concept of nationalism is largely derived from Tibi's book.

82. Tibi, *Arab Nationalism*, p. 122. The quote is from Sati' al-Husri.

83. Cleveland, *The Making of an Arab Nationalist*, pp. 123–126.

84. Quoted in Elie Kedourie, "The Kingdom of Iraq: A Retrospect," in his *The Chatham House Version and Other Middle Eastern Studies*, p. 274.

85. Great Britain, Foreign Office 624/24, 448/3/41, July 29, 1941. British Foreign Office documents are henceforth cited as F.O.

86. United States Department of State 890g.00, General Conditins/12, Knabenshue to Secretary of State, Baghdad, August 18, 1933. United States Department of State documents are henceforth cited as U.S. Dept. of State. Knabenshue was of the

opinion that the interest in a league formed on the lines of the Nazi party, wherein its inherents would wear brown shirts and would be trained to defend the country, would be short-lived and was due to the impact of the Assyrian troubles.

87. Wilhelm II was very interested in the Middle East. He encouraged Orientalists and held frequent congresses in Germany. Vernier, *La Politique Islamique de l'Allemagne*, pp. 26–28.

On July 29, 1914, Wilhelm II convinced Liman von Sanders, who wanted to go home, to remain in Turkey to work to stir up anti-British agitation. Under-Secretary of State Arthur Zimmermann mobilized German academics and Middle East specialists under Professor Max von Oppenheim, whom he recalled to the Foreign Ministry from retirement. Von Oppenheim, an Arabist and an expert on Islam which he studied in Cairo, had served there as attaché to the Consulate General from 1896 to 1910. Now his job was to direct the "Information Service for the East." His directive on the efficiency of turning pan-Islamism against the British by instigating a *jihad* (holy war) in the Middle East, an abortive plan to attack the Suez Canal, subventions to the Egyptian khedive, the sharif of Mecca (before the British thought of the idea), and Ibn Sa'ud and Ibn Rashid—the competing shaykhs of Arabia—were some of the attempts the Germans used to subvert British influence in the Arab world. Fritz Fischer, *Germany's Aims in the First World War*, pp. 122–130; on von Oppenheim see p. 123, n.2.

Both Joachim von Ribbentrop and Franz von Papen, who later dealt with the Iraqis during World War II, received experience in the Middle East during the Great War. C. L. Sulzberger, "German Preparations in the Middle East," pp. 664–665; Vernier, *La Politique Islamique de l'Allemagne*, p. 95.

88. F.O. 624/18, Germany: Propaganda 133/16/40. Dr. Herbert Melzig, who had been press advisor to the Near Eastern Department of the German Ministry of Propaganda, transmitted this memorandum to the British in 1940. He had received it from advisors to the German Ministry of Propaganda, and subsequently published the memo in Turkish in order to alert the Turks to the danger: Melzig, *Yakin Sarkta Alman Propagandasi Hakkinda Bir Muhtira*.

89. U.S. National Archives, RG 338: MS. #P–207, "German Exploitation of Arab Nationalist Movements in World War II" (n.d.).

90. F.O. 624/18, Germany: Propaganda 133/16/40, p. 8.

91. *Ibid.*, p. 9.

92. Z. A. B. Zeman, *Nazi Propaganda*, pp. 69–70.

93. Vernier, *La Politique Islamique de l'Allemagne*, pp. 36, 40–41, and 28.

94. Virginia Vacca, "Ar-Radyo: Le Radio Arabe d'Europa e d'Oriente e le Loro Pubblicazioni," *Oreinte Moderno* (1940), 20:444–451; Callum A. MacDonald, "Radio Bari: Italain Wireless Propaganda in the Middle East and British Countermeasures 1934–1938;" Seth Arsenian, "Wartime Propaganda in the Middle East," pp. 417–418.

95. Nevill Barbour, "Broadcasting to the Arab World," p. 63; Arsenian, "Wartime Propaganda in the Middle East," pp. 419–420.

96. U.S. Dept. of State 890g.00, General Conditions/150, #1293, Knabenshue to Secretary of State, Baghdad, May 12, 1939.

97. U.S. National Archives RG 208: "Progaganda and the Near East," by Anne Fuller, June 26, 1941.

98. Arsenian, "Wartime Propaganda in the Middle East," p. 428.

99. U.S. National Archives RG 84: #1812, Knabenshue to Secretary of State, Baghdad, January 13, 1942. British broadcasting from Jerusalem and Cairo had been

described as "singularly inept" (U.S. National Archives RG 208: "Propaganda and the Near East"). The British Air Liaison Officer in Mosul, A. H. Marsack, presented similar views in his report written in 1940 (F.O. 624/18/133 "Enemy and Allied Publicity and Propaganda).

100. Fritz Grobba, *Männer und Mächte im Orient: 25 Jahre diplomatischer Tatigkeit im Orient.*

101. Majid Khadduri, *Independent Iraq*, p. 172.

102. Lord Birdwood, *Nuri as-Said: A Study in Arab Leadership*, pp. 164–166; F.O. 406/77, "Report on Heads of Foreign Missions at Baghdad, 1939.

103. U.S. Dept. of State 890g.00/474, telegram, Knabenshue to Secretary of State, Baghdad, April 18, 1939.

104. H. H. Kopietz, "The Use of German and British Archives in the Study of the Middle East: The Iraqi Coup d'Etat of 1936," p. 56.

105. Vernier, *La Politique Islamique de l'Allemagne*, p. 49.

106. See below. On Dr. Jordon see F.O. 406/77 E2817/77/93, Houstoun-Boswall to Halifax, Baghdad, April 11, 1939; U.S. National Archives RG 84: #1294, Knabenshue to Secretary of State, Baghdad, May 12, 1939.

107. Gerald de Gaury, *Three Kings in Baghdad, 1921–1958*, p. 114.

108. Sir Maurice Peterson, *Both Sides of the Curtain*, pp. 144–145.

109. F.O. 624/24 448/3/41, "Nazi Propaganda in Iraq."

110. U.S. Dept. of State 890g.00, General Conditions/19, Knabenshue to Secretary of State, Baghdad, December 6, 1933; 890g.00, General Conditions/33, Diplomatic #341, Knabenshue to Secretary of State, Baghdad, July 11, 1934.

111. U.S. Dept. of State 890g.00, General Conditions/55, Diplomatic #491, Knabenshue to Secretary of State, Baghdad, June 11, 1935; 890g.00, General Conditions/70 #573, Knabenshue to Secretary of State, Baghdad, January 23, 1936.

112. U.S. Dept. of State 762.90G/7 #1252, Knabenshue to Secretary of State, Baghdad, March 9, 1939. Grobba circulated copies in English of Hitler's January 30, 1939, speech to the Reichstag. See also: U.S. Dept. of State 740.0011, European War 1939/4269, Knabenshue to Secretary of State, Baghdad, May 29, 1940; F.O. 624/24 448/3/41, "Nazi Propaganda in Iraq"; Albert Viton, "Britain and the Axis in the Near East," p. 380.

113. F.O. 624/24 448/3/41, "Nazi Propaganda in Iraq." The German Ministry of Propaganda set up professional societies to entertain guests from the Middle East—"Oriental Verein" (F.O. 624/18, Germany: Propaganda 133/16/40, n.11).

114. "A Short History of Enemy Subversive Activity in Iraq, 1935–1941," in the American Christian Palestine Committee, *The Arab War Effort: A Documented Account*, p. 31.

115. Sir Harry C. Sinderson, *Ten Thousand and One Nights*, pp. 167–168; Peterson, *Both Sides of the Curtain*, p. 144; F.O. 406/74, #89 E708/708/65, "German Economic Penetration in the Middle East, January 1936."

116. F.O. 624/9, Scott to (?) #317, Baghdad, July 31, 1937.

117. U.S. National Archives RG 165: Government of Iraq, Ministry of Economics, *Statistical Abstract 1939*, Section 5, table 80, p. 59.

118. F.O. 624/22 87/5/41, "Notes on the Iraqi Educational Mission to Germany."

119. F.O. 624/17 E5620/474/93, Newton to Halifax, Baghdad, August 10, 1939.

120. Vernier, *La Politique Islamique de l'Allemagne,* pp. 92–93; *Oreinte Moderno,* December 1938, pp. 10–11.

121. "Document: German Ideas on Iraq—Grobba, 1937–1938."

122. Kopietz, "The Use of German and British Archives in the Study of the Middle East," pp. 58–60, 55, and 60.

123. Sinderson, *Ten Thousand and One Nights,* p. 170; Abd al-Razzaq al-Hasani also notes that Dr. Shawkat was present. Abd al-Razzaq al-Hasani, *Ta'rikh al-Wizarat al-Iraqiyyah,* 5:74–75.

124. U.S. National Arvhives RG 84: #1294, Knabenshue to Secretary of State, Baghdad, May 12, 1939.

125. Sinderson, *Ten Thousand and One Nights,* p. 170.

126. F.O. 406/77 E2817/77/93, Houstoun-Boswall to Halifax, Baghdad, April 11, 1939; U.S. National Archives RG 84: #1294, Knabenshue to Secretary of State, Baghdad, May 12, 1939 and enclosure. Grobba gave Knabenshue a copy.

127. Grobba, *Männer und Mächte im Orient,* pp. 179–181.

128. al-Hasani, *Ta'rikh al-Wizarat al-Iraqiyyah,* 5:73, n. 1; Mushtaq, *Awraq Ayyami,* pp. 314 ff.

129. U.S. National Archives RG 165: Iraq 2930, "Berlin in Arabic," March 23, 1944, 9:30 PM; Freya Stark, *Dust in the Lion's Paw,* p. 77.

The British were also accused of murdering Faysal in Switzerland. The Iraqi nationalists do not consider the cases closed.

3. The Officers in Iraq

1. B.C. Busch, *Britain, India, and the Arabs 1914–1921,* pp. 56–109.

2. Ghassan R. Attiyah, *Iraq 1908–1921: A Political Study,* p. 109–110.

3. Busch, *Britain, India, and the Arabs,* p. 175; Lord Birdwood, *Nuri as-Said: A Study in Arab Leadership,* p. 49; Attiyah, *Iraq 1908–1921,* p. 102; Birdwood, *Nuri as-Said,* pp. 18, 48–49; and Busch, *Britain, India, and the Arabs,* p. 175.

4. Phebe A. Marr, "Yasin al-Hashimi: The Rise and Fall of a Nationalist."

5. Abdul Wahhab Abbas al-Qaysi, "The Impact of Modernization on Iraqi Society during the Ottoman Era: A Study of Intellectual Development in Iraq 1869–1917," p. 106.

6. Busch, *Britain, India, and the Arabs,* pp. 175–176.

7. Attiyah, *Iraq 1908–1921,* p. 103.

8. Mohammad Tarbush, *The Role of the Military in Politics: A Case Study of Iraq to 1941,* p. 237.

9. For detailed studies of the British occupation of Mesopotamia, see Peter Sluglett, *Britain in Iraq 1914–1932,* and P. W. Ireland, *Iraq: A Study in Political Development.*

10. On Wilson, see his own account: A. T. Wilson, *Loyalties: Mesopotamia 1914–1917* and *Mesopotamia 1917–1920: A Clash of Loyalties.*

11. M. I. Darwazah, *Hawl al-Harakah al-'Arabiyyah al-Hadithah* 1:74–79.

12. Marr, "Yasin al-Hashimi," pp. 69–86.

13. Amal Vinogradov, "The 1920 Revolt in Iraq Reconsidered: The Role of the Tribes in National Politics," p. 134.

14. Attiyah, *Iraq 1908–1921,* pp. 272–273.

15. For the text and the signatories, see Tawfiq al-Suwaydi, *Mudhakkirati* pp. 53–57; see also 'Ali Jawdat, *Dhikriyat 'Ali Jawdat, 1900–1958,* pp. 88–89.

16. Birdwood, *Nuri al-Said,* p. 109. Nuri told the British that leading figures in Baghdad and Mosul authorized six of the men in Damascus to speak for them: Faysal, Ja'far al-'Askeri, Naji al-Suwaydi, Mawlud Mukhlis, Yasin al-Hashimi, and 'Ali Jawdat.

17. Phebe Marr, *The Modern History of Iraq,* p. 33.

18. Vinogradov, "The 1920 Revolt."

19. Khaled A. M. al-Ani, *Encyclopedia of Modern Iraq,* 1:127–128.

20. Elie Kedourie, "The Kingdom of Iraq: A Retrospect," *The Chatham House Version and Other Middle Eastern Studies,* pp. 250–252.

21. Vinogradov, "The 1920 Revolt," p. 124. Hanna Batatu says that "at bottom" the revolt was a "shaykhs affair." Hanna Batatu, *The Old Social Classes and the Revolutionary Movements: A Study of Iraq's Old Landed and Commercial Classes and of its Communists, Ba'thists, and Free Officers,* p. 119.

22. Attiyah, *Iraq 1908–1921,* pp. 275–278.

23. Walid Khadduri, "Social Background of Modern Iraqi Politics," p. 175.

24. Sluglett, *Britain in Iraq,* p. 45.

25. On the Cairo Conference, see A. S. Klieman, *Foundations of British Policy in the Arab World: The Cairo Conference of 1921.*

26. Sluglett, *Britain in Iraq,* p. 67.

27. *Ibid.,* p. 93, n. 3.

28. S. H. Longrigg, *Iraq 1900–1950,* p. 133.

29. Kedourie, "The Kingdom of Iraq," p. 241.

30. Gerald de Gaury, *Three Kings in Baghdad,* p. 25.

31. Quoted in Sluglett, *Britain in Iraq,* p. 77.

32. Marr, *The Modern History of Iraq,* p. 45.

33. Ayad al-Qazzaz, "Power Elite in Iraq, 1920–1958: A Study of the Cabinet."

34. Marr, "*The Modern History of Iraq,*" p. 51.

35. U.S. Dept. of State 890g.001, Faisal/36, #259, Sloan to Secretary of State, Baghdad, July 22, 1932.

36. U.S. Dept. of State 890g/001/176, Diplomatic Series #119, Sloan to Secretary of State, Baghdad, February 3, 1932; U.S. Dept. of State 890g.00/181, Diplomatic Series #139, Sloan to Secretary of State, Baghdad, February 29, 1932. See also Marr, "Yasin al-Hashimi," pp. 193–194, where she refers to an article in *al-'Iraq,* the government organ, in which the editor advocates national dictatorship under an enlightened despot, presumably Faysal.

37. Marr, "Yasin al-Hashimi," p. 195.

38. U.S. Dept. of State 890g.00/184, Sloan to Secretary of State, Baghdad, March 16, 1932.

39. Great Britain, Foreign Office, F.O. 371/15324, telegram #304 from Acting HC to S/S Col. July 11, 1931. British documents henceforth cited as F.O.

40. U.S. Dept. of State 890g.00/154, Diplomatic Series #29, Sloan to Secretary of State, Baghdad, July 21, 1931.

41. Marr, "Yasin al-Hashimi," pp. 212–219.

42. F.O. 371/16903, Minute 105/105/93, Hall, January 9, 1933.

43. U.S. Dept. of State 890g.00/250, Doc. File #118, Knabenshue to Secretary of State, Baghdad, June 10, 1933.

44. *Ibid.*

45. U.S. Dept. of State 890g.00/176, Dipl. Series #119, Sloan to Secretary of State, Baghdad, February 3, 1932.

46. On Nuri al-Sa'id, see Majid Khadduri, *Arab Contemporaries: The Role of Personalities in Politics;* Birdwood, *Nuri as-Said.*

47. Marr, "Yasin al-Hashimi," pp. 69–86.

48. *Ibid.,* pp. 116–191.

49. De Gaury, *Three Kings in Baghdad,* pp. 49 and 37.

50. Kedourie, "The Kingdom of Iraq," p. 279. He cites Gertrude Bell as the reporter of this episode.

51. Sluglett, *Britain in Iraq,* pp. 159–160.

52. De Gaury, *Three Kings in Baghdad,* pp. 49 and 66.

53. On Nuri, see U.S. Dept. of State 890g.002/36, Doc. File #50, "Confidential Biographical Report," Baghdad, Sloan to Secretary of State, April 1, 1931; Birdwood, *Nuri as-Said.* On Yasin al-Hashimi, see Marr, "Yasin al-Hashimi," pp. 44–45.

54. F.O. 371/18946, Clark-Kerr to Eden, Baghdad, December 6, 1935.

55. Marr, "Yasin al-Hashimi," p. 236.

56. Ahali, a group of social reformers influenced by socialist democracy, who advocated social and economic rather than mere political reform. By 1935 the group included a number of former Ikha members. The group was called by the name of its newspaper, *al-Ahali* (The People).

57. Marr, "Yasin al-Hashimi," p. 318.

58. U.S. Dept. of State 890g.00, General Conditions/67, #561, Knabenshue to Secretary of State, Baghdad, December 4, 1935.

59. U.S. Dept. of State 890g.00/248, Doc. File #110, Knabenshue to Secretary of State, Baghdad, June 3, 1933.

60. U.S. Dept. of State 890g.00, General Conditions/55, #491, Knabenshue to Secretary of State, Baghdad, June 11, 1935; 890g.00, General Conditions/58, #511, Slavens to Secretary of State, Baghdad, July 25, 1935; 890g.00/516, #1651, Mattison to Secretary of State, Baghdad, October 17, 1940.

61. U.S. Dept. of State 890g.00, General Conditions/163, #1438, Knabenshue to Secretary of State, Baghdad, November 15, 1939; 890g.00, General Conditions/122, #976, Knabenshue to Secretary of State, Baghdad, March 4, 1938; 890g.00, General Conditions/115, #903, Knabenshue to Secretary of State, Baghdad, November 27, 1937.

62. U.S. Dept. of State 890g.00/167, Baghdad, February 12, 1931.

63. Reeva S. Simon, "The Hashemite 'Conspiracy': Hashemite Unity Attempts, 1921–1958."

64. Khaldun S. Husry, "King Faysal I and Arab Unity, 1930–1933."

65. F.O. 406/74 #99, Bateman to Eden, Baghdad, August 17, 1936, Enclosure: "Report on the Repercussions in Iraq of the Creation of a National Home for the Jews in Palestine." Henceforth cited as "Report."

66. Sluglett, *Britain in Iraq,* p. 160.

67. U.S. Dept. of State 867n 404, Wailing Wall/247, Dispatch #957, Randolph to Secretary of State, Baghdad, September 7, 1929.

68. See, for example, U.S. National Archives RG 84: confidential telegram, Knabenshue to Secretary of State, Baghdad, January 14, 1938 and subsequent correspondence.

69. On the 1936 Palestine Arab strike, see: Y. Porath, *The Palestinian Arab National Movement 1929–1939: From Riots to Rebellion;* Norman A. Rose, "The Arab Rulers and Palestine: The British Reaction;" Gabriel Sheffer, "The Involvement of the Arab States in the Palestine Conflict and British-Arab Relationship Before World War II."

70. Elie Kedourie, "The Bludan Congress on Palestine, September 1937;" Y. Taggar, "The Iraqi Reaction to the Partition Plan for Palestine, 1937," pp. 195–213.

71. J. C. Hurewitz, *The Struggle for Palestine;* Barry Rubin, *The Arab States and the Palestine Conflict.*

72. F.O. 406/74, E1173/381/65, Clark-Kerr to Eden, Baghdad, February 24, 1936

73. F.O. 406–74, #99, "Report."

74. F.O. 406/74, E2653/94/31, Clark-Kerr to Eden, Baghdad, May 4, 1936.

75. *Ibid.*

76. *Ibid.* Clark-Kerr advised the reader of the despatch to disregard the wording of the memorandum which he enclosed. "It [the wording] is not so happy, but I think allowance must be made for habitual oriental hyperbole in such *clichés* as 'bloody calamities' and 'extermination of a nation.'"

77. U.S. Dept. of State 890g.00, General Conditions/78, #628, Knabenshue to Secretary of State, Baghdad, May 20, 1936.

78. F.O. 406/74, #99 "Report."

79. *Ibid.*

80. The Jews of Baghdad consisted of approximately one-third of the total population of the city. Since the institution of the French-Jewish schools of the Alliance Israélite Universelle in the 1880s, Jews had access to Western education and concentrated on language study, especially English and French, but later Turkish when the Young Turks came to power, and Arabic with Iraqi independence. Their language proficiency plus their involvement in commerce made them a natural middle class in the new state. Under the British many filled civil service jobs, but were expelled in Yasin's purge of the civilian bureaucracy carried out in 1935. As a community they were not interested in politics.

Zionist organizations were legal in Iraq in the early 1920s but they suffered from lack of participation by the community at large. From 1929, when the Iraqi government officially forbade Zionist activity, until 1935, there was underground cultural activity. In 1935 the last two Jewish schoolteachers of Palestinian origin were deported and contact with the Jews from Palestine, whether by visit, importation of Jewish books, newspapers or teachers was halted. Sylvia Haim, "Aspects of Jewish Life in Baghdad Under the Monarcy," *Middle Eastern Studies* (1976), 12:188–208; Hayyim J. Cohen, *Ha-Pe'ilut Ha-Ziyyonit b'Iraq* (Jerusalem: Hasifriyah ha-Ziyyonit, 1969); F.O. 406/74 #99 "Report".

81. U.S. Dept. of State 890g.00/379 Doc. File #707, Moose to Secretary of State, Baghdad, 1 October 1936; 890g.00 General Conditions/87 #703, Moose to Secretary of State, 20 September 1936; 890g.4016 Jews/12, Moose to Secretary of State, Baghdad, October 14, 1936.

82. *Ibid.*

83. U.S. Dept. of State 890g.4016/Jews/20, #1112, Barbour to Secretary of State, Baghdad, August 16, 1938.

84. Muhammad Mahdi Kubbah, *Mudhakkirati fi Samim al-Ahdath 1918-1958,* pp. 59–60; F.O. 406/76, E796/10/31, Morgan to Eden, Baghdad, February 4, 1938.

85. U.S. Dept. of State 890g.00, General Conditions/81, #658, Knabenshue to Secretary of State, Baghdad, July 5, 1936.

86. Michael Assaf, *Toldot Hitorerut ha-Aravim b'Eretz Yisrael u-Virikhatam*, 3:293-294, n. 1,647.

87. See the letter reproduced in U.S. National Archives RG 84: #1302, Knabenshue to Secretary of State, Baghdad, May 26, 1939; and #1310, June 8, 1939; also protests in F.O. 406/76, E796/10/31, Morgan to Eden, Baghdad, February 4, 1938.

88. Rubin, *The Arab States and the Palestine Conflict*, p. 75.

89. Batatu, *The Old Social Classes and the Revolutionary Movements of Iraq*, pp. 457–458.

90. F.O. 406/77, E1255/6/31, Sir R. Bullard to Viscount Halifax, Jedda, February 18, 1939.

91. ESCO Foundation for Palestine, *Palestine: A Study of Jewish, Arab, and British Policies*, 2:795.

92. F.O. 406/74, #99, "Report."

93. Ann Mosely Lesch, "The Palestine Arab Movement Under the Mandate," pp. 23–24.

94. Interview with Fawzi al-Qawuqji in U.S. National Archives RG 84: #872, Dipl., Satterthwaite to Secretary of State, Baghdad, September 16,l937.

95. See series of correspondence F.O. 406/78, #283, Halifax to Newton, London, August 14, 1940; #290, Nuri al-Sa'id to Newton, Baghdad, September 9, 1940; #291, Newton to Halifax Baghdad, September 26, 1940.

96. Kubba, *Mudhakkirati*, p. 55. See also U.S. Dept. of State 890g.9111/17, #1740, Knabenshue to Secretary of State, Baghdad, April 28, 1941.

97. F.O. 624/17, 489/2/39, S. to Viscount Halifax, Baghdad, July 29, 1939.

98. After World War II the membership of the club reconstituted itself under Kubba's leadership into the nationalist al-Istiqlal party.

99. Kubbah, *Mudhakkirati*, pp. 54–57; William L. Cleveland, *The Making of an Arab Nationalist: Ottomanism and Arabism in the Life and Thought of Sati' al-Husri*, p. 74.

100. U.S. Dept. of State 890g.00, General Conditions/87, #703, Moose to Secretary of State, September 30, 1936.

101. Kedourie, "The Bludan Congress on Palestine, September 1937," pp. 121–125. Kedourie reproduces the memorandum of the Congress and the annexes.

4. Education

1. 'Ajjan al-Hadid, "Le Développement de l'éducation nationale en Iraq," p. 236.

2. The biographical material on Sati' al-Husri is drawn from William L. Cleveland, *The Making of an Arab Nationalist: Ottomanism and Arabism in the Life and Thought of Sati' al-Husri*.

3. Niyazi Berkes, *The Development of Secularism in Turkey*, pp. 409–410; L. M. Kenny, "Sati' al-Husri's Views on Nationalism," p. 232.

4. Cleveland, *The Making of an Arab Nationalist*, p. 62.

5. Na'im 'Attiyah, "Ma'alim al-Fikr al-Tarbawi fi al-Bilad al-'Arabiyyah fi al-Mi'at al-Sanah al-Akhirah," p. 527.

6. Sati' al-Husri, "Al-Khidmah al-'Askariyyah wa-al-Tarbiyuah al-Ammah."

7. 'Attiyah, "Ma'allim al-Fikr al-Tarbawi," p. 528.

8. Matta Akrawi, *Curriculum Construction in the Public Primary Schools of Iraq*, p. 180. Akrawi examined the French primary school curriculum of 1887 and maintains that al-Husri took his curriculum directly from it.

Akrawi, a colleague of Mohammed Fadhil al-Jamali, finished his thesis in the early 1930s; it was not published until 1943. Almost every study of Iraqi education relies on its detailed analysis of Iraqi history and social conditions.

9. The ideological clash within the Ministry of Education concerned pedagogical methodology more than political doctrine. Sati' al-Husri represented the European academic approach to education, which based the curriculum on reading by the phonetic method and the traditional subjects (arithmetic, geography, language, history), requiring that the student master a prescribed body of knowledge. Al-Jamali and those who followed him to Columbia University Teachers College, such as Matta Akrawi and the educators who were involved in Iraqi education after 1941, wished to introduce the "Progressive" ideas of John Dewey; namely, reading using the whole word method, practical subjects such as home economics and shop, and education geared to minorities, bedouin, girls, a philosophy directed toward the development of individual potential.

10. 'Attiyah, "Ma'alim al-Fikr al-Tarbawi," p. 525. As a concession for Iraqi entrance into the League of Nations, the local languages law was passed in 1931, allowing Kurdish or Turkish to be used in the school where the majority of the students spoke Kurdish or Turkish.

11. Edward H. Reisner, *Nationalism and Education Since 1789: A Social and Political History of Modern Education*, p. 82. Sami Shawkat also picked this up. In his address to Baghdad school teachers, "On Nationalist History," he mentions that Bismarck answered well-wishers that it was not he who united Germany, but the teachers. Sami Shawkat, "Ta'rikhna al-Qawmi," in *Hadhihi Ahdafuna*, p. 42.

12. *Ibid.*, p. 127. For Fichte's influence on al-Husri, see Bassam Tibi, *Arab Nationalism: A Critical Inquiry*.

13. *Ibid.*, p. 169.

14. *Ibid.*, pp. 82–83.

15. Carlton J. H. Hayes, *France: A Nation of Patriots*, pp. 53 and 373. The story of "The Torn Flag" is in a composition and reading book in use at the beginning of World War I.

16. *Ibid.*, p. v. Hayes describes the text of *Tu seras soldat: Histoire d'un soldat français* (Paris: Colin, 1916), a book of readings and patroitic lessons for military instruction widely used between 1880 and 1900. From the preface:

"This book is designed for the youth of the schools. . . . In speaking to young people of all the griefs inflicted upon France in 1870, when she was subjected to foreign invasions, in acquainting them with what the defeat has cost us, I have desired to show them to what frightful misfortunes a people is exposed which does not keep on guard and is not sufficiently armed to defend its frontiers *always menaced*. . . . To sum up my thought, I would wish that in all the schools of France the teachers would repeat often to each of his or her pupils the words which I have inscribed in large letters at the head of this modest little book: You will be a soldier" (p. 365).

See also Hayes's analysis of *Précis d'histoire de France a l'usage du cours supérieur des écoles primaires élémentaires, des écoles primaires supérieurs* (Paris: Gedalge, 1915), a narrative of French history which shows that France is remarkable because of the Republic which repaired French disasters after 1870 and conquered a vast colonial domain (p. 371).

17. Akrawi, *Curriculum Construction*, p. 180.

18. Abdul Amir al-Rubaiy, "Nationalism and Education: A Study of Nationalistic Tendencies in Iraqi Education," p. 88.

19. Akrawi attributed the drop-out rate in Iraqi schools to: the lack of a compulsory education law, the expense, suspicions of Shi'i and tribesmen that the schools were merely preparation for military service, the mullah's dissuading parents from sending children to secular government schools, incomplete schools—children, especially in rural areas, were forced out of school because not all schools had all grades—and a large failure rate in government exams. Akrawi, *Curriculum Construction*, pp. 165–169.

20. Abdul Wahhab Abba al-Qaysi, "The Impact of Modernization on Iraqi Society During the Ottoman Era," p. 72.

21. Akrawi, *Curriculum Construction*, pp. 126–131.

22. The Turks blew up the technical school and the equipment, and mobs looted the primary schools. Gertrude Bell, *Review of the Civil Administration of Mesopotamia* (London: His Majesty's Stationery Office, 1920), p. 12.

23. John J. Diskin, S.J., "The Genesis of the Governmental Educational System in Iraq," p. 233.

24. Akrawi, *Curriculum Construction*, p. 132.

25. Humphrey Bowman, *Middle East Window*, p. 193. Bowman set up education in Iraq for the occupation administration.

26. Akrawi, *Curriculum Construction*, p. 132.

27. Peter Sluglett, *Britain in Iraq 1914–1932*, pp. 273-275.

28. Philip W. Ireland, *Iraq: A Study in Political Development*, pp. 446-447.

29. United States Department of State 890g.01/12, #185, Sloan to Secretary of State, Baghdad, April 16, 1932. United States Department of State documents will henceforth be cited as U.S. Dept. of State.

30. Sati' al-Husri, *Mudhakkirati fi al-'Iraq*, 1:65–71.

31. Sluglett, *Britain in Iraq*, pp. 281–282.

32. Great Britain, Colonial Office, *Report by His Britannic Majesty's Government to the Council of the League of Nations on the Administration of Iraq for the Year 1927*, p. 159. See also E. C. Hodgkin, "Lionel Smith on Education in Iraq," *Middle Eastern Studies* (April 1983), 19(2):259.

33. Cleveland, *The Making of an Arab Nationalist*, pp. 66–67.

34. Talib Mushtaq, *Awraq Ayyami, 1908–1958*, pp. 129–130.

35. U.S. Dept. of State 890g.02/11, #183, Sloan to Secretary of State, Baghdad, April 15, 1932.

36. Al-Husri, *Mudhakkirati*, 1:65–71.

37. Cleveland, *The Making of an Arab Nationalist*, pp. 71–72

38. U.S. Dept. of State 890g.01/12, #185, Sloan to Secretary of State, Baghdad, April 16, 1932. Sloan made the comment about Abd al-Husayn al-Chalabi who held the post frequently.

39. The biographical detail on Jamali is derived from U.S. National Archives RG 84: C.I.C.I. S.56/119, December 14, 1942, Personality Sheet No. IRQ/10.

40. Muhammad Fadhil al-Jamali, *The New Iraq: Its Problems of Bedouin Education*.

41. Muhammad Fadhil al-Jamali, "John Dewey, the Philosopher Educator," pp. 75–89.

42. Muhammad Fadhil al-Jamili, *Ittijahat al-Tarbiyah wa-al-Ta'alim fi Al-maniyyah wa-Inkiltirah wa-Faransah.*

43. U.S. National Archives RG 84: C.I.C.I. S.56/119, December 14, 1942; al-Jamali, *Ittijahat,* pp. 25–26.

44. F.O. 371/17869, Humphreys to Rendel, Baghdad, February 8, 1934. There were discussions throughout February and March concerning the elite school.

45. Al-Jamali, *Ittijahat,* pp. 12–16.

46. U.S. National Archives RG 84: O.S.S. Report #41854, "Who's Who in Iraq," July 24, 1943; RG 226; O.S.S. Report #43221, "Enemy Activities in Iraq," August 6, 1943.

47. Sami Shawkat, "Sinat al-Mawt," in *Hadhihi Ahdafuna* pp. 1–3; for a translation, see S. G. Haim, *Arab Nationalism,* pp. 97–99.

48. U.S. Dept. of State 890g. 00/483, #1307, Knabenshue to Secretary of State, Baghdad, June 7, 1939.

49. Majid Khadduri, *Independent Iraq,* p. 167; Shawkat, "Ahdaf al-Futuwwah al-Ulyah," in *Hadhihi Ahdafuna,* p. 7.

50. 'Attiyah, "Ma'alim al-Fikr al-Tarbawi," pp. 520–522.

51. Sati' al-Husri, *Naqd Taqrir Lajnat Monroe,* Introduction.

52. Government of Iraq, *Report of the Education Inquiry Commission.* At least two long analytical articles were written about the Monroe report and published in Europe. Both criticized Monroe's disdain for "Latin" education. See al-Hadid, "Le Développement de l'éducation nationale en Iraq," and Paul Catrice, "Le Développement du sens national et de l'éducation en Irak."

53. Al-Husri, *Naqd,* Introduction.

54. *Ibid.,* pp. 18–19.

55. *Ibid.,* pp. 125–129.

56. *Ibid.,* p. 4; In 1928 the Director General of Education issued two circulars containing modifications in these areas which amounted to more hours of object lessons and home economics for girls. Akrawi, *Curriculum Contruction,* pp. 196–197.

57. Elie Kedourie, "The Kingdom of Iraq: A Retrospect," in *The Chatham House Version and Other Middle Eastern Studies,* p. 273.

58. Al-Husri, *Naqd,* p. 136.

59. *Ibid.,* pp. 87, 8–9, and 18.

60. U.S. Dept. of State 890g.00/81, #139, Sloan to Secretary of State, Baghdad, February 29, 1932.

61. U.S. Dept. of State 890g.01/11, #183, Sloan to Secretary of State, April 15, 1932.

62. Kedourie, "The Kingdom of Iraq," pp. 283–285.

63. U.S. National Archives RG 84: U.S. Dept. of State Division of Biographic Information, "Jamali, Muhammad Fadhil (Dr.), October 8, 1946.

64. Al-Husri, *Mudhakkirati,* 2:320–322.

65. U.S. National Archives RG 226: O.S.S. Report #807220, July 11, 1944; U.S. Dept. of State 890g.00, General Conditions/62, #528, Slavens to Secretary of State, September 18, 1935.

66. Al-Husri, *Mudhakkirati,* 2:320–369.

67. Shawkat, "Ta'rikhna al-Qawmi," *Hadhihi Ahdafuna,* p. 43. The translation is by S. G. Haim in "Islam and the Theory of Arab Nationalism," p. 282.

68. Kenny, "Sati' al-Husry's Views on Arab Nationalism," pp. 253–254.

69. Shawkat, *Hadhihi Ahdafuna*, p. 14, The translation is by S. G. Haim in "Islam and the Theory of Arab Nationalism," p. 281, Sati al-Husri called Shawkat a fanatic and a heretic for making this statement. Ibn Khaldun did not refer to the Arabs; he referred to bedouin. al-Husri, *Mudhakkirati*, 2:160–161.

70. Al-Husri, *Mudhakkirati*, 1:215. Sati' al-Husri reproduced most of his 1922–23 curriculum in his memoirs.

71. Iraq, Ministry of Education, *Manhaj al-Dirasah al-Ibtida'iyyah*, pp. 65–66. Curriculum guides for the elementary schools will be cited as *Manhaj*.

72. *Manhaj* (1936), p. 46.

73. *Manhaj* (1940), p. 66.

74. Akram Zu'aytir and Darwish al-Miqdadi, *Ta'rikhuna bi Uslub Qisasi*, p. 3; *Manhaj* (1940), p. 66.

75. Adnan Mohammad Abu-Ghazaleh, *Arab Cultural Nationalism in Palestine during the British Mandate*, pp. 70–74.

76. Al-Husri, *Mudhakkirati*, 1:557. On the Nasuli incident see al-Husri, *Mudhakkirati*, 1:557-575; 'Abd al-Razzaq al-Hasani, *Ta'rikh al-Wizarat al-'Iraqiyyah*, 2:84–85.

77. Great Britain, Foreign Office, FO 624/22, 87/5/41, "Notes of the Iraqi Educational Mission to Germany" (n.d.). Foreign Office documents henceforth cited as F.O.

76. F.O. 624/17, 489/2/39, extract from *al-Istiqlal*, August 8, 1939, note by translator; F.O. 624/17, Syrian Visas: 489/2/39, July 29, 1939; Ya'akub al-'Awrat, 'Alam al-Fikr wa al-Adab fi Filastin, pp. 239–240.

77. U.S. National Archives, RG 84: #619, "The Jewish Minority in Iraq," enclosure #1, February 7, 1945, pp. 5–6

78. Al-Husri, *Mudhakkirati*, 1:215; *Manhaj* (1936), p. 44.

79. *Manhaj* (1940), p. 65.

80. David Kushner, *The Rise of Turkish Nationalism, 1876–1908;* Bernard Lewis, "History Writing and National Revival in Turkey," pp. 224–225; H. E. Allen, *The Turkish Transformation*, pp. 95–96; Andreas M. Kazamias, *Education and the Quest for Modernity in Turkey*, pp. 220–225.

81. Anwar G. Chejne, "The Use of History by Modern Arab Writers," pp. 394–395.

82. Shawkat, *Hadhihi Ahdafuna*, p. 11. The translation is by S. G. Haim in "Islam and the Theory of Nationalism," pp. 280–281.

83. *Ibid.*, Zu'aytir and al-Miqdadi, *Ta'rikhuna bi-Uslub Qisasi*, p. 3; Muhammad 'Izzat Darwazah, *Durus al-Ta'rikh*, pp. 1–8, 9–10.

84. *Manhaj* (1940), p. 70.

85. Darwazah, *Durus al-Ta'rikh*, pp. 297–299.

86. *Manhaj* (1936), pp. 44, 49.

87. Talib Mushtaq, *Durus al-Ta'rikh*, p. 121.

88. Elie Kedourie, "The Kingdon of Iraq," pp. 274–275.

89. F.O. 624/24, Germany: Propaganda 448/3/41. July 26, 1941, "Nazi Propaganda in Iraq," p. 3.

90. Mushtaq, *Durus al-Ta'rikh*, pp. 67 and 132.

91. F.O. 371/20014 Minute, J. G. Ward, November 21, 1936; telegram #794, Rendel to Clark-Kerr, London (?), December 1936.

92. F.O. 624/17, Education: 375/9/39, Sir Basil Newton to Viscount Halifax, Baghdad, July 29, 1939.

93. Darwazah, *Durus al-Ta'rikh*, p. 287.

94. Darwish al-Miqdadi, *Ta'rikh al Ummah al-'Arabiyyah*, pp. 380–381.

95. F.O. 624/24, Germany: Propaganda 448/3/41, p. 2.

96. Al-Miqdadi, *Ta'rikh al-Ummah al-'Arabiyyah* (1936), p. 511; (1939), p. 379.

97. Zu'aytir and al-Miqdadi, *Ta'rikhuna bi-Uslub Qisasi*, p. 17.

98. F.O. 624/17, Education 375/19/39, September 12, 1939, enclosure, p. 2.

99. Zu'aytir and al-Miqdadi, *Ta'rikhuna bi-Uslub Qisasi*, pp. 258–260.

100. Al-Miqdadi, *Ta'rikh al-Ummah al-'Arabiyyah* (1939), p. 378.

101. Darwazah, *Durus al-Ta'rikh*, p. 286.

102. Al-Miqdadi, *Ta'rikh al-Ummah al-'Arabiyyah* (1939), p. 379.

103. U.S. Dept. of State 890g.00, General Conditions/67, #561, Knabenshue to Secretary of State, Baghdad, December 4, 1935; 890g.00, General Conditions/89, #717, Knabenshue to Secretary of State, Baghdad, November 6, 1936; U.S. National Archives RG 84: "Copy of Civil Schools Instructions," January 4, 1938.

104. U.S. National Archives RG 84; note by Sami Shawkat published in *al-Zaman*, June 9, 1939.

105. This law caused complications with the foreign schools, especially those established by American organizations which were guaranteed independence by treaty. The entire correspondence has been reproduced in U.S. Dept. of State, *Foreign Relations of the United States*, 1939 (4), 1940 (3). Similar laws were passed in Turkey, in Argentina under Peron, and in Japan before World War II. I. L. Kandel, "Nationalism and Education," *The Yearbook of Education*, p. 42.

106. F.O. 624/21, Secondary School 396/2/40 May 13, 1940, "The Central Secondary School, Baghdad."

107. F.O. 624/4, Germany: Propaganda 448/3/41, July 26, 1941.

108. Al-Husri, *Mudhakkirati*, 1:557–575; 'Abd al-Razzaq al-Hasani, *Ta'rikh al-Wizarat al-'Iraqiyyah* 2:84–85.

109. Great Britain, Colonial Office, *Report by His Britannic Majesty's Government to the Council of the League of Nations on the Administration of 'Iraq for the Year 1927*, p. 159.

110. Mushtaq, *Awraq Ayyami*, pp. 188–194.

111. F.O. 624/24, Germany: Propaganda 448/3/41. July 26, 1941. Sluglett, *Britain in Iraq*, pp. 159–160. Mushtaq mentions in his memoirs that the British thought erroneously that the Iraqis did not understand the significance of Zionism. Mustaq, *Awraq Ayyami*, p. 188.

112. F.O. 624.24, Germany: Propaganda 448/3/41, July 26, 1941.

113. U.S. Dept. of State 890g.00/181, Sloan to Secretary of State, Baghdad, February 29, 1932; F.O. 624/21, Secondary School 396/2/40, May 13, 1940.

114. F.O. 624/21, Secondary School 396/2/4, May 13, 1940.

115. Kedourie, "The Kingdom of Iraq," pp. 275–276.

116. See, for example, the circular from the Ministry of Education to all district officers and principals requesting that all students, teachers, and officials be urged to donate and to send their donations to the Society for the Defense of Palestine. *Filastin*, April 21, 1936; reported in U.S. National Archives RG 84: "Review of the Palestine Press for the Period ending 18 April 1936.

117. U.S. Dept. of State 890g.42/33, Dispatch #1183, December 5, 1938.

118. U.S. Dept. of State 890g.42/17, #284, Hughes to Secretary of State, September 17, 1932; U.S. National Archives RG 165: "Regional File, Current Events for Period December 1–15, 1934," Baghdad, December 16, 1934 al-Husri, *Mudhakkirati*, 2:380–382. According to Sati' al-Husri, the idea was first suggested to him in 1924 by Minister of Education al-Shabibi who wanted to replace the term "scouts" with "futuwwah" in order to evoke the historic Islamic organization.

119. U.S. National Archives RG 165: "Military Regulations for Training Iraqi Boys," Baghdad, January 6, 1936.

120. U.S. National Archives RG 84: Enclosure to Diplomatic Dispatch #596: "Current Events for Period 16 February to 29 February 1936," Baghdad, March 5, 1936.

121. Al-Husri, *Mudhakkirati*, 1:231–234.

122. F.O. 624/13 525/1/38, Boy Scouts, Hubert S. Martin to W. E. Houstoun-Boswall, London, September 14, 1938.

123. U.S. Dept. of State 890g.00, General Conditions.133, #1114, Barbour to Secretary of State, August 1–15, 1938; *Oriente Moderno*, (1938), 18:10–11; U.S. Dept. of State 890g.00, General Conditions/134, #1128, Satterthwaite, Baghdad, September 6, 1938; U.S. Dept. of State 890g.00, General Conditions/135, #1137, Satterthwaite, Baghdad, September 19, 1938.

124. U.S. National Archives RG 338: MS. #P-207 "German Exploitation of Arab Nationalist Movements in World War II, Supplement Grobba, p. 33.

125. U.S. Dept. of State 890g.00/483. #1307, Knabenshue to Secretary of State, Baghdad, June 7, 1939.

126. Al-Husri, *Mudhakkirati*, 2:382–383.

127. *Ibid.;* U.S. Dept. of State 890g.00/483, #1307, Knabenshue to Secretary of State, Baghdad, June 7, 1939; F.O. 624/17, Education 375/6/39, July 4, 1939. On the regulations: Iraq, Ministry of Education, *Nidham al-Futuwwah wa-al-Kashafah* (Baghdad: Matba'ah al-Hukumah, 1939), and the article by E. Rossi, "L'Istituzione scolastica militare al-Futuwwah nell' 'Iraq." U.S. Dept. of State 890g.00, General Conditions/150, #1293, Knabenshue to Secretary of State, Baghdad, May 12, 1939.

128. U.S. Dept. of State 890g.00, General Conditions.156, #1352, Mattison to Secretary of State, Baghdad, August, 8, 1939.

129. U.S. Dept. of State 890g.00, General Conditions/164, #1449, Knabenshue to Secretary of State, Baghdad, November 30, 1939.

130. U.S. Dept. of State 890g.00, General Conditions/170, #1520, Knabenshue to Secretary of State, Baghdad, March 14, 1940.

131. U.S. Dept. of State 890g.00/155, #1344, Knabenshue to Secretary of State, Baghdad, July 26, 1939.

132. *Ibid.;* U.S. Dept. of State 890g.00, General Conditions/157, #1360, Mattison to Secretary of State, Baghdad, August 23, 1939; 890g.00, General Conditions/159, #1386, Knabenshue to Secretary of State, Baghdad, September 20, 1939.

133. F.O. 624/17, Education 375/6/39, July 4, 1939.

134. Cleveland, *The Making of an Arab Nationalist*, pp. 167–169.

135. Al-Husri, *Mudhakkirati*, 2:381–387, 160.

136. Khadduri, *Independent Iraq*, p. 167.

137. U.S. Dept. of State 890g.00/483, #1307, Knabenshue to Secretary of State, Baghdad, June 7, 1939.

138. Shawkat, *Hadhihi Ahdafuna*, pp. 1–3 and 5; see also Elsa Marston, "Fascist Tendencies in Pre-War Arab Politics," pp. 19–22, 33.

139. Khadduri, *Independent Iraq*, p. 167.

5. The Army

1. Peter Sluglett, *Britain in Iraq 1914–1932*, pp. 259–270.

2. Great Britain, Naval Intelligence Division, *Iraq and the Persian Gulf*, p. 295; Mohammad Tarbush, *The Role of the Military in Politics: A Case Study of Iraq to 1941*, pp. 75–77.

3. B. Vernier, *Le Role extra-militaire de l'armée dans le Tiers Monde*, p. 139.

4. Tarbush, *The Role of the Military in Politics*, p. 237.

5. Phebe A. Marr, "Yasin al-Hashimi: The Rise and Fall of a Nationalist."

6. Tarbush, *The Role of the Military in Politics*, p. 83.

7. Great Britain, Colonial Office, *report on Iraqi Administration October 1920–March, 1922*, p. 56; and *Report by His Britannic Majesty's Government to the Council of the League of Nations on the Administration of 'Iraq for the Year 1926*, pp. 100–101; S. H. Longrigg, *Iraq 1900–1950*, pp. 246–247.

8. Great Britain, Colonial Office, *Report on the Administration of Iraq for 1926*, pp. 100–102.

9. Hanna Batatu, *The Old Social Classes and the Revolutionary Movements of Iraq: A Study of Iraq's Old Landed and Commercial Classes and of its Communists, Ba'thists, and Free Officers*, p. 26. Batatu quotes 'Abd al-Razzaq al-Hasani, *Ta'rikh al-Wizarat al-'Iraqiyyah*, 3:228–289.

10. Marr, "Yasin al-Hashimi," pp. 173–175.

11. Sati' al-Husri, "Al-khidmah al-'Askariyyah wa-al-Tarbiyyah al-Ammah." This article, like much of al-Husri's work was reprinted in other sources. See, for example, the anthology, *Ahadith fi al-Tarbiyyah wa-al-'Ijtima'* (Beirut, 1962).

12. Great Britain, Colonial Office, *Report by His Majesty's Government in the United Kingdom of Great Britain and Northern Ireland to the Council of the League of Nations on the Administration of 'Iraq for the Year 1928*, pp. 15–17.

13. Tarbush, *The Role of the Military in Politics*, pp. 73–79. Longrigg, *Iraq 1900–1950*, p. 38; Sluglett, *Britain in Iraq*, p. 144.

14. Great Britain, Colonial Office, *Report by His Britannic Majesty's Government to the Council of the League of Nations on the Administration of 'Iraq for the Year 1927*, p. 19. When a group of Shi'i troops were taken to the Mosque of Kadhimayn to participate in the mourning and witness the processions, was ministerpreted as a provocation. Overt hostility to the soldiers ensued, a soldier and a considerable number of civilians were killed. The king tried to placate the Shi'i by including two Shi'is in the cabinet; but Shi'i antipathy toward the government was so great that candidates could not be found.

15. United States, Department of State 890g.00/170, Sloan to Secretary of State, Baghdad, December 19, 1931. In April 1932, Sloan wrote that it was difficult to get the true facts regarding government military campaigns against the Kurds as the government always exaggerated victories and was silent on defeats (890g.00/191, #188, April 20, 1932). Department of State documents are henceforth cited as U.S. Dept. of State.

16. U.S. Dept. of State 890g.42/17, #284, Hughes to Secretary of State, Baghdad, September 17, 1932.

17. U.S. Dept. of State 890g.00, General Conditions/5, Knabenshue to Secretary of State, Baghdad, May 3, 1933; 890g.00, General Conditions/6, Knabenshue to Secretary of State, Baghdad, May 24, 1933.

18. R. S. Stafford, *The Tragedy of the Assyrians;* A. Toynbee, *Survey of International Affairs, 1934,* pp. 115–174.

19. The Assyrians had been used frequently against the Kurds.

20. This view has been expressed by Khaldun Sati' al-Husry's two-part article in *International Journal of Middle East Studies:* "The Assyrian Affair of 1933."

21. *Ibid.,* p. 353.

22. U.S. National Archives RG 165: #251, Knabenshue to Secretary of State, Baghdad, January 25, 1934.

23. U.S. Dept. of State 890g.00/365, #626, Knabenshue to Secretary of State, May 3, 1936.

24. Phebe A. Marr, *The Modern History of Iraq,* p. 62.

25. U.S. Dept. of State 890g.00, General Conditions/60, #519, Slavens to Secretary of State, Baghdad, August 21, 1935; 890g.00, General Conditions/66, #553, November 19, 1935.

26. Longrigg, *Iraq 1900–1950,* p. 88.

27. Marr, *The Modern History of Iraq,* p. 67.

28. Husry, "The Assyrian Affair of 1933," p. 352.

29. Gerald de Gaury, *Three Kings in Baghdad 1921–1958,* p. 94. Soon after, Ghazi promoted Colonel Bakr Sidqi to Brigadier General. U.S. Dept. of State 890g.00, General Conditions/17, Knabenshue to Secretary of State, Baghdad, November 6, 1933.

30. U.S. Dept. of State 890g.00/181, #139, Sloan to Secretary of State, Baghdad, February 29, 1932.

31. De Gaury, *Three Kings in Baghdad,* p. 99.

32. On Ghazi, see: U.S. Dept. of State 890g.001, Ghazi/43, #1275, Knabensue to Secretary of State, Baghdad, April 12, 1939; F.O. 406/74 (E172/172/93), #30, Clark-Kerr to Eden, Baghdad, January 1, 1936; Sir Maurice Peterson, *Both Sides of the Curtain,* pp. 150–152; de Gaury, *Three Kings in Baghdad,* pp. 95–97, 104–105; Mahmud al-Durrah, *al-Harb al-'Iraqiyyah al-Britaniyyah 1941,* pp. 39–40; Khayri al-'Umari, *al-Khilaf bayn al-Bulat al-Mulki wa-Nuri al-Sa'id,* pp. 39–64.

33. Sir Harry Sinderson, *Ten Thousand and One Nights: Memories of Iraq's Sherifian Dynasty,* pp. 160–162.

34. Al-Durrah, *al-Harb al-'Iraqiyyah al-Britaniyyah 1941,* pp. 39–40; Taha al-Hashimi, *Mudhakkirat Taha al-Hashimi,* p. 159.

35. Sinderson, *Ten Thousand and One Nights,* pp. 160–162; F.O. 406/74 (E172/172/93), Clark-Kerr to Eden, Baghdad, January 1, 1936.

36. On the marriage scandal: the elopement of Princess Azzah in May 1936, see F.O. 371/20017, Wakefield Harrey, Consulate Rhodes, May 30, 1936. On the reaction in Baghdad: F.O. 371/20017 (E4057/3089/93), Clark-Kerr to Eden, Baghdad, June 19, 1936. On discussions to replace Ghazi with Amir Zayd: F.O. 371/20017, Minute by D. S. Box, Baghdad, June 23, 1936.

37. On curbing Ghazi's private life: F.O. 406/74 (E4361/3089/93), Bateman to Eden, Baghdad, July 2, 1936; F.O. 371/20017, Clark-Kerr to Eden, Baghdad, June 19, 1936. On Ghazi's role in the Bakr Sidqi coup: F.O. 371/20801 (E4057.3089/93), Secret Memo, J. G. Ward, Baghdad, January 21, 1937.

38. F.O. 371/20017, Minute by D. S. Box, Baghdad, June 23, 1936.

39. Peterson, *Both Sides of the Curtain,* pp. 150–151.

40. Batatu, *The Old Social Classes and the Revolutionary Movements of Iraq,* pp. 342–344.

41. Peterson, *Both Sides of the Curtain,* pp. 150–152. Grobba denied the charge (Robert L. Melka, "The Axis and the Arab Middle East," p. 89, n.4; Tawfiq al-Suwaydi also thought Ghazi irresponsible (*Mudhakkirati,* pp. 309–312).

42. F.O. 406/77, Sir M. Peterson to Viscount Halifax, Baghdad, March 8, 1939. U.S. Dept. of State 790B.90G/3, #1247, Knabenshue to Secretary of State, Baghdad, February 28, 1939; al-Hasani, *Ta'rikh al-Wizarat al-'Iraqiyyah,* 5:57.

43. Sati' al-Husri, *Mudhakkirati fi al-'Iraq,* 1:395–400.

44. Peterson, *Both Sides of the Curtain,* pp. 150–151.

45. De Gaury, *Three Kings in Baghdad,* p. 96.

46. U.S. Dept. of State 890g.00, General Conditions/123, #987, Knabenshue to Secretary of State, Baghdad, March 17, 1938.

47. U.S. Dept. of State 890g.00, General Conditions/56, #493, Knabenshue to Secretary of State, Baghdad, June 26, 1935.

48. Al-Suwaydi, *Mudhakkirati,* p. 309.

49. Khaldun al-Husry's introduction to Taha al-Hashimi's *Mudhakkirati,* pp. 29–30; and al-Suwaydi, *Mudhakkirati,* pp. 313–315.

50. Tawfiq al-Suwaydi, *Mudhakkirati,* pp. 313–315.

51. On the coups from 1936 to 1941 I have generally relied on Tarbush, *The Role of the Military in Politics,* and Khadduri, *Independent Iraq 1932–1958: A Study in Iraqi Politics.*

52. On the coup, see also Khalil Kanna, *al-'Iraq Amsuha wa Ghaduha,* pp. 50–51, al-Hasani, *Ta'rikh al-Wizarat al-'Iraqiyyah,* 4:207–218, from which Majid Khadduri's account in *Independent Iraq* is largely derived. See also Majid Khadduri, "The Coup d'Etat of 1936: A Study in Iraqi Politics."

53. The politicans who supported amnesty were Jamil al-Midfa'i and the king (Ghazi was a supporter of Bakr). Husayn Fawzi and Amin al-'Umari wanted amnesty also, even though they were involved in the conspiracy to kill Bakr. Nuri al-Sa'id and Rashid 'Ali had the support of Rustam Haydar, Taha al-Hashimi, and Yunis al-Sab'awi. They courted the young pan-Arab officers.

54. Al-Hashimi, *Mudhakkirati,* pp. 174 ff.

55. U.S. Dept. of State 890g.00/475, Knabenshue to Secretary of State, Baghdad, March 15, 1939.

56. Although most writers agree that the plot probably existed only in the mind of the accused and that Nuri used it to wreak vengeance upon Hikmat Sulayman, Hirszowicz reports that Hikmat proposed a plan for a pro-Turkish pro-German coup to the German ambassador. Lukasz Hirszowicz, *The Third Reich and the Arab East,* pp. 52–53.

57. Khadduri relates that Grobba thought that Rustam Haydar was killed because of his pro-German sympathies, while Salih Jabr, Shi'i political leader, maintained that his mentor was assassinated because he was a pro-British Shi'i (Khadduri, *Independent Iraq,* pp. 150–151). The convicted man, Husayn Fawzi Tawfiq, who shot Rustam Haydar in his office at point blank range, was a ne'er-do-well who floated from job to job and who did have pro-Nazi proclivities. George Kirk describes him as a "half-wit" *The Middle East in the War,* p. 61).

58. Salah al-Din al-Sabbagh, *Fursan al-'Urubah fi al-'Iraq,* pp. 18–22; Quotation on p. 301. Al-Sabbagh's memoirs, published posthumously, are one of the

best expressions of the pan-Arab point of view. See also Sami Shawkat, *Hadhihi Ad-hafuna*, discussed in chapter 4.

59. Mahmud al-Durrah, *Hayah 'Iraqi*, p. 44.

60. Great Britain, Colonial Office, *Report by His Britannic Majesty's Government-to-the-Council of the League of Nations on the Administration of 'Iraq for the Year 1925*, p. 105. The comment is by C. J. Edmonds: F.O. 624/24 (448/3/41), C. J. Edmonds to British ambassador, Baghdad, July 24, 1941.

61. When the British contended that the Iraqis were training Palestinians, Nuri told Sir Basil Newton that training non-Iraqis was against the law. F.O. 406/78 (E2355/31), #290, "Enclosure," Nuri al-Sa'id to Sir Basil Newton, Baghdad, September 9, 1940.

62. Tarbush, *The Role of the Military in Politics*, p. 78.

63. Mahmud al-Durrah, *al-Harb al-'Iraqiyyah al-Britaniyyah 1941*, pp. 47–52.

64. *Ibid.*

65. *Ibid.*, pp. 48–49.

66. Al-Sabbagh, *Fursan al-'Urubah fi al-'Iraq*, p. 29.

67. Iraq, *al-Dalil al-'Iraqi al Rasmi li-Sanah 1936* (Baghdad, 1936), p. 553.

68. Taha al-Hashimi, *Mudhakkirati*, p. 165; al-Sabbagh, *Fursan al-'Urubah fi al-'Iraq*, p. 17.

69. Isma'il Ahmad Yaghi, *Harakat Rashid 'Ali al-Kaylani*, p. 23; Khadduri, *Independent Iraq*, pp. 107–108.

70. Sabbagh, *Fursan al-'Urubah fi al-'Iraq*, p. 76; Tarbush, *The Role of the Military in Politics*, p. 258.

71. F.O. 371/20796, Minute, General Hay, December 1936.

72. Fritz Grobba, *Männer und Mächte im Orient: 25 Jahre diplomatischer Tatigkeit im Orient*, pp. 158–159; Khadduri, *Independent Iraq*, p. 107.

73. Al-Sabbagh, *Fursan al-'Urubah fi al-'Iraq*, p. 17; al-Hashimi, *Mudhakkirati*, pp. 152, 156.

74. The officers who resented Bakr Sidqi's policies were contacted by Jamil al-Midfa'i (also an ex-Ottoman officer) and by Tawfiq al-Suwaydi. Some had personal motives for their opposition: Nuri al-Sa'ids brother-in-law, Ja'far al-'Askari, while on a mission to speak with the rebel officers, was killed by Bakr's order; Fahmi Sa'id's wife was related to Nuri's wife.

75. U.S. Dept. of State 890g.4016/32, #730, Knabenshue to Secretary of State, Baghdad, December 3, 1936.

76. Khaldun al-Husry, "Introduction," to Taha al-Hashimi, *Mudhakkirati* p. 26. Hirszowicz, *The Third Reich and the Arab East*, p. 34.

77. U.S. Department of State, *Documents on German Foreign Policy*, series D (1938), 5:787–797, henceforth cited as *DGFP*; al-Hashimi, *Mudhakkirati*, p. 314; al-Suwaydi, *Mudhakkirati*, pp. 311–312.

78. Khadduri, *Independent Iraq*, p. 152.

79. U.S. Dept. of State, *Foreign Relations of the United States*, (1940), 3:703–708, henceforth cited as *FRUS*.

80. U.S. National Archives RG 84: Enclosure to dispatch #1572, May 29, 1940. While the text of the dispatch is reprinted in *FRUS*, the translations of these editorials were not included. Editorials appeared in *al-Istiqlal*, May 23, 1940; *al-Zaman*, May 24, 1940; and *al-'Iraq*, May 24, 1940.

81. The diplomatic intricacies have been detailed in the following sources which have digested German, Arabic, and British documents: Hirszowicz, *The Third Reich and the Arab East*; Robert L. Melka, "The Axis and the Arab Middle East, 1930–1945;" Yaghi, *Harakat Rashid 'Ali al-Kaylani*; Geoffrey Warner, *Iraq and Syria*, B. P. Schröder, *Deutschland und der Mittlere Osten im Zweiten Weltkrieg*; Heinz Tillmann, *Deutschlands Araberpolitik im Zweiten Weltkrieg* (East Berlin, 1965).

82. Khadduri, *Independent Iraq*, p. 172.

83. Francis Nicosia, "Arab Nationalist and Nationalist Socialist Germany, 1933–1939." F.O. 371/20797 (E1692/19/93), Minute, J. G. Ward, Baghdad, March 29, 1937; F.O. 371/20797 (E1925/19/93), Minute, J. G. Ward, Baghdad, April 10, 1937.

84. Nicosia, "Arab Nationalism and National Socialist Germany," p. 363.

85. Khaldun al-Husry, "Introduction," to Taha al-Hashimi, *Mudhakkirati*, p. 31.

86. *Ibid.*; Nicosia, "Arab Nationalism and National Socialist Germany," p. 363; F.O. 371/20798 (E6016/19/93) Minute, Williams, Baghdad, October 19, 1937.

87. F.O. 406/75 (E3399/2/93), Eden to Clark-Kerr, Foreign Office, June 24, 1937; telegram #119, July 3, 1937.

88. Al-Sabbagh, *Fursan al-'Urubah fi al-'Iraq*, p. 63; Peterson, *Both Sides of the Curtain*, p. 143; Lord Birdwood, *Nuri al-Said: A Study in Arab Leadership*, p. 165. In July 1940, von Papen suggested using Herr Steffan as the link with the officers because he had connections with al-Sabbagh.

89. Joseph B. Schechtman, *The Mufti and the Fuehrer: The Rise and Fall of Haj Amin el-Husseini* p. 95. Al-Durrah tells us that the Colonels invited the Mufti (*al-Harb al-'Iraqiyyah al-Britaniyyah 1941*, p. 136), and 'Ali Jawdat says that Iraq had no prior knowledge (*Dhikriyat 'Ali Jawdat, 1900–1958*, pp. 241–241).

90. U.S. National Archives RG 84: Memo, Knabenshue to Secretary of State, October 24, 1939; *FRUS* (1939), 4:808–809.

91. U.S. National Archives RG 84: #1161, November 14, 1939.

92. Al-Suwaydi, *Mudhakkirati*, p. 380.

93. Sinderson, *Ten Thousand and One Nights*, p. 174; de Gaury, *Three Kings in Baghdad*, p. 117.

94. Freya Stark, *The Arab Island*, p. 159.

95. Eliezer Be'eri, *Army Officers in Arab Politics and Society*, p. 30.

96. Batatu, *The Old Social Classes and the Revolutionary Movements of Iraq*, pp. 456–457; al-Hashimi, *Mudhakkirati*, pp. 254ff.

7. Al-Sabbagh, *Fusan al-'Urubah fi al-*'Iraq, p. 109.

98. *FRUS* (1940), 3:842; U.S. National Archives RG 84: O.S.S. R7A 1090.116, "The Near East and the War Crimes Problems," June 23, 1945.

Grobba maintains that the Germans via the Abwehr had been subsidizing the Mufti since October 1938. (U.S. National Archives RG 338: MS #P-207, Supplement, pp. 29–30). See also American Christian Palestine Committee, *The Arab War Effort*, p. 36; Kirk, *The Middle East in the War*, p. 63.

99. Sinderson reports that before the Mufti arrived in Baghdad, he tried to have a Syrian physician, who visited the king without Sinderson's permission, practice in Baghdad (*Ten Thousand and One Nights*, p. 174).

100. American Christian Palestine Committee, *The Arab War Effort*, p. 36.

101. See, for example, the "White Society" of Mosul, which was directed by Taha al-Hashimi, but was under the Mufti's control in F.O. 624/23 (214/2/41), V. Holt to

Cook, Baghdad, January 20, 1941. See also the "Society of the Arab Union Guards" in Basra, in F.O. 624/23 Ex-Mufti: (214/1/41), Holt to Weld Forester, Baghdad, January 20, 1941. The British saw these groups as centers for Fifth Column activity.

     102. Yunis al-Bahri had been in Berlin off and on since 1924. Yaghi, *Harakat Rashid 'Ali al-Kaylani,* p. 196.

     103. Khadduri, *Independent Iraq,* pp. 162–163.

     104. Al-Sabbagh, *Fursan al-'Urubah fi al-'Iraq,* p. 111.

     105. Grobba, *Männer und Mächte im Orient,* p. 195. Grobba reports that the "Committee" was formed in April 1940; it is unclear when Rashid 'Ali became a member.

     106. Al-Sabbagh, *Fursan al-'Urubah fi al-'Iraq,* pp. 136–138.

     107. *FRUS* (1940), 3:710.

     108. On the diplomacy, see Uthman Kemal Haddad, *Harakat Rashid 'Ali al-Kaylani 1941,* in addition to the sources cited in n.81 above.

     109. Majid Khadduri, "General Nuri's Flirtation with the Axis Powers;" see also the "Appendix" in his *Arab Contemporaries: The Role of Personalities in Politics.*

     110. Jon Kimche, *The Second Arab Awakening: The Middle East 1914–1970,* pp. 148–150.

     111. *DGFP,* Series D (1940), 10:515–516.

     112. U.S. National Archives RG 84: telegram #112, Knabenshue to Secretary of State, Baghdad, December 2, 1940.

     113. U.S. Dept. of State 890g.00, General Conditions/182, #1631, Knabenshue to Secretary of State, September 20, 1940; 890g.00/515, #1648, Mattison to Secretary of State, Baghdad, October 16, 1940.

     114. U.S. Dept. of State 890g.00, General Conditions/189, #1697, Knabenshue to Secretary of State, Baghdad, January 24, 1941. General Amin Zaki Sulayman's speech, which was printed in *al-Bilad* on January 13, 1941, is herein translated.

     115. U.S. Dept. of State 890g.00, General Conditions/175, #175, Knabenshue to Secretary of State, Baghdad, May 29, 1940.

     116. Al-Suwaydi, *Mudhakkirati,* pp. 343 ff.

6. The Rashid 'Ali Coup

     1. On Rashid 'Ali see George Kirk, *The Middle East in the War,* pp. 62–63; Hanna Batatu, *The Old Social Classes and the Revolutionary Movements of Iraq,* pp. 205–209.

     2. Batatu, *The Old Social Classes and the Revolutionary Movements of Iraq,* p. 456.

     3. *The Times* (London), June 28, 1941, p. 5.

     4. Sir Maurice Peterson, *Both Sides of the Curtain,* p. 151.

     5. Batatu, *The Old Social Classes and the Revolutionary Movements of Iraq,* p. 206.

     6. Majid Khadduri, *Independent Iraq 1932–1958: A Study in Iraqi Politics,* p. 197.

     7. Geoffrey Warner, *Iraq and Syria 1941,* p. 66.

     8. Salah al-Din al-Sabbagh, *Fursan al-'Urubah fi al-'Iraq,* pp. 218–220. There is some confusion concerning the nature of some of the meetings al-Hajj Amin chaired. When Rashid 'Ali and the Mufti were in Germany, there was discussion of the existence

of a pan-Arab committee, which included representatives from Syria and Palestine. Hirszowics maintains that the meetings cited here were concerned with local Iraqi politics. Lucasz Hirszowicz, *The Third Reich and the Arab East*, p. 135.

9. S. H. Longrigg, *Iraq 1900–1950*, p. 288.

10. Winston S. Churchill, *The Second World War*, 3:254.

11. The diplomatic story has been drawn to a large degree from the following studies: Hirszowicz, *The Third Reich and the Arab East*; Khadduri, *Independent Iraq*; Kirk, *The Middle East in the War*; Warner, *Iraq and Syria, 1941*; Robert Melka, "The Axis and the Arab Middle East."

12. Hirszowicz, *The Third Reich and the Arab East*, p. 141.

13. Elie Kedourie, "The Sack of Basra and the *Farhud* in Baghdad," *Arab Political Memoirs and Other Studies*, p. 292.

14. Tawfiq al-Suwaydi, *Mudhakkirati*, pp. 355–358; Hirszowicz reports this from the German documents (p. 141).

15. Warner, *Iraq and Syria, 1941*, p. 23.

16. On the British plan to assassinate the Mufti, see Philip Mattar, "Al-Hajj Amin al-Husayni: A Political Biography;" Joseph Nevo, "Al-Hajj Amin and the British in World War II," *Middle Eastern Studies* (1984), 20:3–16.

On *Irgun* involvement, see Yitshaq Ben-Ami, *Years of Wrath, Days of Glory: Memoirs from the Irgun* p. 245:

"At this point, incredibly, the British who had for years supported the Arab cause to the detriment of the Jews, approached the Hebrew Underground to help them battle against the Iraqis. David Raziel was asked by British headquarters in Cairo whether the *Irgun* could help to destroy the stocks of aviation fuel in Baghdad. Raziel promptly answered yes, provided the *Irgun* might also have a chance to "acquire" the Jerusalem Mufti, who had taken refuge in Baghdad. The British answered that they themselves could not participate in such a venture; but they implied that they would not interfere if the *Irgun* tried to capture him."

See also David Levine, "David Raziel: The Man and His Times," and J. Bowyer Bell, *Terror Out of Zion*, pp. 54–55.

17. See Woermann's memorandum to the Foreign Ministry dated March 7, 1941, in U.S. Department of State, *Documents on German Foreign Policy*, (1941), 12:234–243. This collection of documents is henceforth cited as *DGFP*.

18. The letter is reprinted in Khadduri, *Independent Iraq*, pp. 378–380.

19. Woermann's memorandum to the Foreign Minister dated March 7, 1941, in *DGFP* (1941), 12:234–243.

20. Warner, *Iraq and Syria, 1941*, p. 83.

21. Melka, "The Axis and the Arab Middle East," pp. 215–220.

22. Warner, *Iraq and Syria, 1941*, p. 98.

23. Hirszowicz, *The Third Reich and the Arab East*, p. 145.

24. *Ibid.*, p. 146.

25. Al-Suwaydi, *Mudhakkirati*, pp. 366–368. According to Khadduri, the landing of British troops at Basra in April 1941 "forced the Four Colonels, against the advice of Rashid 'Ali, into premature action (*Independent Iraq*, p. 234).

26. Quoted from *al-Bilad*, May 3, 1941, in Khadduri, *Independent Iraq*, p. 223.

27. Abraham Twena, *The Pogrom in Baghdad*, p. 26.

28. Khadduri, *Independent Iraq*, p. 224.

29. Melka, "The Axis and the Arab Middle East," p. 280.

30. U.S. National Archives RG 338: MS. #P-207, Walter Warlimont, "German Exploitation of Arab Nationalist Movements in World War II," part 2, p. 59.

31. Sir Harry C. Sinderson, *Ten Thousand and One Nights,* p. 191.

32. Twena, *The Pogrom in Baghdad,* p. 26.

33. Sylvia G. Haim, "Aspects of Jewish Life in Baghdad under the Monarchy," pp. 192–193.

34. Twena, *The Pogrom in Baghdad,* pp. 23–25.

35. Haim, "Aspects of Jewish Life in Baghdad," p. 192.

36. Freya Stark, *Dust in the Lion's Paw,* p. 112.

37. Haim, "Aspects of Jewish Life in Baghdad," p. 193.

38. Twena, *The Pogrom in Baghdad,* p. 33.

39. Mahmud al-Durrah, *Hayah 'Iraqi,* pp. 140–141.

40. Freya Stark, *The Arab Island,* p. 168.

41. Longrigg, *Iraq 1900–1950,* p. 295; see also Great Britain Foreign Office 624/24 (448/3/41), July 24, 1941. Foreign Office documents are henceforth cited as F.O.

42. Phebe A. Marr, *The Modern History of Iraq,* p. 85.

43. The Arab Legion fought well, but the Transjordan Frontier Force revolted at the H3 pumping station of the oil pipeline. Hirszowicz, *The Third Reich and the Arab East,* p. 168. Note the article by Glubb Pasha in the "Appendix" of Somerset de Chair, *The Golden Carpet,* pp. 239–244.

44. Hirszowicz, *The Third Reich and the Arab East,* p. 167.

45. Grobba maintained that British planes flying overhead shot down the plane. Another interpretation held that overjoyed Iraqis, shooting in the air, hit the plane.

46. On the German agreement with Vichy concerning the integrity of French possessions, see Robert O. Paxton, *Vichy France;* Isaac Lipschits, *La Politique de la France au Levant 1939–1941.*

47. Uthman Haddad, *Harakat Rashid 'Ali al-Kaylani 1941,* pp. 120–122.

48. On their sojourn in Turkey, see Paul Leverkeuhn, *German Military Intelligence.*

49. Al-Sabbagh, *Fursan al-'Urubah fi al-'Iraq,* pp. 255–257.

50. Mahmud al-Durrah, *Hayah 'Iraqi,* pp. 144–148.

51. Hirszowicz, *The Third Reich and the Arab East,* p. 169; Eliezer Be'eri, *Army Officers in Arab Politics and Society,* pp. 38–39.

52. See Glubb's report on the Arab Legion's performance in the 1941 war, F.O. 624/26 (589/1/41).

53. De Chair, *The Golden Carpet,* pp. 241–242.

54. John Bagot Glubb, *Great Britain and the Arabs,* pp. 240–241.

55. De Chair, *The Golden Carpet,* pp. 133–134.

56. U.S. National Archives RG 226: MID Military Attaché Report, August 3, 1943; see also de Chair, *The Golden Carpet,* pp. 133–134.

57. U.S. National Archives RG 338: MS. #P-207, "German Exploitation of Arab Nationalist Movements in World War II."

58. Ernst von Weizsäcker, *Memoirs of Ernst von Weizsäcker,* p. 247.

59. Reports by generals Felmy and Worlimont in MS. #P-207, "German Exploitation of Arab Nationalist Movements in World War II."

60. U.S. National Archives RG 226: MID Military Attaché Report, August 3, 1943.

61. "Document—German Ideas on Iraq—Grobba."

62. Tawfiq al-Suwaydi, *Mudhakkirati*, pp. 378–380.

63. On the "farhud," see U.S. National Archives RG 84: dispatches from Edward Kennedy, Associated Press; Government of Iraq, "Report of the Committee Investigation of the Events of June 1–2, 1941," in Abd al-Razzaq al-Hasani, *Ta'rikh al-Wizarat al-'Iraqiyyah*, 5:272–282; Hayyim J. Cohen, "The Anti-Jewish Farhud in Baghdad 1941."

64. Elie Kedourie, "The Sack of Basra and the *Farhud* in Baghdad," *Arabic Political Memoirs*, pp. 303–304. According to Kedourie, only after London received inquiries from the Jewish agency concerning the events in Baghdad did Cornwallis respond to London's request for information. He replied on July 12. Knabenshue sent a telegram to Washington on June 4, 1941. U.S. Dept. of State 890g.1115/36, telegram, Kanbenshue to Secretary of State, Baghdad, June 4, 1941.

65. The report is reproduced in al-Hasani, *Ta'rikh al-Wizarat al-'Iraqiyyah*, 5:272–282.

66. Al-Durrah, *al-Harb al-'Iraqiyyah al-Britaniyyah 1941*, pp. 409–410.

67. Stark, *Dust in the Lion's Paw*, p. 115.

68. Twena, *The Pogrom in Baghdad*, pp. 27–28. Twena also reports the testimony of a man who said that a friend at the British Embassy gave him a gun on the morning of June 1, warning him that he would need it. The man told him that he had given guns to other friends (p. 38).

Longrigg and Stark thought that the riots were part of a counter-revolution. Longrigg, *Iraq 1900–1950*, pp. 296–297; Stark, *The Arab Island*, p. 177.

69. Al-Durrah, *al-Harb al-'Iraqiyyah al-Britaniyyah 1941*, p. 411; Kedourie, "The Sack of Basra and the *Farhud* in Baghdad;" Stark attributes the riot to the longstanding influence of Palestine (*The Arab Island*, p. 177).

70. Twena, *The Pogrom in Baghdad*, p. 26.

71. This reasoning comes from Kedourie.

72. Khadduri, *Independent Iraq*, p. 227; Kedourie, "The Sack of Basra and the *Farhud* in Baghdad," p. 295.

73. De Chair, *The Golden Carpet*, p. 128.

74. *The New York Times*, February 3, 1942.

75. Iraq, Ministry of Education, *Manhaj al-Dirasah al-Ibtida'iyyah*, pp. 68–74.

76. Batatu, *The Old Social Classes and the Revolutionary Movements of Iraq*, p. 645.

77. U.S. Dept. of State 890g.00/6-2145, CS/MA #783, Moreland to Secretary of State, Baghdad, June 21, 1945.

78. Marr, *The Modern History of Iraq*, p. 89.

79. U.S. National Archives RG 84: October 7, 1941. Letter from Bayard Dodge to Paul Knabenshue decrying the fact that the British do not want graduates of the American University in Beirut to teach in Iraq. Those who caused the trouble, said Dodge, were students the Iraqis chose because of their politics.

80. U.S. National Archives RG 226: Military Attache Report, Baghdad, August 6, 1943.

81. Jamali claims that the British put him into Foreign Affairs to remove him from education. F.O. 624/26 (800/1/41), Stewart Perowne to W. J. Farrell, Baghdad, November 17, 1941.

82. Marr, *The Modern History of Iraq*, pp. 89–90.

83. Be'eri, *Army Officers in Arab Politics and Society*, p. 40.

7. Conclusion

1. Majid Khadduri, *Republican Iraq: A Study in Iraqi Politics Since the Revolution of 1958*, p. 51; Khalil Kannah, *al-'Iraq Amsuhu wa Ghaduhu*, pp. 69–70; Eliezer Be'eri, *Army Officers in Arab Politics and Society*, p. 172.

2. Amazia Baram, "Saddam Hussein: A Political Profile," pp. 115–116.

3. Majid Khadduri, *Socialist Iraq: A Study in Iraqi Politics Since 1968*, pp. 72–73.

4. Khaldun al-Husry, "Introduction," to Taha al-Hashimi, *Mudhakkirat*, p. 39.

Bibliography

Primary Sources

I. *Archives*

Great Britain: Foreign Office series 371, 406, 624

Combined Intelligence Command Iraq (CICI) reports transmitted to U.S. Intelligence

United States: U.S. Department of State series 890g, 1920–1945

O.S.S. Research and Analysis Reports, 1940–1945

Records of the O.S.S. (RG226)

Records of the War Department General and Special Staffs (RG 165)

Records of the Office of War Information (RG 208)

Records of the Foreign Service Posts of the Department of State (RG 84)

II. *Published Official Documents*

"Document—German Ideas on Iraq—Grobba, 1937–1938." *Middle East Journal* (1958), 12:196–203.

Gooch, G. P. and H. Temperley, eds. *British Documents on the Origins of the War 1889–1914*. 13 vols. London: HMSO, 1926–1938.

Great Britain. Colonial Office. *Report on Iraqi Administration, October, 1920–March, 1922*. London: HMSO, 1922.

—— *Report on the Administration of Iraq 1922–1923*. London: HMSO, 1924.

—— *Report by His Britannic Majesty's Government on the Administration of 'Iraq for the Period April, 1923–December, 1924*. London: HMSO, 1925.

—— *Report by His Britannic Majesty's Government to the Council of the League of Nations on the Administration of 'Iraq for the year 1925*. London: HMSO, 1926.

—— *Report by His Britannic Majesty's Government to the Council of the League of Nations on the Administration of 'Iraq for the Year 1926*. London: HMSO, 1927.

—— *Report by His Britannic Majesty's Government to the Council of the League of Nations on the Administration of 'Iraq for the Year 1927*. London: HMSO, 1928.

—— *Report by His Majesty's Government in the United Kingdom of Great*

Britain and Northern Ireland to the Council of the League of Nations on the Administration of 'Iraq for the Year 1928. London: HMSO, 1929.

—— Report by His Majesty's Government in the United Kingdom of Great Britain and Northern Ireland to the Council of the League of Nations on the Administration of 'Iraq for the Year 1929. London: HMSO, 1930.

—— Report by His Majesty's Government in the United Kingdom of Great Britain and Northern Ireland to the Council of the League of Nations on the Administration of 'Iraq for the Year 1930. London: HMSO, 1931

—— Report by His Majesty's Government in the United Kingdom of Great Britain and Northern Ireland to the Council of the League of Nations on the Administration of 'Iraq for the Period January to October, 1932. London: HMSO, 1933

—— Special Report by His Majesty's Government to the Council of the League of Nations on the Progress of Iraq during the Period 1920–1931. London: HMSO, 1931.

Great Britain. Naval Intelligence Division. Iraq and the Persian Gulf. Geographical Handbook Series, 1944.

Hurewitz, J. C., ed. The Middle East and North Africa in World Politics: A Documentary Record. Vol. 2: British-French Supremacy, 1914–1945. 2d ed. New Haven: Yale University Press, 1979.

Iraq. Government of Iraq. Report of the Education Inquiry Commission. Survey directed and report edited by Paul Monroe. Baghdad: Government Press, 1932.

Iraq. Ministry of Education. Manhaj al-Dirasah al-Ibtida'iyyah. Baghdad: Government Press, 1936.

—— Manhaj al-Dirasah al-Ibtida'iyyah. Baghdad: Government Press, 1940.

—— Manhaj al-Dirasah al-Ibtida'iyyah. Baghdad: Government Press, 1943.

Italy. Ministero Degli Affari. I Documenti Diplomatici Italiani, 1861– Rome, 1952–   .

Statement of Policy of H. E. Hikmat Suleiman's Cabinet. Baghdad, 1936.

U.S. Department of State. Documents on German Foreign Policy. Series D: 1937–1945. Washington, D.C.: GPO, 1949–1966.

—— Foreign Relations of the United States, 1961–   . Washington, D.C.: GPO, 1962–

Secondary Sources

Abu-Ghazalah, Adnan Mohammad. Arab Cultural Nationalism in Paletstine During the British Mandate. Beirut: Institute for Palestinian Studies, 1973.

Abuu Nasr, 'Umar. al-'Iraq al–Jadid. Beirut, 1937.

Ahmad, Feroz. The Young Turks: The Committee of Union and Progress in Turkish Politics 1908–1914. Oxford: Clarendon, 1969.

Akrawi, Matta. "The Arab World: Nationalism and Education." *The Yearbook of Education* (1949), pp. 422–439.

—— *Curriculum Construction in the Public Primary Schools of Iraq.* New York: Columbia Teachers College, 1943.

—— "Educational Growth in Iraq in Fifty Years." *al-Amilun fi al-Naft* (1967), no. 62, pp. 2–8.

—— "The New Educational System in Iraq." *The Open Court* (1935), 49: 162–176.

'Ali Jawdat. *Dhikriyat 'Ali Jawdat, 1900–1958.* Beirut: Matbat'a al-Wafa', 1967.

Allen, Henry E. *The Turkish Transformation: A Study in Social and Religious Development.* Chicago: University of Chicago Press, 1935.

American Christian Palestine Committee. *The Arab War Effort: A Documented Account.* New York, 1947.

Ani, Khaled A. M. al-. *Encyclopedia of Modern Iraq: English-Arabic.* 3 vols. Baghdad: Arab Encyclopedia House, 1977.

Antonius, George. *The Arab Awakening: The Story of the Arab National Movement.* New York: 1965.

Arsenian, Seth. "Wartime Propaganda in the Middle East." *Middle East Journal* (1948), 2: 417–429.

'Askeri, Ja'far al-. "Five Years Progress in Iraq." *Journal of the Central Asian Society* (1927), 14:62–72.

Assaf, Michael. *Toldot Hitorerut ha-Aravim b'Eretz Yisrael u-Vrikhatam.* Tel Aviv: Tarbut ve-Khinukh, 1967.

Attiyah, Ghassan R. *Iraq 1908–1921: A Political Study.* Beirut: Arab Institute for Research and Publishing, 1973.

'Atiyyah, Na'im. "Ma-'alim al-Fikr al Tarbawi fi al-Bilad al-'Arabiyyah fi al-Mi'at al-Sanah al-Akhirah." Fu'ad Sarruf and Nabih Amin Faris, eds., *al-Fikr al-'Arabi fi Mi'at Sanah.* Beirut: American University in Beirut, 1967.

'Awdat, Ya'akub, al. *Al-Fikr wa al-Adab f: Filastin.* Amman: al-Matabi'al-Ta'awuniyya, 1976.

Baram, Amazia. "Saddam Hussein: A Political Profile." *Jerusalem Quarterly* (1980), no. 17, pp. 115–144.

Barbour, Nevill, "Broadcasting to the Arab World." *Middle East Journal* (1951), 5:57–69.

Basgoz, Ilhan and Howard E. Wilson. *Educational Problems in Turkey 1920–1940.* Bloomington: Indiana Univerisity Press, 1968.

Batatu, Hanna. *The Old Social Classes and the Revolutionary Movements of Iraq: A Study of Iraq's Old Landed and Commercial Classes and of its Communists, Ba'thists, and Free Officers.* Princeton: Princeton University Press, 1978.

Be'eri, Eliezer. *Army Officers in Arab Politics and Society.* New York: Praeger, 1970.

Bell, J. Bowyer. *Terror Out of Zion.* New York: St. Martin's Press, 1977.

Ben Yaakov, Avraham. *Yehudei Bavel Misof T'kufah ha-Gaonim ad Yamaynu.* 2d ed. Jerusalem, 1979.

Berkes, Niyazi. *The Development of Secularism in Turkey.* Montreal: McGill University Press, 1964.

—— *Turkish Nationalism and Western Civilization: Selected Essays of Ziya Gökalp.* New York, 1959.

Bilinski, A. de. "The Turkish Army." *Contemporary Review* (1907), 92:403–409.

Birdwood, Lord. *Nuri as-Said: A Study in Arab Leadership.* London: Cassell, 1959.

Bourdieu, Pierre. "Systems of Education and Systems of Thought." *International Social Science Journal* (1967), 19:338–358.

Bowdon, Tom. "The Politics of the Arab Rebellion in Palestine 1936–1939." *Middle Eastern Studies* (1975), 11:147–174.

Bowman, Humphrey. *Middle East Window.* London: Longman's Green, 1942.

Busch, Briton Coper. *Britain, India, and the Arabs 1914–1921.* Berkeley: University of California Press, 1971.

Carsten, F. L. *The Rise of Fascism.* Berkeley: University of California Press, 1971.

Catrice, Paul. "Le Développement du sens national et de l'éducation en Irak." *Bulletin des Missions* (Bruges) (1934), 13:149–156.

Chair, Somerset de. *The Golden Carpet.* New York: Harcourt Brace, 1945.

Champol, Claude. "L'Essor de l'Irak." *En Terre d'Islam* (1941), Année 6, pp. 157–72.

Chejne, Anwar G. *The Arabic Language: Its Role in History.* Minneapolis: University of Minnesota Press, 1968.

—— "The Use of History by Modern Arab Writers." *Middle East Journal* (1960), 14:382–396.

Churchill, Winston S. *The Second World War. Vol. 3: The Grand Alliance.* Boston: Houghton Mifflin, 1950.

Clausewitz, Carl von. *On War.* Michael Howard and Peter Paret eds. and trs. Princeton: Princeton University Press, 1976.

Cleveland, William L. *The Making of an Arab Nationalist: Ottomanism and Arabism in the Life and Thought of Sati' al-Husri.* Princeton: Princeton University Press, 1971.

Cohen, Hayyim J. "The Anti-Jewish Farhud in Baghdad 1941." *Middle Eastern Studies* (1966–1967), 3:2–17.

—— *Ha-P'elut ha-Zionit b'Iraq.* Jerusalem, 1969.

Cohen, Michael. "British Strategy and the Palestine Question 1936–1939." *Journal of Contemporary History* (1972), 7:157–184.

Cooper, Elias. "Forgotten Palestinian: The Nazi Mufti Roots of Bitterness in the Arab-Israeli Conflict." *American Zionist* (1978), 68:5–36.

Dann, Uriel. *Iraq Under Qassem: A Political History, 1958–1963.* New York, 1969.

Darwazah, Muhammad 'Izzat. *Durus al-Ta'rikh al-'Arabi min Aqdam al-Azmanah ila al-An.* Damascus: 1939.

—— *Hawl al-Harakah al-'Arabiyyah al-Hadithah.* 5 vols. Beirut, 1959.

Davison, Roderic. *Reform in the Ottoman Empire 1856–1876.* Princeton: Princeton University Press, 1963.

—— "Westernized Education in Ottoman Turkey." *Middle East Journal* (1961), 15:289–301.

Dawn, E. "The Question of Nationalism in Syria and Lebanon." In W. Sands, *Tension in the Middle East.* Washington D.C.: 1956.

—— From Ottomanism to Arabism: *Essays on the Origins of Arab Nationalism.* Urbana: University of Illinois Press, 1973.

Diskin, John J., S.J. "The Genesis of the Governmental Education System in Iraq." Ph.D. dissertation, University of Pittsburgh, 1971.

Djemal Pasha, Ahmed. *Memoirs of a Turkish Statesman 1913–1919.* London: n.p., 1922.

Dubois-Richard, M. P. "L'Etat d'esprit des étudiants Egyptiens et leur role dans la vie politique." *Entrètiens sur l'Evolution des Pays de Civilisation Arabe.* Paris, 1936.

Dujaili, Hassan al-. *Taqqadum al-Ta'alim al-'Ala fi al-'Iraq.* Baghdad, 1963.

Durrah, Mahmud al-. *al-Harb al-'Iraqiyyah al-Britaniyyah 1941.* Beirut: Dar al Tali'ah, 1969.

—— *Hayah 'Iraqi.* Cairo: al-Hay'ah al-Misriyyah al-'Ammahli-l Kuttab, 1976.

Earle, E. M. *Turkey, the Great Powers and the Bagdad Railway: A Study in Imperialism.* New York: Macmillan, 1924.

Edmonds, C. J. *Kurds, Turks, and Arabs.* New York, 1957.

Eliraz, David. "Markiviah shel ha-Leumiyat shel ha-'Aravit shel Sati' al-Husri." *Hamizrah Hehadash* (1972), 22:152–169.

Emin (Yalman), Ahmed. *Turkey in My Time.* Norman: University of Oklahoma Press, 1956.

—— *Turkey in the World War.* New Haven: Yale University Press, 1930.

ESCO Foundation for Palestine. *Palestine: A Study of Jewish, Arab, and British Policies.* New Haven, Yale University Press, 1974.

Farago, Ladislas. *The Game of the Foxes: British and German Intelligence Operations and Personalities Which Changed the Course of the Second World War.* London, 1972.

Far'an, Farik al-Mazhir al-. *al-Haka'ik al-Nas'a fi al-Thawra al–'Iraqiyyah Senat 1920 wa-Nata'ijaha.* Baghdad, 1952.

Faris, Nabih Amin. "The Arabs and Their History." *Middle East Journal* (1954), 8:155–162.

Felmy, Hellmuth and Walter Warlimont. *German Exploitation of Arab Nationalist Movements in World War II.* Historical Division, U.S. Army, Europe, n.d.

Fernea, Elizabeth, W. *Guests of the Sheik: An Ethnography of an Iraqi Village.* Garden City, 1969.

Fichte, Johann Gottlieb. *Addresses to the German Nation.* G. A. Kelley, ed. New York; 1968.

Fischer, Fritz. *Germany's Aims in the First World War.* New York: Norton, 1967.

—— *War of Illusions: German Policies from 1911 to 1914.* Norton; New York: 1975.

Fischer-Werth, Kurt. *Amin al-Husseini—Grossmufti von Palästina.* Berlin, 1943.

Fisher, Sydney N., ed. *The Military in the Middle East: Problems in Society and Government.* Columbus; Ohio State University Press, 1963.

Foster, Henry A. *The Making of Modern Iraq.* Norman; Unversity of Oklahoma Press, 1935.

Frey, Frederick W. *The Turkish Political Elite.* Cambridge, Mass.; MIT Press, 1965.

—— "Education." In R. E. Ward and D. A. Rustow, eds. *Political Modernization in Japan and Turkey.* Princeton: Princeton University Press, 1968.

Gallman, W. J. *Iraq Under General Nuri.* Baltimore; Johns Hopkins University Press, 1964.

Gaury, Gerald de. *Three Kings in Baghdad, 1921–1958.* London: Hutchinson, 1961.

Gibb, Sir Hamilton A. R. "The Islamic Congress at Jerusalem in December 1931." In A. J. Toynbee, *Survey of International Affairs 1934.* London, 1935.

Gibson, Hugh. *The Ciano Diaries 1939–1943.* New York: 1946.

Gillet, Marcel. "L'Irak et L'Unité Islamique." *En Terre d'Islam* (Lyon) (1934), Année 9.

Glubb, John Bagot. *Great Britain and the Arabs.* London: Hodder and Stoughton, 1959.

—— *The Story of the Arab Legion.* London, 1948.

Goerlitz, Walter. *History of the German General Staff 1657–1945.* New York, 1967.

Goltz, Colmar von der. *The Army of Rejuvenated Turkey.* Lt. W. J. Buttgenback, tr. Berlin, 1912.

—— *The Conduct of War: A Short Treatise on its Most Important Branches and Guiding Rules.* Major G. F. Leverson, tr. London, 1899.

—— *The Nation in Arms: A Treatise on Modern Military Systems and the Conduct of War.* Philip A. Ashworth, tr. Rev. ed. London, 1906.

Grandjouan, M. "Le Scoutisme chez les Musulmans." *Entrètiens sur l'Evolution du Pays de Civilisation Arabe* (1936), pp. 106–116.

Grey, Edward, *Twenty-Five Years 1892–1916.* New York; 1925.

Griffiths, Merwin A. "The Reorganization of the Ottoman Army under Abdulhamid II, 1880–1897." Ph.D. dissertation, University of California, Los Angeles, 1966.

Grobba, Fritz. *Männer und Mächte im Orient.* 25 Jahre diplomatischer Tatigkeit im Orient. Göttingen: Musterschmitt, 1967.

Guerreau, Alain and Anita Guerreau-Jalabert. *L'Irak: Dévévloppement et contradictions.* Paris, 1978.

Haddad, Uthman Kemal. *Harakat Rashid 'Ali al-Kaylani 1941.* Sidon, al-Maktabah al-'Asriyyah, n.d.

Haddad, William W. and William Ochsenwald, eds. *Nationalism in a Non-National State: The Dissolution of the Ottoman Empire.* Columbus: Ohio State University Press, 1977.

Hadid, 'Ajjan al-. "Le Dévéloppement de l'éducation nationale en Iraq." *Revue des Etudes Islamiques* (1932), 6:231–267.

Haim, Sylvia. "The Arab Awakening, a Source for Historians?" *Die Welt des Islams* (1953), 2:237–250.

—— *Arab Nationalism.* Berkeley: University of California Press, 1962.

—— "Arabic Antisemitic Literature." *Jewish Social Studies* (1955), 17:307–312.

—— "Aspects of Jewish Life in Baghdad uner the Monarchy." *Middle Eastern Studies* (1976), 12:188–208.

—— "Islam and the Theory of Arab Nationalism." In W. Laqueur, ed. *The Middle East in Transition.* New York; Praeger, 1958.

Halls, W. D. *The Youth of Vichy France.* New York, 1981.

Harris, G. L. *Iraq, Its People, Its Society, and Its Culture.* New Haven: Yale University Press, 1958.

Harrison, Austin. *The Pan-Germanic Doctrine.* London: Harper, 1904.

Hasani, Abd al-Razzaq, al-. *Ta'rikh al-Wizarat al-Iraqiyyah.* 10 vols. Sidon: Matba'ah al-Irfan, 1953–1967.

Hashimi, Taha al-. *Mudhakkirat Taha al-Hashimi 1919–1943.* Beirut: Dar al-Tali'a, 1967.

Hassun, Abdur Rahman al-. "The Social Studies Program in the Iraqi Public Secondary Schools." Ed.D. dissertation, Stanford University, 1956.

Hayes, Carlton J. H. *France: A Nation of Patriots.* New York: Columbia University Press, 1930.

Henderson, W. O. "German Economic Penetration in the Middle East, 1870–1914." In *Studies in German Colonial History,* pp. 74–86. London: Frank Cass, 1962.

Heyd, Uriel. *Foundation of Turkish Nationalism.* London: Luzac, 1958.

Hilali, Abd al-Razzaq al-. *Ta'rikh al-Ta'alim fi al-'Iraq.* 2 vols. Baghdad, 1959, 1975.

Hirszowicz, Lukasz. *The Third Reich and the Arab East.* London: Routledge and Kegan Paul, 1966.

Hourani, Albert. *Arabic Thought in the Liberal Age, 1798–1939.* New York: Oxford University Press, 1962.

Hurewitz, J. C. *Middle East Politics: The Military Dimension.* New York: Praeger, 1969.

—— *The Struggle for Palestine.* New York: Schocken, 1976.

Husri, Abu Khaldun Sati'al-. *The Day of Maysalun.* Sidney Glazer, tr. Washington, D.C.: Middle East Institute, 1966.

—— "The Historical Factor in the Formation of Nationalism." In Kemal H. Karpat, ed., *Political and Social Thought in the Contemporary Middle East*. New York: 1968.

—— "Al-Khidmah al-'Askariyyah wa al-Tarbiyyah al-Ammah." *al-Mu'allim al-Jadid* (1936), 1:273–278.

—— *Mudhakkirati fi al-'Iraq*. 2 vols. Beirut, Dar al-Tali'ah, 1966–1968.

Husry, Khaldun S. "The Assyrian Affair of 1933." *International Journal of Middle East Studies* (1974), 5:161–76; 344–60.

—— "King Faysal I and Arab Unity, 1930–1933." *Journal of Contemporary History* (1975), 10:323–340.

Ireland, Philip W. *Iraq: A Study in Political Development*. New York: Macmillan, 1938.

Iskandar, Amir, *Saddam Husayn*. Paris, 1980.

Izzidien, Yousif. *Modern Iraqi Poetry: Social and Political Influence*, Cairo, 1971.

Jackh, Ernest. *The Rising Crescent: Turkey Yesterday, Today, and Tomorrow*. New York: Farrar and Rinehart, 1944.

Jamali, Muhammad F. al-. *Ittijahat al-Taribiyyah wa-al-Ta'alim fi Almaniyyah wa Inkiltira wa Faransah*. Baghdad: Matba'ah al-Hukumah, 1938.

—— "John Dewey, the Philosopher Educator." *Middle East Forum* (1969), 45:75–89.

—— *The New Iraq: Its Problems of Bedouin Education*. New York: Columbia Teachers College, 1934.

Jankowski, James P. *Egypt's Young Rebels*. Stanford: Stanford University Press, 1975.

Jwaideh, Albertine. "Midhat Pasha and the Land System of Lower Iraq." *Middle Eastern Affairs*, No. 3 (St. Antony's Papers #16). London, 1963.

Kandel, I. L. *The Making of Nazis*. New York, 1935.

—— "Nationalism and Education," *The Yearbook of Education*. London: University of London, Institute of Education, 1949.

Karpat, Kemal H. "The Transformation of the Ottoman State, 1789–1908." *International Journal of Middle East Studies* (1972), 3:243–281.

Kanna, Khalil. *al-Iraq Amsuha wa Ghaduha*. Beirut, 1966.

Kazamias, Andreas M. *Education and the Quest for Modernity in Turkey*. Chicago: University of Chicago Press, 1966.

Kedourie, Elie. *Arabic Political Memoirs and Other Studies*. London: Frank Cass, 1974.

—— "The Bludan Congress on Palestine, September 1937." *Middle Eastern Studies* (1981), 17:102–125.

—— *The Chatham House Version and Other Middle Eastern Studies*. London: Frank Cass, 1970.

—— "Continuity and Change in Modern Iraqi History." *Asian Affairs* (1975), 62:140–146.

—— *England and the Middle East: The Destruction of the Ottoman Empire 1914–1921.* London, 1956.

Kelidar, Abbas, ed. *The Integration of Modern Iraq.* London, 1979.

Kenny, L. M. "Sati' al-Husri's Views on Arab Nationalism," *Middle East Journal* (1963), 17:231–256.

Kerner, Robert J. "The Mission of Liman von Sanders." *Slavonic Review* (1927), 6:12–27, 344–63, 543–60; (1928), 7:90–112.

Khadduri, Majid. *Arab Contemporaries: The Role of Personalities in Politics.* Baltimore: Johns Hopkins University Press, 1973.

—— "The Coup d'Etat of 1936: A Study in Iraqi Politics." *Middle East Journal* (1948), 3:270–292.

—— "General Nuri's Flirtation with the Axis Powers." *Middle East Journal* (1962), 16:328–336.

—— *Independent Iraq 1932–1958: A Study in Iraqi Politics.* London: Oxford University Press, 1960.

—— *Political Trends in the Arab World: The Role of Ideas and Ideals in Politics.* Baltimore: Johns Hopkins University Press, 1970.

—— *Republican Iraq: A Study in Iraqi Politics Since the Revolution of 1958.* London: Oxford University Press, 1969.

—— "The Role of the Military in Middle Eastern Politics." *American Political Science Review* (1953), v. 47:511–524.

—— *Socialist Iraq: A Study in Iraqi Politics Since 1968.* Washington, D.C.: Middle East Institute, 1978.

—— *War and Peace in the Law of Islam.* Baltimore: Johns Hopkins University Press, 1955.

Khaddouri, Rose. "Suggestions for the Improvement of Instruction in the Urban Primary Schools." Ed.D. dissertation, Columbia Teachers College, 1951.

Khadduri, Walid. "Social Background of Modern Iraqi Politics." Ph.D. dissertation, Johns Hopkins University, 1970.

Khalid, Abdul Rahman Mohamed. "Science Education in Iraqi Society." Ph.D. dissertation, Columbia Teachers College, 1954.

Khalidi, Rashid. "Arab Nationalism in Syria—The Formative Years, 1890–1914." William W. Haddad and William Ochsenwald, eds., *Nationalism in a Non-National State: The Dissolution of the Ottoman Empire.* Columbus: Ohio State University Press, 1977.

Khoury, Philip. "Factionalism among Syrian Nationalists During the French Mandate." *International Journal of Middle East Studies* (1981), 13: 441–469.

Kimche, Jon. *The Second Arab Awakening: The Middle East 1914–1970.* New York: Holt, Rinehart, and Winston, 1970.

Kirk, George. *The Middle East in the War.* London: Oxford University Press, 1952.

Kitchen, Martin. *The German Officer Corps 1908–1914.* New York: Oxford University Press, 1968.

Klieman, Aaron S. *Foundations of British Policy in the Arab World: The Cairo Conference of 1921.* Baltimore: Johns Hopkins University Press, 1970.

Kohn, Hans. *Nationalism: Its Meaning and History.* Princeton: Van Nostrand, 1955.

Kopietz, H. H. "The Use of German and British Archives in the Study of the Middle East: The Iraqi Coup d'Etat of 1936." Abbas Kelidar, ed. *The Integration of Modern Iraq.* London: Croom and Helm, 1971.

Kubbah, Muhammad Mahdi. *Mudhakkirati fi Samim al-Ahdath 1918–1958.* Beirut: Dar al-Tali'ah, 1965.

Kushner, David. "Expressions of Turkish National Sentiment During the Time of Abdulhamid II, 1876–1908." Ph.D. dissertation, University of California, Los Angeles, 1968.

—— *The Rise of Turkish Nationalism 1876–1908.* London: Frank Cass, 1977.

Lacey, Robert. *The Kingdom: Arabia and the House of Sa'ud.* New York: Harcourt Brace Jovanovich, 1981.

Lerner, Daniel and Richard D. Robinson. "Swords and Ploughshares: The Turkish Army as a Modernizing Force." *World Politics* (1960), vol. 13.

Lesch, Ann Mosely. *Arab Politics in Palestine: The Foundation of a Nationalist Movement.* Ithaca: Cornell University Press, 1979.

—— "The Palestine Arab Movement Under the Mandate." In W. Quandt et al., *The Politics of Palestinian Nationalism.* Berkeley: University of California Press, 1973.

Leverkuehn, Paul. *German Military Intelligence.* R. H. Stevens and C. Fitzgibbon, trs. New York: Praeger, 1954.

Levine, David. "David Raziel: The Man and His Times." Ph.D. dissertation, Yeshiva University, 1969.

Lewin, Evans. *The German Road to the East: An Account of the "Drang Nach Osten" and of Teutonic Aims in the Near and Middle East.* London: Heinemann, 1916.

Lewis, Bernard. *The Emergence of Modern Turkey.* 2d ed. New York: Oxford University Press, 1968.

—— "History Writing and National Revival in Turkey." *Middle Eastern Affairs* (1953), 4:218–227.

Liman von Sanders, Otto. *Five Years in Turkey.* Annapolis, Md.: 1927.

Lipschits, Isaac. *La Politique de la France au Levant 1939–1941.* Amsterdam, 1962.

Longrigg, S. H. *Iraq 1900–1950.* New York: Oxford University Press, 1954.

Lugol, Jean. *Egypt and World War II.* Cairo: Société d'Orientale de Publicité, 1945.

Luks, Harold Paul. "Iraqi Jews During World War II." *The Wiener Library Bulletin* (1977), 30(N.S. 43/44):30–39.

McClelland, David. "National Character and Economic Growth in Turkey and Iran." Lucian W. Pye, ed., *Communications and Political Development.* Princeton: Princeton University Press, 1963.

MacDonald, A. D. *Euphrates Exile*. London, G. Bell and Sons, 1936.

——"Political Developments in Iraq Leading up to the Spring of 1935." *Journal of Royal Central Asia Society* (1936), 23:27–44.

MacDonald, Callum A. "Radio Bari: Italian Wireless Propaganda in the Middle East and British Countermeasures 1934–1938." *Middle Eastern Studies* (1977), 13:195–207.

McGarity, James M. "Foreign Influence on the Ottoman Turkish Army 1880–1918." Ph.D. dissertation, American University, 1968.

Main, E. *Iraq from Mandate to Independence*. London, 1935.

Majid, Hammoudi A. "Guides for the Improvement of Teacher Education: Iraq." Ph.D. dissertation, Columbia Teachers College, 1953.

Malleterre, Col. "L'Armée Jeune-Turque," *Revue des Sciences Politiques* (1911), 26:734–755.

Mardin, Serif. *The Genesis of Young Ottoman Thought: A Study in the Modernization of Turkish Political Ideas*. Princeton: Princeton University Press, 1962.

—— "Ideology and Religion in the Turkish Revolution." *International Journal for Middle East Studies* (1971), 2:197–211.

Marr, Phebe A. "The Iraqi Revolution: A Case Study of Army Rule." *Orbis* (1970), 14: 714–739.

—— "Iraq's Leadership Dilemma: A Study in Leadership Trends 1948–1968." *Middle East Journal* (1970), 2:283–301

—— *The Modern History of Iraq*. Boulder: Westview Press, 1985.

—— "The Political Elite in Iraq." G. Lenczowski, ed., *Political Elites in the Middle East*. Washington, D.C.: 1975. 109–149.

—— "Yasin al-Hashimi: The Rise and Fall of a Nationalist." Ph.D. dissertation, Harvard University, 1966.

Marston, Elsa. "Facist Tendencies in Pre-War Arab Politics." *Middle East Forum* (1959), 35:19–22.

Mattar, Philip. "Al-Hajj Amin al-Husayni: A Political Biography." Ph.D. disseration, Columbia University, 1981.

Matthews, Roderic and Matta Akrawi. *Edication in Arab Countries of the Near East*. Washington, D.C.: American Council on Education, 1949.

Mejcher, Helmut. *Imperial Quest for Oil: Iraq 1910–1928*. London: Ithaca Press, 1976.

——"Iraq's External Relations 1921–1936." *Middle Eastern Studies* (1977), 13:340–358.

Melka, Robert L. "The Axis and the Arab Middle East 1930–1945." Ph.D. dissertation, University of Minnesota, 1966.

—— "Nazi Germany and the Palestine Question." *Middle Eastern Studies* (1969), 5:221–233.

Melzig, Herbert. *Yakin Sarkta Alman Propagandasi Hakkinda Bir Muhtira*. New York: Europa Verlag, 1940.

Meyer, Henry Cord. *Mitteleuropa in German Thought and Action 1815–1945*. The Hague, 1955.

Miqdadi, Darwish al-. *Ta'rikh al-Ummah al-'Arabiyyah,* Baghdad: Matba-ah al-Hukumah, 1939.

Mitchell, Allan. "French Military Reorganization." *American Historical Review* (1981), 36:49–62.

Monroe, Elizabeth. *Britain's Moment in the Middle East 1914–1956.* Baltimore: Johns Hopkins University Press, 1963.

Moosa, M. I. "General Reforms of Midhat Pasha in Iraq 1869–1872." *Islamic Literature* (1966), 12:17–28.

Mousa, Sulaiman. "The Role of Syrians and Iraqis in the Arab Revolt." *Middle East Forum* (1967), 43:5–18.

Mushtaq, Talib. *Awraq Ayyami, 1908–1958.* Beirut: Dar al-Tali'ah, 1968.

—— *Durus al-Ta'rikh.* Baghdad, 1936.

Nicosia, Francis. "Arab Nationalism and National Socialist Germany 1933–1939." *International Journal of Middle East Studies* (1980), 12:351–372.

Nishi, Toshio. *Unconditional Democracy: Education and Politics in Occupied Japan, 1945–1952.* Standord: Hoover Institution Press, 1982.

Parla, Taha. "The Social and Political Thought of Ziya Gökalp." Ph.D. dissertation, Columbia University, 1980.

Patton, John S. "The Historical Background of the 'Iraqi Revolution and Internal and International Problems, 1918–1945." Ph.D. dissertation, American University, 1963.

Paxton, Robert O. *Vichy France: Old Guard and the New Order 1940–1944.* New York: Norton, 1972.

Pearlman, Maurice. *Mufti of Jerusalem: The Story of Haj Amin el Husseini.* London: Victor Gollancz, 1947.

Pears, Sir Edwin. *A Life of Abdul Hamid.* London: Constable, 1917.

Peterson, Sir Maurice. *Both Sides of the Curtain.* London: Constable, 1950.

Penrose, Edith and E. F. Penrose. *Iraq.* Boulder, Col.: Westview Press, 1978.

Playfair, I. S. O. *The Mediterranean and the Middle East.* London H.M.S.O., 1956.

Polk, William R. "Social Modernization: The New Man." Georgiana G. Stevens, ed., *The United States and the Middle East.* Englewood Cliffs, N.J.: Prentice Hall, 1964.

Pool, David. "From Elite to Class: The Transformation of Iraqi Leadership 1920–1939." *International Journal of Middle East Studies* (1980), 12:331–350.

—— "The Politics of Patronage: Elites and Social Structure in Iraq." Ph.D. dissertation, Princeton University, 1972.

Porath, Y. *The Emergence of the Palestinian-Arab National Movement 1918–1929.* London: Frank Cass, 1974.

—— "Al-Hajj Amin al-Husayni, Mufti of Jerusalem—His Rise to Power and the Consolidation of His Position." *Asian and African Studies* (1971), 7:121–156.

—— "Palestinian and Pan-Arab Nationalism 1918–1939." *The Wiener Library Bulletin* (1978), 31 (N.S. 45/46):29–39.

—— *The Palestinian Arab National Movement 1929–1939: From Riots to Rebellion.* London: Frank Cass, 1977.

Preston, Richard A. and Sydney F. Wise. *Men in Arms: A History of Warfare and Its Interrelationships with Western Society.* 2d rev. ed. New York: Praeger, 1970.

Qaysi, Abdul Wahhab Abbas al-. "The Impact of Modernization on Iraqi Society During the Ottoman Era: A Study of Intellectual Development in Iraq 1869–1917." Ph.D. dissertation, University of Michigan, 1958.

Qaysi, Sami Abd al-Hafidh al-. *Yasin al-Hashimi.* 2 vols. Basra: Matba'a Hadad, 1975.

Qazzaz, Ayad al-. "The Changing Patterns of the Politics of the Iraqi Army." Paper delivered at MESA Conference, 1969.

—— "The Iraqi-British War of 1941: A Review Article." *International Journal of Middle East Studies* (1976), 7:591–596.

—— "Power Elite in Iraq, 1920–1958: A Study of the Cabinet." *Muslim World* (1971), 61:267–282.

Ramsaur, Ernest E. *The Young Turks: Prelude to the Revolution of 1908.* Princeton: Princeton University Press, 1957.

Rawi, Ibrahim al-. *Min al-Thawrah al-'Arabiyyah al-Kubra ila al-'Iraq al-Hadith: Dhikriyat.* Beirut, 1969.

Reisner, Edward H. *Nationalism and Education since 1789: A Social and Political History of Modern Education.* New York: Macmillan, 1929.

Ridha, Mohammad Jawad. "Compulsory Education for Iraq." Ph.D. dissertation, University of Michigan, 1959.

Rohrbach, Paul, *German World Policies.* Edmund von Mach, tr. New York: Macmillan, 1915.

Rose, Norman A. "The Arab Rulers and Palestine: The British Reaction." *Journal of Modern History* (1972), 44:213–31.

Rossi, E. "L'Istituzione scolastica militare 'al-Futuwwah' nell 'Iraq." *Oriente Moderno* (1940), 20:297–302.

Rubaiy, Abdul Amir al-. "Nationalism and Education: A Study of Nationalistic Tendencies in Iraqi Education." Ph.D. dissertation, Kent State University, 1972.

Rubin, Barry. *The Arab States and the Palestine Conflict.* Syracuse: Syracuse University Press, 1981.

Rustow, Dankwart A. "The Army and the Founding of the Turkish Republic." *World Politics* (1959), 12:513–552.

—— "The Military in Turkey." R. E. Ward and D. A. Rustow, eds. *Political Modernization in Japan and Turkey.* Princeton: Princeton University Press, 1968.

Saab, Hassan. *The Arab Federalists of the Ottoman Empire.* Amsterdam: Djambatan, 1958.

Sabbagh, Salah al-Din al-. *Fursan al-'Urubah fi al-'Iraq.* Damascus, n.p., 1956.

Sachar, Howard M. *The Emergence of the Middle East: 1914–1924.* New York: Knopf, 1969.

—— *Europe Leaves the Middle East: 1936–1954.* New York: Knopf, 1972.

Salve de. "L'Enseignement en Turquie: Le lycée imperial de Galata Serai." *Revue des Deux Mondes* (1874), 5:836–853.

Sayigh, Anis. *al-Hashimiyyun wa-Qadiyyat Filastin.* Sidon, 1966.

Schechtman, Joseph B. *The Mufti and the Fuehrer: The Rise and Fall of Haj Amin el-Husseini.* New York: Thomas Yoseloff, 1965.

Schmidt, H. D. "The Nazi Party in Palestine and the Levant 1932–1939." *International Affairs* (1952), 28:460–469.

Schröder, Bernd Philipp. *Deutschland und der Mittlere Osten im Zweiten Weltkrieg.* Frankfurt: Musterschmidt Göttigen, 1975.

Shamir, S. "National Philosophy in Contemporary Arab Thought." *Asian and African Studies* (1965), vol. 1.

Sharabi, Hisham. *Arab Intellectuals and the West: The Formative Years 1875–1914.* Baltimore: Johns Hopkins University Press, 1970.

Shaw, Stanford J. *History of the Ottoman Empire and Modern Turkey.* 2 vols. Cambridge: 1976.

Shawkat, Naji. *Awraq Naji Shawkat.* Baghdad, 1977.

—— *Sira wa-Dhikriyat Thamanin 'Amman 1894–1974.* Beirut: Matba'at Dar al-Kutub.

Shawkat, Sami. *Hadhini Ahdafuna.* Baghdad: 1939.

Sheffer, Gabriel. "The Involvement of the Arab States in the Palestine Conflict and British-Arab Relationship Before World War II." *Asian and African Studies* (1974–1975), 10:59–77.

Shimoni, Ya'kov. *Arvei Eretz Yisrael.* Tel Aviv, 1947.

Simon, Reeva S. "The Hashemite 'Conspiracy': Hashemite Unity Attempts, 1921–1958." *International Journal of Middle East Studies* (1974), 5:314–327.

—— "The Teaching of History in Iraq Before the Rashid 'Ali Coup of 1941." *Middle Eastern Studies,* Winter, (1986).

Sinderson, Sir Harry C. *Ten Thousand and One Nights: Memories of Iraq's Sherifian Dynasty.* London: Hodder and Stoughton, 1973.

Sluglett, Peter. *Britain in Iraq 1914–1932.* Oxford: Ithaca Press, 1976.

—— "Some Reflections on Sunni Shi'a Question in Iraq." *British Society for Middle Eastern Studies Bulletin* (1978), 5:79-87.

Stark, Freya. *The Arab Island.* New York: Knopf, 1945.

—— *Baghdad Sketches.* New York: E. P. Dutton, 1938.

—— *Dust in the Lion's Paw.* London: John Murray, 1961.

Stafford, R. S. *The Tragedy of the Assyrians.* London: Allen and Unwin, 1935.

Sulzberger, D. L. "German Preparations in the Middle East." *Foreign Affairs* (1942), 20:663–678.

Suwaydi, Tawfiq al-. *Mudhakkirati*. Beirut: Dar al-Kitab al-'Arabi, 1969.

Swanson, Glen W. "Enver Pasha: The Formative Years." *Middle Eastern Studies* (1980), 16:193–199.

——— "War, Technology, and Society in the Ottoman Empire from the Reign of Abdulhamid II to 1913: Mahmud Sevket and the German Military Mission." V. J. Parry and M. E. Yapp, eds. *War, Technology, and Society in the Middle East*. London: Oxford University Press, 1975.

Taggar, Y. "The Iraqi Reaction to the Partition Plan for Palestine, 1937." Gabriel Ben-Dor, ed. *The Palestinians and the Middle East: Studies in their History, Sociology, and Politics*. Haifa: Turtle Dove Publishing, 1976.

Tamkoc, Metin. *The Warrior Diplomats: Guardians of the National Security and Modernization of Turkey*. Salt Lake City: University of Utah Press, 1976.

Tantwai, 'Ali al-. *Baghdad Mushahadat wa Dhikriyat*. Damascus, 1960.

Tarbush, Mohammad A. *The Role of the Military in Politics: A Case Study of Iraq to 1941*. London: Kegan Paul, 1982.

Thomson, David. *Democracy in France since 1870*. 5th ed. New York: Oxford University Press, 1969.

Thorpe, James A. "The United States and the 1940–1941 Anglo-Iraqi Crisis: American Policy in Transition." *Middle East Journal* (1971), 25:79–89.

Tibi, Bassam. *Arab Nationalism: A Critical Inquiry*. Marion Farouk-Sluglett and Peter Sluglett, eds. and trs. New York: St. Martin's Press, 1981.

Tillmann, Heinz. *Deutschlands Araberpolitik im Zweiten Weltkrieg*. East Berlin: Veb Deutscher Verlag der Wissenschaften, 1965.

Townsend, Mary. *The Rise and Fall of German Colonial Empire 1884–1918*. 1930; New York: Howard Fertig, 1966.

Townshend, Arthur Fritz Henry. *A Military Consul in Turkey*. London: Seeley and Co., ltd, 1910.

Toynbee, Arnold. *Survey of International Affairs, 1934*. London: Royal Institute of International Affairs, 1935.

Trumpener, Ulrich. *Germany and the Ottoman Empire 1914–1918*. Princeton: Princeton University Press, 1968.

Twena, Abraham H. *Jewry of Iraq: Dispersion and Liberation*. Part 6: *The Program in Baghdad*. Ramla: Geoula Synagogue Committee, 1977.

Vagts, Alfred. *A History of Militarism: Civilian and Military*. Rev. ed. New York: Free Press, 1959.

Vambery, Arminius. "Personal Recollections of Abdul Hamid and His Court. *Ninetenth Century*. (1909), 66:69–88.

——— *The Story of My Struggles*. London: Nelson, [1900?]

Van Dusen, M. "Political Integration and Regionalism in Syria." *Middle East Journal* 1972), 26:123–136.

Vatikiotis, P. J. *The Egyptian Army in Politics: Pattern for New Nations?* Bloomington: Indiana University Press, 1961.

Vernier, Bernard. *Armée et Politique au Moyen-Orient*. Paris: Payot, 1966.

—— L'Irak d'aujourd'hui. Paris: Armand Colin, 1963.

—— La Politique Islamique de l'Allemagne. Paris: Centre d'Etudes de Politique Etrangère, 1939.

—— "Le Role de l'armée Irakienne dans l'état." Le Role extra-militaire de l'armée dans le Tiers Monde. Paris: Preses Universitaires de France, 1966.

Vinogradov, Amal. "The 1920 Revolt in Iraq Reconsidered: The Role of the Tribes in National Politics." International Journal of Middle Eastern Studies (1972), 3:123–139.

Viton, Albert. "Britain and the Axis in the Near East." Foreign Affairs (1941), 19:371–384.

Wallach, Jehuda L., ed. Germany and the Middle East 1835–1939. Tel Aviv: Jahrbuch des Institut für Dentsche Geschichte Beiheft 1, 1975.

Warner, Geoffrey. Iraq and Syria 1941. London: Davis-Poynter, 1974.

Weber, Frank G. Eagles on the Crescent: Germany, Austria and the Diplomacy of the Turkish Alliance 1914–1918. Ithaca, N.Y.: Cornell University Press, 1970.

—— The Evasive Neutral. Colombia: University of Missouri Press, 1979.

Weizsäcker, Ernst von. Memoirs of Ernst von Weizsäcker. John Andrews, tr. London: Victor Gollancez, 1951.

Wertheimer, M. S. The Pan-German League. New York: Columbia University, 1924.

Wiesenthal, Simon. Grossmufti-Grossagent der Achse. Salzburg: Ried Verlag, 1947.

Wild, Stefan. "Mein Kampf in Arabischer Ubersetzung." Welt des Islams (1964), 9:207–211.

Wile, F. W. Men Around the Kaiser. Philadelphia: Lippincott, 1913.

Wilson, A. T. Loyalties: Mesopotamia 1914–1917. London: Oxford University Press, 1930.

—— Mesopotamia 1917–1920: A Clash of Loyalties, London: Oxford University Press, 1931.

Winstone, H. V. Gertrude Bell. London, Jonathan Cape, 1978.

Woolbert, R. G. "Pan-Arabism and the Palestine Problem." Foreign Affairs (1938), 16:309–322.

Yafi, 'Abd al-Fattah al-. al-'Iraq bayn Inqilabayn. Beirut, al-Makshuf, 1938.

Yaghi, Isma'il Ahmad. Harakat Rashid 'Ali al-Kaylani. Beirut, Dar al-Tali'ah, 1974.

Yasin, Mohammad Hussain. "Education for all Iraqi Youth." Ph.D. dissertation, Columbia Teachers College, 1947.

Yisraeli, David. Ha-Reich ha-Germani v'Eretz Yisrael. Ramat-Gan, Universitat Bar-Ilan, 1974.

—— "The Third Reich and Palestine." Middle Eastern Studies (1971), 7:343–354.

Young, H. *Independent Arab*. John Murray, London, 1933.

Zeine, Zeine N. *Arab-Turkish Relations and the Emergence of Arab National-ism*. Beirut, Khayat, 1958.

—— *The Emergence of Arab Nationalism*. Delmar, Caravan Books, N.Y., 1973.

Zeman, Z. A. B. *Nazi Propoganda*. London: Oxford University Press, 1964.

Zu'aytir, Akram and Darwish al-Miqdadi. *Ta'rikhuna bi-Uslub Qisasi*. Baghdad, 1939.

Index

'Abd al-Ilah, 66, 129, 130, 146, 153, 159, 160, 164, 165, 167
'Abdallah of Transjordan, 53, 66
Abdulhamid II, 8, 10, 15, 20, 23, 24
Abwehr, 138, 150
Ahali, 64, 127
'Ahd, al-, 29, 30, 47, 49, 50, 52, 61
Akrawi, Matta, 84, 89
'Alam al-Akhdar, al-, 29
'Ali, 'Ali Muhmud al Shaykh, 164
'Ali, Rashid, see Kaylani, Rashid 'Ali, al-
American University of Beirut, 94, 95
Anglo-French Declaration, 1918, 48, 49
Anglo-Iraq Treaty, 53–58, 62
Arab Higher Committee, 69
Arab nationalism, 26–33, 54; see also Pan-Arabism
Arab Revolt, 47, 48, 61
'Arif, 'Abd al-Salam, 167
Army, Iraqi, 115–43; conscription, 55, 117–22; development of, 64, 115–22; education, 9, 131–33, 184; pan-Arabism, 133–52; in politics, 62, 126, 127–52; societies, 126
Army, Ottoman, 8, 9, 15–19, 23–24, 116
Arndt, Ernst Moritz, 32
'Asil, Naji, al-, 50
'Askari, Ja'far, al-, 46, 49, 50, 78, 108, 117, 128, 129, 131, 134, 179
Assyrian Crisis, 65, 119–22
Assyrians, 3, 59

Baghdad, 1, 2, 3, 48
Bagley, William C., 89
Bahri, Yunis, al-, 36
Basra, 1, 3, 46, 48
Bassam, Sadiq, al-, 78, 94
Ba'th, 51, 167

Bell, Gertrude, 1
Bernhardi, General Friedrich von, 11
Bismarck, Otto von, 10
Blomberg, Axel von, 156
Bludan Conference, 67
Boy Scouts, 111
Braham, Dr. Noel, 42
Bustani, Butrus, al-, 28

Cairo Conference, 1921, 1, 53
Chair, Somerset de, 157
Chalabi, 'Abd al-Husayn, al-, 78
Christians, 3, 54, 65
Churchill, Sir Winston, 1, 54, 147–49
Clark-Kerr, Sir Archibald, 63, 64, 68, 69, 104, 138
Colonial Office, 1
Columbia University, Teachers College, 85, 89
Committee of Union and Progress (CUP), Iraq, 28, 29
Congress of Berlin, 1878, 9, 11
Cornwallis, Sir Kinahan, 1, 119, 148–52, 160
Cox, Sir Percy, 1, 47, 48, 49, 54, 82, 105
Czechoslovakia, 64

Darwazah, Muhammad Izzat, 49, 98, 101, 102–3, 104
Demirhan, Pertev, 25
Dewey, John, 85
Dreysée, Colonel, 10
Dulaymi, 'Abdallah, al-, 46
Durrah, Mahmud, al-, 132, 154, 156, 159

Eden, Anthony, 143
Education, 75–114; France, 26, 79–81; Germany, 18, 19, 39, 79, 86; mili-

Education (*Continued*)
tary, 14–19; Ottoman, 7, 8, 14–19,
21–23, 81; Young Turks, 81–82; in
Iraq; 39–40, 55, 75–113, 194; civics,
95; curriculum, 79, 89–107, 162–63;
heroes, 96–98, 162; history, 92,
95–108; pan-Arabism 98–103,
107–10; para-military training, 95,
110–14, 133, 146, 154, 159; politics, 110–14; teachers, 72, 164;
textbooks, 95–107, 162
Enver Pasha, 25

Farhud, 158–61
Farrell, Jerome, 83
Fatat, al-, 29, 46, 48, 49
Fawzi, Husayn, 127, 128, 129, 130,
136, 179
Faysal, 1, 30, 46, 47, 49, 50, 52,
53–60, 61, 62, 66, 119
Felmy, General Helmuth, 34, 150, 158
Fichte, Johann Gottlieb, 32, 79
Four Colonels (Golden Square),
129–31, 141, 143, 145–47, 157, 159
France, 8, 26, 79
Free Officers, 167
Futuwwah, 95, 110–14, 133, 146, 154,
159

Gaury, Gerald de, 62
German General Staff, 11
Germany, 7, 9, 10, 64; education,
18–19, 79, 86; and Middle East,
7–43, 187; National Socialism, 8,
34; officer corps, 16–17; and Ot-
toman military, 14–19, 24, 25; and
World War I, 8–15, 34, 187
Germany and Iraq, 34, 35, 36–43,
140–65; arms, 41, 71, 137–38, 149,
150; foreign policy, 136–41; Rashid
'Ali coup, 149–65; trade, 64
Ghazi, 38, 39, 41–43, 59, 64, 67, 72,
73, 94, 113, 122–26, 129
Ghury, Emile, 68
Glubb, Major John Bagut (Glubb Pasha),
157
Goebbels, Joseph, 34
Gokalp, Ziya, 22, 76

Goltz, Colmar Freiherr von der, 10, 11,
15–17, 19, 22, 23
Great Britain and Iraq, 4–6, 45–57,
82–83, 103–6, 108–14, 115–17,
136–65
Grobba, Fritz, 37–43, 111, 135, 137,
150, 156, 157

HABFORCE, 155, 160
Haddad, 'Uthman Kemal, 142, 150
Hajj, 'Abd Allah, al-, 89
Hamid, 'Abd al-Haqq, 27
Hamley, H. R., 162
Hashimi, Taha, al-, 30, 40, 49, 70, 78,
94, 125, 127, 128, 129, 130, 132,
133, 137, 139, 141, 143, 146, 148,
179
Hashimi, Yasin, al-, 16, 46–47, 49, 55,
57–65, 67, 68, 78, 94, 109, 116,
117, 124, 125, 126, 127, 128, 145,
179
Hashimites, 59, 61, 167
Hassan, 'Abd al- Razzaq, al-, 59
Haydar, Rustam, 89, 129, 202
Hayes, Carleton J. H., 80
Herder, Johann Gottfried von, 32
Hitler, Adolph, 156, 157
Hitler Youth, 86
Humphreys, Sir Francis, 64
Husayn, Muhammad Abs, al-, 89
Husayn, Saddam, 167
Husayn, Tawfiq, 132
Husayni, al-Hajj Amin, al-, 36, 38, 49,
130, 138–41, 143, 146, 147, 149,
151, 158–59, 161
Husayn-Mac Mahon Correspondence,
48
Husri, Sati', al-, 30–33, 49, 73, 75–85,
88, 89–93, 96, 98, 113, 117, 164,
181

Ibn Khaldun, 32, 96
Ikha al-'Arabi al-Uthmani, al-, 29
Ikha al-Watani, al-, 57, 58, 125
Islam, 65
Istanbul, 9
Istiqlal, al-, 49
Italy, 36, 39, 138, 142; Rashid 'Ali

coup, 146, 147, 150, 151
Izzat, Ahmad, 25

Jabr, Salih, 78, 112
Jamali, Muhammad Fadhil, al-, 39, 65,
　75, 78, 84–87, 88, 89, 93–95,
　112–14, 164, 181
Janabi, Mahmud Fadhil, al-, 179
Japan, 64, 132, 146, 150
Jawdat, 'Ali, 27, 46, 125, 131, 179
Jews, 3, 43, 54, 65, 67, 70–71, 73,
　154, 158–60, 192, 206, 208
Jordan, Dr. Julius, 38, 42

Karbala, 3, 51, 53
Kata'ib al-Shabab, al-, 154
Kawakibi, 'Abd al-Rahman, al-, 28
Kaylani, Rashid 'Ali, al-, 36, 59, 109,
　122, 125, 128, 129, 130, 136, 139,
　141, 143, 145–65
Kemal, Mustafa (Atatürk), 22, 23, 87
Kemal, Namik, 27
Khalidi, Tawfiq, al-, 62
Khuja, Rashid, al-, 28
Knabenshue, Paul, 65, 113, 121, 136
Knight, Edward, 84, 89, 93
Kressenstein, General Kress von, 37
Kubbah, Muhammad Mahdi, 72
Kurdistan, 3
Kurds, 54, 119, 121, 122

Lawrence, T. E., 1
League of Nations, 57, 58
Liman von Sanders, Otto, 10, 13–14, 23
London Conference, 68

Mardam, Jamil, 141
Marschall von Bieberstein, 11
Mashnuq, 'Abdallah, al-, 108
Midfa'i, Jamil, al-, 41, 46, 50, 122,
　125, 128, 129, 135, 161, 164, 179
Military College, Iraq, 131
Military College, Istanbul, 9, 61,
　131–33
Ministry of Education, 68, 75, 78, 83,
　84, 92, 107, 110
Minorities, 92
Miqdadi, Darwish, al-, 40, 72, 98–99,

104–6, 108, 164
Misri, 'Aziz 'Ali, al-, 29, 45
Moltke, Helmuth, 10
Monck-Mason, G. E. A. C., 42, 113
Mond, Sir Alfred (Lord Melchet), 62,
　109
Monroe, Paul, 85, 89
Monroe Commission, 84, 89–95
Mosul, 1, 3
Mudarris, Fahmi al-, 152
Muhammad, 97–98
Mukhlis, Mawlud, 46, 50, 179
Mulkiye, 9
Mushtaq, Talib, 9, 84, 103, 108
Muslim Defense League, 69
Mussolini, Benito, 57
Mu'tamar al- 'Iraqi, 50
Muthanna Club, 70, 72–73, 76, 88, 99,
　146

Nadi al-Adabi al-, 29
Najaf, al-, 3, 51, 52
Najib, Sabih, 128, 129, 179
Naqib, Talib al-, 28
Nasuli, Anis al-, 98, 108
Nationalism, Arab, 26–27 (see also
　Pan-Arabism); France, 20; Germany,
　8, 20, 32, 33; Iraq, 50 (see also Pan-
　Arabism); Turkey, 20, 21
Newcombe, Colonel S. F., 141, 149
Newton, Sir Basil, 72, 104, 143, 148
Nur, Thabit 'Abd al-, 50
Nuremberg Rally, 112
Nuri, 'Abd al-Latif, 127, 179

Ottoman Empire, 7–26, 46, 81–82, 100

PAIFORCE, 161, 163
Palestine, 2, 36, 65–73, 110, 131, 135,
　136, 139, 141, 142; revolt
　1936–1939, 67, 68, 110, 136
Palestine Defense Committee, 70, 71,
　73, 99, 135, 140
Palestinians, Iraq, 67–69, 72, 95, 132,
　140, 164
Pan-Arabism, 48, 56, 65–73, 87–88,
　98–110, 133–35, 139–65
Papen, Franz von, 141, 187

Peterson, Sir Maurice, 38, 40, 143, 145
Princess Azzah, 201
Public Education Law, 1940, 107, 198

Qahtaniyya, al-, 29
Qasim, 'Abd al-Karim, 167
Qawuqji, Fawzi, al-, 71, 133, 135, 141
Quwwatli, Shukri, al-, 141

Rashid 'Ali coup, 95, 145–65
Rawi, Ibrahim al-, 179
Rendel, George, 104
Ribbentrop, Joachim von, 150, 187
Riza, 'Ali, 25
Rohrbach, Paul, 12, 13
Rumaytha, 51
Rusafi, Ma'ruf al-, 28
Ruwayha, Amin, 38, 71–72

Sab'awi, Yunis al-, 71, 139, 146, 149,
    159, 160, 164, 165, 181
Sabbagh, Salah al-Din al-, 71, 127,
    128, 130, 131, 132, 133, 134, 138,
    139, 145, 146, 149, 151, 156, 165,
    167, 180
Sabians, 3
Sadr, Muhammad al-, 130
Sa'dun, 'Abd al-Muhsin al-, 180
Sa'id, Fahmi, 127, 128, 130, 146, 165,
    180
Sa'id, Nuri al-, 16, 38, 41, 46, 49, 50,
    55, 56, 57–65, 67, 94, 108, 128,
    129, 130, 131, 141, 142, 143, 145,
    167, 180
Salman, Mahmud, 127, 128, 139, 146,
    180
Salman, Dr. Muhammad Hassan, 78
San Remo Conference, 1920, 2, 50–51
Schiemann, Theodor, 11
Schirach, Baldur von, 40, 111
Shabib, Kamil, 127, 128, 130, 143,
    180
Shabibi, Ridha, al-, 78
Shanshal, Siddiq, 153
Sharifians, 1, 2, 116, 118
Sharif of Mecca, 45, 47, 48, 50, 52
Shawkat, Mahmud, 25, 28
Shawkat, Naji, 139, 141, 146, 180

Shawkat, Dr. Saib, 42, 72
Shawkat, Dr. Sami, 39, 43, 72, 75, 78,
    84, 87–88, 96, 101, 107, 112–14,
    164, 180
Shi'a, 3, 49, 50, 52, 54–55, 57, 59, 65,
    84, 89, 93–94, 108, 155, 200; con-
    scription, 118–22
Shidyak, Faris, al-, 27
Sidqi, Bakr, 41, 122, 123, 125, 127,
    133, 134, 137, 180
Sinderson, Dr. Harry C., 42, 123
Smith, Lionel, 83
Stark, Freya, 155
Strikes, 58
Sulayman, Hikmat, 41, 67, 72, 78,
    125, 127, 128, 129, 134, 135, 181
Sunni, 2, 3, 55, 59, 61
Suwaydi, Naji, al-, 50, 67, 69, 139,
    141, 181
Suwaydi, Tawfiq, al-, 50, 67, 78, 135,
    138, 143, 145, 149, 152, 158, 181
Sykes-Picot Agreement 1916, 48
Syria, 2, 30, 31 46, 49, 50, 52, 61–62;
    Faysal, 66; Vichy France, 156

Talfah, Khayr Allah, 167
Talib, Sayyid, 53
Tantawi, 'Ali, al-, 103, 110
Tanzimat, 21, 81
Teachers Training College, 68, 88, 98
Textbooks, 95–107, 162
Thabit, Sa'id, 70, 71, 72, 139
Turkman, 3

'Umari, Amin, al-, 127, 128, 129, 130,
    180
'Umari, Arshad, al-, 159
Umayyads, 97, 98, 108

Wakil, Mustafa, al-, 152
Waldersee, General Alfred von, 11
Wangenheim, Baron Hans von, 12–13,
    17, 18
Warlimont, General Walter, 34, 153
Washburn, Carleton, 89
Wilhelm II, 9, 10, 11, 13, 14, 23, 24,
    41, 47
Wilson, Sir Arnold, 47–50, 105

Wilson, President Woodrow, 48
World War I, 14, 34, 61
World War II, 36, 37, 135–65

Yad al-Sawda, al-, 29
Yamulki, 'Aziz, 127, 128, 129, 130, 181
Yazidis, 3, 64

Young Turks, 10, 24, 25, 27, 81
Youth movements, 86–87, 88

Zahawi, Jamil, al-, 28
Zaki, Amin, 130, 164, 181
Zayd, Amir, 129
Zionism, 62, 66, 70, 106–7, 109
Zu'aytir, Akram, 72, 98–99, 101, 105–6